The Dybbuk

SUNY series in Western Esoteric Traditions

David Appelbaum, editor

The Dybbuk

Its Origins and History

MORRIS M. FAIERSTEIN

Cover: Dybbuk illustration from the Book of Job, appearing in *Die Bucher Der Bibel*, Ephraim Moses Lilien (1874–1925). Source: Wikimedia Commons

Published by State University of New York Press, Albany

© 2024 State University of New York

All rights reserved

Printed in the United States of America

No part of this book may be used or reproduced in any manner whatsoever without written permission. No part of this book may be stored in a retrieval system or transmitted in any form or by any means including electronic, electrostatic, magnetic tape, mechanical, photocopying, recording, or otherwise without the prior permission in writing of the publisher.

For information, contact State University of New York Press, Albany, NY
www.sunypress.edu

Library of Congress Cataloging-in-Publication Data

Name: Faierstein, Morris M., author.
Title: The dybbuk : its origins and history / Morris M. Faierstein.
Description: Albany, New York : State University of New York Press, [2024] | Includes bibliographical references and index.
Identifiers: LCCN 2023045139 | ISBN 9781438497952 (hardcover : alk. paper) | ISBN 9781438497976 (ebook)
Subjects: LCSH: Dybbuk—History. | Mysticism—Judaism.
Classification: LCC BM729.D92 F35 2024 | DDC 296.3/1—dc23/eng/20231026
LC record available at https://lccn.loc.gov/2023045139

For Prof. Zeev Gries
Friend, Colleague, and Mentor

Contents

Acknowledgments	ix
Introduction	1
1 The Theoretical Origins of the *Dybbuk* Concept	7
2 *Dybbuk* Possession in Safed in the Sixteenth Century	31
3 The Published *Dybbuk* Accounts in the First Half of the Seventeenth Century	47
4 The *Dybbuk* in the Second Half of the Seventeenth Century: The Age of the *Ba'alei Shem*	63
5 Rabbi Israel Ba'al Shem Tov and Hasidism	71
Conclusions	75
Appendix to Chapter 2	81
Appendix to Chapter 3	89
Appendix to Chapter 4	121
Appendix to Chapter 5	185
Notes	189
Bibliography	211
Index	221

Acknowledgments

This project had its origins twenty-five years ago when Professor Moshe Idel of the Hebrew University asked me to translate a Hasidic text, *Megillat Setarim* (Book of Secrets) by Rabbi Yitzhak Isaac of Komarno, a nineteenth-century Hasidic master and kabbalist. This request ultimately led to the publication of *Jewish Mystical Autobiographies: Book of Visions and Book of Secrets*. *Sefer Hezyonot* (Book of Visions) is the mystical diary of Rabbi Hayyim Vital, the foremost disciple of Rabbi Isaac Luria, the central figure of Safed kabbalah in the sixteenth century. Several years later, I also published a new Hebrew edition of this text. The publication of both of these books was made possible through the support and encouragement of Prof. Idel and I am grateful to him for this and his support of my scholarship more broadly.

The earliest known story of a *dybbuk* possession and exorcism is found in the *Sefer Hezyonot* (Book of Visions), and I explored this and related subjects as part of my study of this work. Several articles resulted from this research, including some relating to the *dybbuk*. The final stage in the evolution of this project was an invitation to participate in the Klutznick Symposium at Creighton University. This was an opportunity to assemble my research on the *dybbuk* into a coherent theory and present it to a scholarly audience. The response to my presentation was positive and encouraged me to complete this monograph. My thanks to Prof. Leonard Greenspoon for the invitation to participate in this symposium and to the other participants for their positive and helpful reception of my presentation.

Like most of my scholarly projects, this study has benefited from the support and encouragement of several friends of long standing, and I would like to thank Zeev Gries of Ben Gurion University of the Negev,

Elliot Ginsburg of the University of Michigan, and Jerry Schwarzbard of the Jewish Theological Seminary Library. The support and encouragement of my spouse, Ruth Anne, has made possible all of my scholarly work. My debt to her is beyond calculation. This study is dedicated to my friend and colleague, Zeev Gries of Ben Gurion University of the Negev. We first met in Jerusalem in the summer of 1988. Since then, our friendship has grown and flourished over the years. Zeev has been a reader, critic, and resource whose contributions can be found in almost everything I have published since our first meeting. This study is dedicated to him as a small token of thanks for his support and encouragement of my scholarly work over the years.

My thanks to James Peltz and the SUNY Press for accepting this volume for publication. My thanks also to Diane Ganeles, Camille Hale, and the others involved in the production of this book.

Earlier versions of aspects of this study of the *dybbuk* appeared in a variety of publications. My thanks to the publishers and editors for publishing these books and articles:

> Faierstein, Morris M. *Jewish Mystical Autobiographies: Book of Visions and Book of Secrets* (Classics of Western Spirituality, 94). New York: Paulist Press 1999.
>
> Faierstein, Morris M. "*Maggidim*, Spirits, and Women in Rabbi Hayyim Vital's *Book of Visions*." In *Spirit Possession in Judaism: Cases and Contexts from the Middle Ages to the Present*. Ed. Matt Goldish. Detroit: Wayne State University Press, 2003, 186–96.
>
> Faierstein, Morris M. "Women as Prophets and Visionaries in Medieval and Early Modern Judaism." In *Studies in Jewish Civilization 14: Women and Judaism*. Ed. L. J. Greenspoon, R. A. Simkins, and J. A. Cahan. Omaha: Creighton University Press, 2003, pp. 247–62.
>
> Faierstein, Morris M. "The First Published Account of a Safed Exorcism" (Hebrew). *Pe'amim*, 104 (Summer, 2005): 11–19.
>
> Faierstein, Morris M. *Sefer Ha-Hezyonot: Yomano ha-Mysti shel Rabbi Hayyim Vital*. Jerusalem: Machon Ben Zvi, 2005.
>
> Faierstein, Morris M. "The *Dibbuk* in the *Mayse Bukh*." *Shofar* 30, 1 (2011): 94–103.

Faierstein, Morris M. "The Possession of Rabbi Hayyim Vital by Jesus of Nazareth." *Kabbalah: Journal for the Study of Jewish Mystical Texts*, 37 (2017): 29–36.

Faierstein, Morris M. "The *Dybbuk*: The Origins and History of a Concept." In *olam ha-zeh v'olam ha-ba: This world and the World to Come in Jewish Belief and Practice* (Studies in Jewish Civilization 28). Ed. L. J. Greenspoon. West Lafayette: Purdue University Press, 2017, 135–50.

Introduction

The popular understanding of the *dybbuk* concept is associated with the play *Between Two Worlds*, better known as *The Dybbuk*, written by the Russian revolutionary activist and Jewish ethnographer Shlomo Zanvil Rapoport (1862–1920), better known by his pen name, S. Anski.[1] It was influenced by the ethnographic expedition he led from 1912 through 1914 to Volhynia and Podolia to study and preserve the Jewish folk traditions that were rapidly disappearing.[2] The conventional wisdom is that the expedition provided the raw material that inspired the play. The play was first presented a month after Anski's death and two years later in a Hebrew translation. It became a great success, translated into many languages, and is considered the greatest Yiddish play of the twentieth century.[3] Of greater importance for this study is that the play with its ethnographic folkloristic patina came to define the concept of the *dybbuk*, not only for popular audiences but also for much that has been written about this subject. Many scholarly and popular studies of the *dybbuk* assume that Anski's play was an accurate representation of the popular folk beliefs of East European Jewry and therefore a historically significant source for the understanding of the *dybbuk*.

My own interest in the *dybbuk* comes from my studies of Rabbi Hayyim Vital's mystical diary, *Sefer Hezyonot* (Book of Visions).[4] Vital was the most important disciple of Rabbi Isaac Luria, the charismatic Safed kabbalist, and a central figure in the earliest accounts of *dybbuk* possession and exorcism that occurred in Safed in the second half of the sixteenth century. Vital's diary and his other writings were the most important primary sources for this phenomenon in Safed. Several years after publishing the English translation of Vital's diary, I edited and published a new Hebrew edition of the *Sefer Hezyonot*.[5] During the years that I worked on these editions I also published several articles relating to the *dybbuk* concept as it was found in Safed.[6] This research motivated me to revisit the origins and history of the *dybbuk* and examine it afresh.

This project differs from most of what has been previously written on this subject in that I begin *ab initio* with a return to the original sources and endeavor to understand the concept of the *dybbuk* from its origins in Safed in the sixteenth century to its later historical evolution. Many of the basic questions about this subject have not been adequately dealt with in previous studies. Is the concept of the *dybbuk* based on earlier sources and concepts? Why did it appear in Safed and not before? What purpose did the *dybbuk* serve in Safed? Does the evidence validate the common assertion that women were the primary victims of *dybbuk* possession as has been assumed? What was the purpose of the *dybbuk* after Safed? How and why were *dybbuk* stories disseminated after Safed? Were the *dybbuk* stories in subsequent centuries records of actual events or fictional accounts published as "folktales" or for other reasons? What is the place of the *dybbuk* story in Hasidism? This study will attempt to answer these questions in a scholarly manner, without privileging any perspective that is not supported by the sources.

Much of what has been written about the *dybbuk* since Anski popularized the concept has taken his play as the starting point and has analyzed or discussed the concept through this prism. Studies of the play, its ideas, and its reception are beyond the purview of this study.[7] The modern scholarly study of the history of the *dybbuk* begins with Gedaliah Nigal.[8] He collected and published the texts of virtually all known *dybbuk* stories with important historical and bibliographical information. Nigal described the when, where, and how of the *dybbuk*, but he does not adequately explain the why. The first scholarly effort to provide a comprehensive understanding of the *dybbuk* in Safed is the monograph by J. H. Chajes.[9] However, it is flawed by the author's assumption that the *dybbuk* concept can be explained by reference to modern feminist interpretations, and his work is a brief in support of this contention. He does not seriously deal with alternative possible approaches to the question of the origins and meaning of the *dybbuk* concept. He begins his study with the appearance of the *dybbuk* in the sixteenth century and does not adequately examine the prehistory of the concept and the kabbalistic teachings that made it possible. To answer the basic question of why the *dybbuk* appears in the sixteenth century, he points to the supposed parallelism with the upsurge of witchcraft trials in Europe at about the same time. The primary point of connection is that the two events are contemporaneous, and women are the focus in both cases. There are two obvious problems with this analysis. Witchcraft trials had been going on for a century before the appearance of the first *dybbuk*, and equally important, gender is not a factor in *dybbuk* possession. The distribution between men and women being possessed by *dybbukim* is roughly equivalent, as will be shown. Chajes ignores the stories about the possession of men and emphasizes the role of women. Additionally, there is no evidence that anyone in Safed was aware of the witchcraft persecutions in Europe or vice versa. Witches were possessed by the devil or Satan, and this phenomenon has been understood by modern scholars in terms of larger social and cultural issues and events that occurred over a long period of time and in many places. In addition, as will be discussed below, the concept of the *dybbuk* and possession by him is a uniquely Jewish phenomenon and has only the most surface relationship to the Christian concept of possession and its causes. These differences will be discussed in chapter 1. There is no evidence that *dybbuk* possession was a form of persecution of a group or a result of larger social issues. Rather, as we will demonstrate, the *dybbuk* is based on the concept of transmigration as it was developed in the medieval kabbalistic tradition. The concept of transmigration is rejected in the whole Christian tradition, Protestant and Catholic, and in the Sunni Islamic tradition. Second, the exorcism of a *dybbuk* was originally the purview of one person in Safed, Rabbi Isaac Luria. Rabbi Hayyim Vital, his disciple, was able to exorcise a *dybbuk* under the direction of Luria with difficulty. The competing exorcism story from Safed, by Elijah Falco, is problematic and will be discussed below in greater detail.

Sara Zfatman, a scholar of early modern Yiddish literature, has made a significant contribution to the reception history of the *dybbuk* concept. She studied several specific episodes of *dybbuk* possession in the second half of the seventeenth century in Central Europe but does not attempt to provide a comprehensive history or analysis of the concept. Her studies have been collected in an important monograph that will be discussed in its appropriate place in the reception history of the *dybbuk*.[10]

As a historian, I have not found social scientific approaches to the *dybbuk*, such as the anthropological approach of Yoram Bilu and the folkloristic methodology of Eli Yassif, to be helpful in answering the questions that concern me.[11] The methodological focus of this study is reception history. The basic questions will be historical and not literary or involving other methodological approaches, such as philosophical, literary, or social scientific perspectives. Another lacuna in many previous studies is that they do not explain the context of the *dybbuk* story in its original setting. What purpose did it serve in Safed? Why does it first occur in Safed and not elsewhere or beforehand?

This work is divided into three sections. The first section explores the prehistory of the *dybbuk*. What are the sources in rabbinic and kabbalistic literature that lay the groundwork for the *dybbuk*? The rabbinic story of "Rabbi Akiva and the Dead Man" and the kabbalistic concept of transmigration are important foundations for its prehistory. The second section is devoted to Safed. The first *dybbuk* possession is recorded in Safed in 1571 and 1572. The first accounts of *dybbuk* possession in Safed were published during the first half of the seventeenth century. This section discusses the events in Safed and the reception history of the published accounts of the Safed events. The third section begins in the second half of the seventeenth century with accounts of *dybbuk* possession that share little with the Safed accounts beyond the basic idea that a person had been possessed by a *dybbuk* and needed to be exorcised. The main actors in these exorcisms were *ba'alei shem*, kabbalists who specialized in what is called "practical kabbalah," the knowledge and use of Divine Names and other rituals that are often considered to be in the realm of magic. The name most often associated with the concept of a *ba'al shem* is Rabbi Israel Baal Shem Tov, the founder of Hasidism. Later generations of hasidic masters who followed in his footsteps were also reported to have exorcised *dybbukim* in the hagiographic literature of Hasidism.

Since my purpose is not to create an encyclopedic overview of every *dybbuk* story in the history of Judaism, but rather to indicate a new direction in understanding this phenomenon and its history, there are many *dybbuk* stories that have not been considered or discussed in this study. A significant category of stories that were not considered are hagiographic accounts that were recorded second or third hand and are part of the genre of miracle stories about holy men. A significant example are the exorcism stories in the hagiographical literature of Hasidism that were published from the middle of the nineteenth century until the first quarter of the twentieth century.

A note on the term *dybbuk*. The soul of the sinner condemned to *gilgul* (transmigration) was originally called an "evil Spirit" (*ruah rah*) in the early possession stories from Safed. This term can also refer to demons and other "spirits" found as early as the writings of Josephus and continued to be mentioned in Jewish literature through the ages. These references to spirits or evil spirits have no connection to the *dybbuk* concept that is the concern of this study. Some authors who translated early texts have been known to change the term "evil Spirit" and use *dybbuk* in its place to make it more comprehensible to the modern reader. The most prominent example is Moses Gaster in his edition of the *Ma'aseh Book*. The title of the story in his collection is changed from "The Evil Spirit" to "The Dibbuk."[12] It has been the conventional wisdom, based on the study of Gershom Scholem that the term *dybbuk*, derived from the Hebrew term *dybbuk* meaning "that which is attached," began to be used instead of "evil Spirit" at the end of the seventeenth century.[13] More recently, Sara Zfatman has demonstrated that this terminological transition took place later, in the first part of the eighteenth century. The first reference to the term *dybbuk* that she found is in a story of an exorcism in Speyer in 1715.[14]

All of the stories discussed in this study will be translated in full, from the primary sources cited, and all translations are my own unless otherwise noted. Many of them are not available in English translation or only short passages have been previously translated. The translations of the stories will appear in an appendix in the back. In several cases, I have translated multiple versions of a given story. The reason for this is that there are significant variations in the different versions that are worthy of consideration. In other places where a text is reprinted without significant variation, I cite the additional sources where the story is cited at the end of the translation of the story.

Chapter 1

The Theoretical Origins of the *Dybbuk* Concept

Tales of people being possessed by demons and other evil spirits[1] can be found in Jewish literature as early as the first century CE. Talmudic and Midrashic literature also contains such stories,[2] but these stories did not attract unusual attention or comments in the post-Talmudic medieval Jewish tradition. They were part of the "normal" supernatural world that surrounded the human world, and the two worlds interacted in a variety of ways sanctioned by tradition and folklore.[3] The classic models of possession in Christianity were the stories of possession of people by demons and by Satan and their exorcism by Jesus in the New Testament.[4] Possession and exorcism were well-known phenomena in the ancient world beyond the Jewish and Christian communities and were widely discussed in a variety of Jewish, Christian, and Greco-Roman sources. The earliest description of the method used to exorcise a demon is found in the writings of Josephus. He describes in the *Antiquities of the Jews* an exorcism of a demon that he witnessed, performed by a Jewish exorcist by the name of Eleazar in the presence of the future emperor Vespasian. Josephus writes:

> God also granted (Solomon) knowledge of the art concerning demons for the benefit and healing of mankind: he composed incantations for the alleviation of illness and left behind modes of exorcism for those in need, to chase out demons such that they would never return. This healing prevails widely among us to the present day: for I have witnessed one of my coun-

trymen, Eleazar, in the presence of Vespasian . . . releasing from demons those possessed by them. The mode of healing was as follows: he would bring his ring up to the nostrils of the demoniac, which had under its seal one of the roots recommended by Solomon, then draw the demon through the nostrils of the patient as he smelled. The person fell at once, and (Eleazar) would adjure (the demon) never to return to him, mentioning Solomon and uttering the incantations that he composed.[5]

Michael Zellmann-Rohrer in his discussion of this topic also cites an ancient account that approaches the concept from the perspective of parody and mockery, but in the process, it offers valuable insights into the Jewish origin of this form of exorcism and its popularity in the ancient world. He writes:

To pass from praise to parody, Lucian, native of neighboring Syria, could speak in the second century of a more general tradition of Palestinian professionals of exorcism absent any explicit confessional affiliation. In and of itself, that is evidence for a diffusion of the technique. But more interesting is the way in which Lucian proceeds to ridicule it. In the *Lovers of Lies*, the sophist describes a fictional gathering of philosophers whose discourse on the paradoxical, and their uncritical attitude towards it, mark them as unworthy of their profession: an account of these "lies" is the occasion for the framing story of the more skeptical Tychiades, who bears witness, and his interlocutor Philocles. Natural remedies involving sympathy, healing incantations, and erotic magic all come in for mockery by Tychiades before one of the philosophers, Ion, who represents the Platonic school, offers an example that he expects will be credible due to how well-known it is. The discussion amounts in the end to an unsuccessful attempt to convince Tychiades of the existence of *daimones*, phantoms, and ghosts, among other supernatural manifestations and magical operations. A professional specializes in the treatment of epilepsy, explicitly associated with the influence of the moon—reflecting a facet of popular belief to be discussed further on—which is diagnosed as a form of demonic possession. From this he makes a large profit. The exorcist engages the demon in dialogue, forcing it to reveal its origin and means of entry in its native tongue, and then compels it to withdraw, applying adjurations and making threats. Witnesses are able to see the demon itself as it departs. The text from Lucian follows:

> *Everyone knows the Syrian from Palestine, the expert in this field, how many patients he takes on, who fall under the influence of the moon and roll their eyes with their mouths full of foam and stands them up and sends them off with sound mind, relieving them of their terrible suffering for a high price. When he stands over the fallen and asks from where (the demons) entered the body, the patient himself is silent, but the demon answers, speaking Greek or a foreign language depending on its origin, how and from where it entered the person. He drives the demon out by applying adjurations, and even, if it does not obey, by making threats. I myself have seen one coming out, with a complexion like dark smoke.*[6]

It is fascinating to put these texts side by side with the materials from later accounts of Jewish exorcisms. One example that will be discussed at length below is the description of an exorcism by Moshe Prager, a famous *ba'al shem* of the late seventeenth century, of a *dybbuk* from a youth in Nikolsburg has many parallels to the exorcism by Eleazar in Josephus's story.[7] The two of them could be colleagues who would understand each other's methods completely. Lucian's parody of an exorcism would be completely accepted as a description of an authentic exorcism if the reader was not told about the source.

All of the exorcisms in Jewish history that preceded the sixteenth century were of demons or other malevolent spirits, and the methods of exorcism followed the Josephus/Lucian model. The *dybbuk* only appears for the first time in Safed, in the second half of the sixteenth century. Yet, the methodology and rituals of the majority of later *dybbuk* exorcism stories are the same as the exorcisms of demons.[8] There are two individuals, Jesus and Rabbi Isaac Luria who were exceptions to the statement that all Jewish exorcisms, from Josephus to the present, follow the outlines of the exorcism strategy first found in Josephus. In both cases, it was their personal charisma that was at the center of their ability to exorcize demons and malevolent spirits in the case of Jesus and *dybbukim* in the case of Luria, without resort to magical rituals and formulas.[9]

Following Jesus's example, stories of possession and exorcism of demons and malevolent spirits were often encountered in the lives of Christian saints. The ability to exorcise or subdue a demonic spirit or even to vanquish the works of Satan was a sure sign of sainthood. Stories of demonic possession and connection to Satanic forces, which came to be known as witchcraft, grew in the course of the medieval period and reached a high point in the sixteenth and seventeenth centuries in the midst of the religious and political conflicts arising from the Protestant Reformation and the Catholic Counter-Reformation. Possession of a person in the Christian tradition was always by a malevolent power, Satan or one of his demonic minions. There is a vast literature on the subject of demonic possession and its relation to witchcraft in early modern Europe. It is interesting that the ritual of exorcism with methods and rituals similar to the Josephus model were formalized by the Catholic Church as late as the fifteenth century, and not earlier.[10]

What Is a *Dybbuk*?

In the ancient world the concept of transmigration or metempsychosis was not mentioned in the Talmud but was known in the Greek philosophical traditions of the Pythagoreans, Platonists, and later the Neoplatonists. On the other hand, Aristotle and the later Aristotelian tradition rejected the possibility of metempsychosis. Aristotle saw the soul as the form of the body and could not transmigrate to another body.[11] As a result of the greater influence of Aristotelian thought on the theological development of the Roman Catholic Church and later Protestantism, both repeatedly rejected the concept of transmigration and the possibility of possession by the souls of the deceased.[12] There are stories about dead people wandering the earth and possessing people in European Christian popular literature in the Middle Ages and the Early Modern period, even though this was contrary to Church doctrine. The existence of this genre in Christian Europe should be noted, but at the same time, it should also be emphasized that any similarities between these stories and *dybbuk* possession are surface phenomena and have no direct connection.[13] There is even a Jewish "*dybbuk*" story in sixteenth-century Italy about a Jewish woman possessed by the soul of an executed Christian criminal. When carefully examined, this story is based on the Christian model of a ghost story rather than the Jewish concept of the *dybbuk*.[14]

Sunni Islam also did not accept the concept of transmigration, as a result of the Aristotelian influence on Islamic thought. However, some offshoots of Shi'ite Islam, like the Druze, Alawites, and Ismailis do accept the concept of transmigration.[15] Similarly, there were Gnostic groups and other Christian offshoots that were more influenced by Neoplatonic ideas, and they accepted the possibility of transmigration. Of course, transmigration is a key concept of Hinduism and Buddhism along with the religious traditions that emanate from them. However, the understanding of this concept in these religions is different from its understanding in Judaism, and an analysis of transmigration in these religious traditions is beyond our present purview. Our interest is only in those religious traditions that interacted with or influenced premodern Judaism.

The traditions of possession by demons and other supernatural entities, like demons, Satan, the devil, or evil spirits, have no real connection or relationship to what we call a *dybbuk*, since a *dybbuk* is a very different being from a demon or other type of supernatural spirit. This applies not only to Christian and Islamic demons and evil spirits of all sorts, but also to the demons and spirits found in rabbinic literature and medieval Jewish traditions. A *dybbuk* is a unique being and is only found in the Jewish tradition. It is defined as the soul of a Jewish man who had died and was being punished for his sins by being forced to wander the earth while being tormented. His sins were so severe that he had been denied entrance to Gehenna, where sinners were normally sent for punishment of their sins. The soul not allowed into Gehenna was trapped between this world and the next and had to wander until expiation was found for the sin. Once expiation was found, the soul could be judged and sent to Gehenna for its punishment and then on to the Garden of Eden for its reward.[16] In the interim, the soul could only find rest by possessing or joining with another entity or being, animate or inanimate. The wandering soul became a *dybbuk* when it possessed another person. It was only in sixteenth-century Safed that we hear of cases of people being possessed by a *dybbuk* and needing exorcism. There is no evidence in the literature of *dybbuk* possessions of a female *dybbuk*. Hayyim Vital explicitly stated that the soul of a woman could not become a *dybbuk* because women did not participate in the process of *gilgul* (transmigration). Rather, their souls were sent directly to Gehenna, where they were punished for their sins.[17] There is also no evidence that the soul of a non-Jew could be a *dybbuk*.[18]

"Rabbi Akiva and the Dead Man"

The primary sources that form the theoretical basis of the *dybbuk* concept are a rabbinic story called "Rabbi Akiva and the Dead Man," and the kabbalistic concepts of *gilgul* (transmigration of the soul), and *ibbur* (spiritual impregnation). The earliest source that discusses the concept of the soul of a deceased sinner wandering the world without finding rest as a form of punishment is a story first found in tractate *Kallah Rabbati*. This tractate is included in a post-Talmudic collection of minor tractates that originated in the Geonic period (approximately seventh–ninth centuries). Known as, "Rabbi Akiva and the Dead Man," this story incorporates a central aspect of the *dybbuk* concept, the idea that the soul of a sinner does not go directly to Gehenna for punishment, but instead it wanders the earth as an integral aspect of its punishment. Moreover, it is considered a worse punishment than Gehenna. In this story, there is a cycle of endless punishment, and it is only the intervention of Rabbi Akiva that breaks the cycle of punishment and brings an end to the deceased person's suffering. Various versions of this story are found in medieval sources,[19] including the *Zohar*.[20] It is usually associated with the halakhic and other discussions relating to the origins and dissemination of the tradition of the prayer for the dead known as the "Mourner's Kaddish." Traditionally, this story has not been explicitly connected to the Safed *dybbuk* stories, but the similarities are suggestive. The version of this story as found in tractate *Kallah Rabbati* is as follows:

> Come and hear; R. Akiba went to a certain place [a cemetery] where he met a man [i.e., a ghost] carrying a heavy load on his shoulder with which he was unable to proceed, and he was crying and groaning. He asked him, "What did you do [in your lifetime]?" He replied, "There is no forbidden act in the world which I left undone, and now guards have been set over me who do not allow me to rest." R. Akiba asked him, "have you left a son?" He answered, "By your life! Do not detain me because I fear the angels who beat me with fiery lashes and say to me, 'Why do you not walk quickly?'" R. Akiba said to him, "Tell me whom have you left?" He replied, "I have left behind my wife who was pregnant." R. Akiba then proceeded to that city and inquired, "Where is the son of So and so?" [The inhabitants] replied, "May

the memory of that wicked person be uprooted." He asked them the reason and they said, "He robbed and preyed upon people and caused them suffering; what is more, he violated a betrothed girl on the Day of Atonement." He made his way to the house and found the wife about to be delivered of a child. He waited until she gave birth to [a son], circumcised him and when he grew up, took him to the Synagogue to join in public worship. Later R. Akiba returned to that [cemetery] and [the ghost] appeared to him and said, "May your mind be [always] at rest because you have set my mind at rest."[21]

The relationship between the *Kallah Rabbati* story and its later versions that are found in later medieval sources have many parallels to what happened in the *dybbuk* stories of Safed. The later versions of the story become more detailed and have similarities to the interrogations of the *dybbuk* found in some of the *dybbuk* tales from the seventeenth century and later in their expansion of and addition of details to the original story. The version of this story that is found in the *Mahzor Vitry* is illustrative of how the story was expanded. Two interesting details found in this version, not found in the earlier version, are the "thorns on his head" and the phrase, "that man (*oto ha-ish*)." Both phrases would trigger images of Jesus in the imagination of a medieval Jew living in a Christian environment. There are many other details in the later version of the story that are specific to the culture of medieval Ashkenazi society. The *Mahzor Vitry* version of this story is:

It once happened that Rabbi Akiva was passing through a cemetery, and he came upon a man who was naked, and black as coal, and carrying a great burden of thorns on his head. Rabbi Akiva thought that the man, who was running like a horse, was alive. Rabbi Akiva commanded and stopped him, and said to him: "Why does that man ['oto ha-'ish] do this difficult work? If you are a servant and your master treats you this way, I will redeem you from his hands; if you are poor and people are treating you unfairly, I will enrich you." [The man] said to him: "Please do not delay me, lest those appointed over me become angry." [Rabbi Akiva] said to him: "What is this, and what are your deeds?" [The man] said to him: "That man is dead, and every day I am sent out to chop trees." [Rabbi Akiva] said to him: "My son, what was your profession in the world from which you came?" [The man] said to him: "I was a tax collector [*gabba'i ha-mekhes*], and I would favor the rich and kill the poor." [Rabbi Akiva] said to him: "Haven't you heard anything from those appointed to punish you about how you might be relieved?" [The man] said: "Please do not delay me, lest those in charge of my punishments become angry, for there is no relief for that man. But I did hear from [those appointed over me] one impossible thing: 'If only this poor man had a son who would stand in front of the congregation and say, "Let us bless God, who is blessed" [*barkhu 'et 'adonai ha-mevorakh*] and have them answer "May His great name be blessed," [*yehe shmeh rabbah mevorakh*] he would be immediately released from his punishments. But that man never had a son—he left his wife pregnant, and I do not know if she had a boy. And even if she did have a boy, who would teach him Torah? That man does not have a friend in the world.'" Immediately, Rabbi Akiva decided to go and see if he had a son, in order to teach him Torah and stand him in front of the congregation. He said to [the man]: "What is your name?" [The man] said to him: "Akiva." "And your wife's name?" [The man] said to him: "Shoshniba." "And the name of your city?" "Laodicea." Immediately Rabbi Akiva was extremely saddened and went to ask after [the man]. When he arrived in that city, he asked after him. [The townspeople] said to him: "May the bones of that man be ground up." [Rabbi Akiva] asked after [the man's] wife. They said to him: "May her memory be erased from the world." He asked about her son. They said to him: "He is uncircumcised—we did not even engage in the commandment of circumcision for him." Immediately, Rabbi Akiva circumcised him, and put a book in front of him. But he would not accept Torah study, until Rabbi Akiva fasted for forty days. A heavenly voice said to him: "For this you are fasting?" [Rabbi Akiva] said: "Master of the Universe! Is it not for You that I am preparing him?" Immediately the Holy One opened [the child's] heart, and [Rabbi Akiva] taught him Torah, and the *Shema*, and grace after meals. He then stood [the child] in front of the congregation, and [the child] recited *"Let us bless,"* and the congregation answered after him "*Blessed be the blessed God.*" In that hour, they freed [the man] from his punishment. Immediately, the man came to Rabbi Akiva in a dream, and said "May it be the will of the Holy One, blessed be He, that you rest in the Garden of Eden, for you have saved me from the judgment of Gehenna." Rabbi Akiva exclaimed: "*God, your name endures forever, your renown, God, through all generations*" (Psalm 135:13).[22]

The aspects of this story that are original and relevant to the *dybbuk* concept are the idea that there are sins that cannot be atoned for through the normal forms of punishment and that the only recourse to relief is through the intercession of a holy man with exceptional powers. If one substitutes Isaac Luria for Rabbi Akiva and a *dybbuk* for the dead man, we have the setting of a classic Safed *dybbuk* event. It is certainly an important component and precursor of the matrix that makes up the backgrounds of the *dybbuk* concept.

The Concept of *Gilgul*[23]

The second concept that makes up the matrix of ideas that forms the background for the *dybbuk* is the doctrine of transmigration of souls (*gilgul neshamot*). It is found in the early medieval kabbalistic work *Sefer ha-Bahir*. Gershom Scholem notes that the concept is taken for granted in the *Bahir*, as if it is well known. He finds this remarkable considering the strong opposition to the concept of transmigration by the Jewish philosophical elite.[24] *Gilgul* was considered to be a widespread phenomenon for Jewish souls in the *Bahir* and had no negative connotation. There was no sense that this was a punishment, but at the same time, there was no explanation or reason for this phenomenon. The doctrine was presented in a series of parables that are open to interpretation. In contrast, the Gerona school of kabbalists treated *gilgul* as a profound mystery. They considered it a hidden mystery of the Torah, and it was forbidden to expound this doctrine in writing but could only be transmitted orally to those worthy to receive the tradition.[25] The important change to this doctrine in the *Zohar* was that *gilgul* was seen as a form of punishment for certain specific sins. The *Zohar* focused on the sin of not fulfilling the commandment of levirate marriage. The soul of the person who failed to fulfill this commandment had to transmigrate into a new body where the soul would have another opportunity to correct this sin. Other sins could be atoned for by a period in Gehenna, but not this sin. The *Zohar* also expanded this punishment to those transgressions for which the punishment was *karet* (being cut off). The rationale given was that the transmigrations would give the person additional opportunities to repent for these sins and avoid being cut off from God permanently.[26] Kabbalists writing on this subject after the period of the *Zohar* expanded the number of sins that qualified for the punishment of *gilgul*.

Another definition of *gilgul* or transmigration entailed the soul being reborn into a new body and being given the opportunity to atone for a sin that had not been completely expiated in the original lifetime of the soul. A famous example is the story of the ten Rabbinic Martyrs who were killed by the Romans at the end of the Bar Kochba rebellion. According to the medieval *Midrash Bereshit Rabbati*, by Rabbi Moses ha-Darshan, the death of the ten martyrs was a punishment for the sin committed by Joseph's ten brothers who were present when they sold him into slavery. The rabbis were the *gilgulim* of the ten brothers, and the martyrdom of the rabbis expiated the sin of the sale of Joseph by his brothers.[27] Hayyim Vital described his own *gilgulim* as described to him by Isaac Luria, and all of them hinged on one sin that needed to be corrected.[28]

The second half of the fifteenth century saw the beginnings of broader interest in kabbalah, in both the Jewish and Christian intellectual communities. Jewish and Christian thinkers, especially in Italy, took an interest in kabbalah as part of their larger project of investigating ancient traditions, like Neoplatonism and Hermeticism.[29] One of the subjects that attracted attention in the course of this interest in kabbalah was the question of transmigration of the soul (*gilgul neshamot*). The first public debate about *gilgul* occurred in Candia on the island of Crete, in 1466. The larger context was the debate between philosophy and kabbalah that was beginning to attract public attention. The immediate cause of the debate was related to the question of whether to authorize levirate marriage in the community. The normative procedure was the ritual of *halizah*, which allowed the widow to marry someone other than her late husband's brother. Those who supported authorizing levirate marriage relied in part on the connection between levirate marriage and *gilgul* in kabbalistic literature. Those who accepted the concept of *gilgul* believed that the levirate marriage allowed not only for the name of the deceased to be preserved, but also the reincarnation of his soul.[30]

The following century saw significant interest in reincarnation and *gilgul*, along with a growing literature that explored this subject. Not only Jewish authors, but also Christian scholars like Marsilio Ficino and Giovanni Pico della Mirandola, were influenced by kabbalah and Neoplatonism and attracted to the idea of *gilgul*.[31] *Galya Raza*, a treatise on the concept of *gilgul*, was composed by an anonymous kabbalist living in the Ottoman Empire in the middle of the sixteenth century. It brought together the ideas about *gilgul* prevalent in his day and is useful as a compendium of the state of the subject at the time.[32] The subject of *gilgul* was also important for Rabbi David ibn Zimra, an important halakhic authority and kabbalist in Egypt. He discussed the subject of *gilgul* at length in his many influential kabbalistic writings.[33] His teachings are of particular interest since Rabbi Isaac Luria, who went on to become the most influential kabbalist in Safed and who made the concept of *gilgul* an important concept in his activities and teachings, was a student of Rabbi David ibn Zimra when both lived in Cairo. It is important to note that there is no evidence that the concept of *gilgul* moved from the realm of theory to one of practical import before its emergence in relation to the concept of the *dybbuk* in Safed. The impact and importance of the concept of the *dybbuk* in Safed will be discussed in the next chapter.

The Concept of *Ibbur*

The concept of *ibbur* (impregnation) is a kabbalistic concept that is the opposite of *gilgul* in many respects. Rather than being considered to be a punishment, it was considered a reward that was accessible only to the most pious and righteous figures. It was mentioned in the writings of Nahmanides but was always called "*sod ha-ibbur*" (the secret of *ibbur*), an esoteric doctrine that should be restricted to initiates.[34] The *Zohar* begins to discuss this concept somewhat more explicitly. As Gershom Scholem described it:

> According to the *Zohar*, the souls of certain pious figures in the Bible were impregnated with the deceased souls of other righteous men from the past at decisive moments in their lives. Hence, the soul of Judah entered that of Boaz,[35] while those of Aaron's two sons, Nadab and Abihu, entered that of Phinehas.[36] It does not state that these phenomena are

subject to the laws of transmigration . . . there is no reason for the *Zohar* to assume this. Rather, at a particular moment, and for the performance of a particular deed (such as Boaz's marriage to Ruth), a soul returns and descends (even from Paradise!) in order to strengthen and encourage another soul in the performance of a given act. This of course requires a certain kinship, either of the souls themselves, or of the situation in which the person finds himself at a given moment that repeats a moment from the life of the deceased soul.[37]

This definition is closer to the concept of souls having affinities and sharing spiritual ancestors and the certain souls for specific reasons. It is the basis of the concept of *shoresh neshamah* (the source of a given soul).[38] In later kabbalah and in the sixteenth century, the term *ibbur* acquired a different meaning. This latter meaning is how it was understood in sixteenth-century Safed. Hayyim Vital gives a clear explanation of the distinction between the two terms as they evolved:

> *Gilgul* is when, as the newborn emerges from its mother's womb, the soul enters the body, and it suffers all the sorrow and sufferings of that body from the moment it came into the world until its death, and it cannot leave until the day of death. But *ibbur* is when the soul exists in this world after a person has been born and grown up; then another soul enters him and that person is like a fetus of a pregnant woman [*ubarrah*] who carries an infant in her womb, and thus it is called *ibbur*.[39]

There are several important differences between *gilgul* and *ibbur*. *Gilgul* implies that a soul is being implanted into a new body at conception, while *ibbur* refers to the temporary introduction of an additional soul into a living person who already has his own soul. Additionally, *gilgul* was for the purpose of punishment and expiation, while *ibbur* was not for the benefit of the righteous person being impregnated, but for the benefit of the person who received the impregnation or to help influence events that would lead to greater holiness and goodness in the world. Like *gilgul*, the *ibbur* remained a theoretical concept that did not have practical consequences until the second half of the sixteenth century in Safed. The concept of *yihud* (unification), an offshoot of *ibbur*, becomes important in Safed. This aspect of *ibbur* refers to the unification of the soul of the kabbalist with the soul of a deceased worthy for the purpose of receiving insights or information from the deceased partner.[40] The chief practitioner of *yihudim* was Rabbi Isaac Luria, who regularly engaged in *yihudim* at the grave of Rabbi Simeon bar Yohai, the purported author of the *Zohar*. Luria taught the practice of *yihudim* to some of his disciples, who had greater or lesser success with this practice. *Yihudim* played a central role in establishing Isaac Luria's religious authority in Safed. This practice and its implementation will be discussed below.

From Tradition to Revelation[41]

Medieval Spanish kabbalah was based on the basic principle of the authority of tradition for the school of Nahmanides and the following generations. The kabbalists who produced the *Zohar* in the late thirteenth century and early fourteenth century attributed the original creation of this large corpus to the revelations received by the early rabbinic figure Rabbi Simeon bar Yohai. When the writings were disseminated, it was assumed that the secrets of the *Zohar* could be made accessible by a variety of hermeneutic methods. At the same time, the idea of direct revelation from the heavenly realms did not end with prophecy or even with the rabbinic *bat kol*, or revelations from encounters with Elijah, and other modes described in rabbinic literature. Visitation by Elijah was a motif that is widely reported in the Jewish mystical tradition. This was particularly true with regard to figures who might be considered innovators or pivotal figures in moving into a new intellectual direction.[42] There were a variety of thinkers in the medieval period who employed a diversity of methods to continue receiving divine revelations that could be called prophetic. A pioneering examination of this phenomenon was the study of divine inspiration in the Middle Ages by Abraham Joshua Heschel.[43] More recently, this subject has also been a focus of Moshe Idel's scholarship.[44] Two medieval examples of "prophetic" activity that have been studied by Idel are Abraham Abulafia[45] and Nehemiah ben Solomon ha-Navi (the prophet).[46] It is beyond the purview of this survey to discuss this important topic in the detail that it deserves.

About 1475, a new kabbalistic school emerged that placed the emphasis on direct revelation of esoteric secrets by a divine being, an angel, or the Shekhinah. The central text of this school was the *Sefer ha-Meshiv* (the Book of the Responding Angel),[47] which first appeared in Spain in the decades before the expulsion of the Jews from Spain in 1492. It recorded a series of revelations by the angel, responding to the inquiries of a kabbalist. The kabbalist who received these revelations may have been Rabbi Joseph Taitazak of Salonika, who was a refugee from Spain.[48] He was a major rabbinic figure in Salonika and author of halakhic works, philosophical writings, and biblical commentaries. Though his name is not explicitly mentioned in the manuscripts of the *Sefer ha-Meshiv*, there are many authors in the sixteenth and seventeenth centuries that attribute a Maggid to him and suggest his authorship of this work. Among Taitazak's students in Salonika were Joseph Karo and his colleague Shlomo Alkabetz. The turn to revelation first found in the *Sefer ha-Meshiv* leads ultimately to Joseph Karo's *maggid* and Isaac Luria and his revelation of new kabbalistic teachings based on his direct contact with the soul of Rabbi Simeon bar Yohai through the process of *yihudim*, when Luria visited his grave in Meron. The concept of *maggidic* revelation was discussed in the Lurianic writings, but there is no evidence Luria or Hayyim Vital utilized or experienced this form of divine revelation.[49] *Yihudim* were Luria's preferred form of contact with the divine world.

Though there were many reports of various forms of divine revelation attributed to figures in Safed, there are two methods that directly relate to *dybbuk* possession, the subject of this study, *maggidic* possession and *yihudim*. The other forms of revelation that do not directly relate to the *dybbuk* will not be considered. In addition to the forms of divine revelation there are many forms of divination, dream interpretation, and people to whom a variety of visionary experience are attributed in the writings of the Safed kabbalists. Among those to whom these experiences are attributed are a number of women who are mentioned in Hayyim Vital's *Sefer Hezyonot*, and other Safed sources.[50]

The *Maggid*

There are two documented incidents of a *maggid* possession that are related to the *dybbuk* concept. The first is the *maggid* attributed to Joseph Karo, and Karo's interactions with his *maggid*, the personification of the Mishnah, are described at length in his book *Maggid Mesharim*. Karo kept a diary of his interactions with his *maggid*. The second recorded possession by a *maggid* is the possession of the daughter of Raphael Anav[51] that took place in Damascus in the summer (*Rosh Hodesh Ab*) of 1609 when Hayyim Vital was living there. This possession was different from that of Karo as the daughter of Raphael Anav was only a medium who served as the host for the *maggid*, who had come down from heaven to bring a message to Hayyim Vital.

Joseph Karo

The first person that we have contemporary accounts of their having received revelations through a *maggid*, a heavenly spiritual guide, was Rabbi Joseph Karo, the great halakhic authority and author of the great code the *Shulhan Arukh*.[52] Karo, Alkabetz, and a group of their disciples gathered to engage in the kabbalistic ritual that became known as Tikkun Leyl Shavuot on the first night of Shavuot, 1534 or 1535 in Adrianople, Turkey.[53] This was also the first time there is a record of anyone engaging in this ritual, though it had been described in the *Zohar*. Shortly after beginning the study of the Mishnah, a voice began to emanate from Karo that was not his own, a form of automatic speech. This voice identified itself as the personification of the Mishnah. Alkabetz and the others present heard the voice, which addressed not only Karo, but also all those who were present, and it encouraged them in their mystical devotions. The *maggid* remained in contact with Karo for the rest of his life. He recorded the messages of the *maggid* in a diary that was published as *Maggid Mesharim* (Lublin, 1646).

Our knowledge of this event comes from a letter that Shlomo Alkabetz sent to the sages of Salonika informing them of the events that had transpired regarding the appearance of Karo's *maggid*. The letter was eventually published as a preface to *Maggid Mesharim*, and shortly afterwards in the popular kabbalistic compendium *Shnei Luhot ha-Berit* (Amsterdam, 1649), authored by Rabbi Isaiah Horowitz.[54]

The relationship between Taitazak's *maggid* and Karo's *maggid* is not entirely clear. R. J. Z. Werblowsky originally suggested that Karo had been aware of Taitazak's *maggid*, and its messages had been transmitted through automatic writing,[55] while Karo's *maggid* had used the higher form of communication, direct speech. In addition, Karo's *maggid* was the Mishnah, and not merely an angel. Gershom Scholem, in his study of Taitazak, suggested that Werblowsky had "over interpreted" some of the evidence and offered an alternative interpretation. First, he suggested that while Taitazak was known as an important mystic, there is no evidence that the *Sefer ha-Meshiv* and his writing of it was publicly known at the time. Scholem further argued that whereas Karo's *maggid* was the Mishnah, which was a symbol of the *shekhinah* in kabbalah, Taitazak claimed to have received his revelations directly from God.[56]

The *maggidim* of both Taitazak and Karo were very personal affairs. In Taitazak's case there is no evidence that his contemporaries were even aware of his *Maggid* or its relation to him. It was only in the twentieth century that these writings and their connection to Taitazak were brought to light. Karo's contemporaries knew about his *Maggid*, and some of them even experienced the visitation of the *maggid*. Alkabetz describes hearing the voice of the *maggid* emanating from Karo's mouth, in his letter. Karo's diary, which recorded the instructions and teachings of the *maggid*, was published less than a century after Karo's death and is a well-known work. Yet, what the *maggidim* of Taitazak and Karo shared was that they were revelations directed to one person and did not have a significant impact on the larger community. They also did not affect or enhance the reputation of either of them in relation to their other works on which their reputations stood. Taitazak was known in his day as an important halakhic authority, biblical commentator, and philosopher.[57] Karo achieved exceptional fame and influence as the author of the *Beyt Yosef* and *Shulhan Arukh*, two works that remain the most basic and important works of halakhah to the present. To the extent that the *Maggid Mesharim* was the subject of discussion, it was about whether it was indeed an authentic work by Karo. Many questioned how it was possible for the author of the great halakhic code, the *Shulhan Arukh* to also be the author of a work that they found exceedingly strange. For many, the answer was that it was a forgery, and it was inconceivable for it to be the work of Karo. However, we do know that Karo did indeed record the revelations that he received from his *maggid*.[58]

The Second *Maggid* and the Daughter of Raphael Anav

An obvious question is what is the relation between these two *maggidic* events? How are they connected? It is clear from his *Book of Visions*, that Vital had a problematic relationship with Joseph Karo and that he felt the need to assert his superiority over Karo in a number of ways.

Vital asserts his importance in relation to some of the great scholars of Safed, but most notably R. Joseph Karo.[59] He reports that in his youth,

Karo was told by his *maggid* that Vital would be his successor (B.V. 1.3).[60] This prediction is fulfilled for Vital in several dreams, both in his youth and old age. The first dream he reports is one in which a wealthy man had died and the whole community, including Karo, attended his funeral. When the cantor told someone to put the deceased's *zizit* on his head, the deceased objected. All the assembled, including Karo, were powerless to do anything, until Vital compelled him to obey (B.V. 2.1). In another early dream, Vital ascends to Heaven where he has a vision of God, who tells him to sit at His right hand. Vital demurs, saying that this place had been reserved for Karo. God agreed, saying that He too had thought so originally but had decided that Karo should sit somewhere else, and Vital should sit there instead (B.V. 2.5).

In his later years (1608), Vital again had three dreams that demonstrated his superiority over Karo. In one dream, Adam is lying ill in the street in Safed near Karo's house, but it is Vital who brings him medications for his weak heart (B.V. 2.25). In another dream, it is Karo himself who is ill, and Vital heals him (B.V. 2.46). In the last dream, Karo tells Vital that the king is sending his viceroy to destroy and pillage the city, and he implores Vital to use his kabbalistic knowledge to save the city. The implication is that Vital's wisdom and powers are greater than Karo's, for he can perform deeds that the greatest halakhic authority is incapable of accomplishing. Vital's kabbalistic knowledge is more highly valued in heaven and more efficacious than halakhic knowledge.[61]

The second instance of a *maggid* possession is found in Hayyim Vital's *Book of Visions* and differs in significant ways from Joseph Karo's possession by a *maggid*. In this case Vital himself was not the one possessed, though he was the intended recipient of the *maggid*'s message. The person who is possessed by the *maggid* is "*the daughter of Raphael Anav.*" Her name is never mentioned, and no more details about her are found in the story. No reason is given why she was chosen to be the medium for this *maggid*. The *maggid* identified himself as the sage Piso, who had been a rabbi in Jerusalem. He told the assembled group that he had died thirty-five years ago but was sent back as a *maggid* to bring a message to Rabbi Hayyim Vital. Piso said that he had been negligent in bringing his community to do a complete repentance, and to atone for this act, he was being sent back to rebuke Hayyim Vital and urge him not to make the same mistake. The possession is an event that took place over a number of weeks and has many twists and turns. In the first event of possession, she was in a coma, and in later possessions, she was awake. We also learn that she had visions and heavenly messages long after her initial possession and continued to have visions and messages through the rest of her life.[62]

It is noteworthy that in the sections of Vital's diary immediately preceding this story, Vital talks about his frustrations with the Jewish community of Damascus who were not listening to preaching of repentance. This incident of the *maggid* is in the larger context of Vital's experiences in Damascus. It took place when Vital was an old man and bitter about his lack of professional success.[63] The *maggid* was not completely finished after he delivered his rebuke to Vital. Vital continues that a short time afterwards, the *maggid* returned and turned his wrath on Vital's nemesis in Damascus, Meir Abulafia, who was the rabbi of the community. Vital blamed his failures in Damascus on Abulafia's opposition, and the *maggid* chastised him for his bad behavior toward Vital.[64] The rebukes of Vital's *maggid* also mirror the key reason for Karo's *maggid*, to rebuke him for his spiritual shortcomings and guide him to the correct spiritual path. The fact is that Vital went to great lengths to discuss his superiority to Karo. Vital's *maggid* may have been another expression of his attempt to outdo Karo, as is seen from the many examples in the *Book of Visions*. In Vital's story, the *maggid*'s possession of the daughter of Raphael Anav is more closely related to the *dybbuk* since it is a possession by the soul of a human being (the sage Piso), as opposed to Karo's possession by the Mishnah, which was an angelic or other form of divine being.

In addition to the *maggid* as a source of mystical revelation, the kabbalists of Safed engaged in several other mystical practices to receive teaching from heavenly sources or the souls of deceased mystical and rabbinic figures who were buried in the vicinity of Safed. For example, Moses Cordovero and Solomon Alkabetz wandered the graves of the ancient sages scattered in the vicinity of Safed, which resulted in their finding themselves involuntarily uttering mystical interpretations of Torah. These teachings were collected in a small book called *Sefer Gerushin* (The Book of Wanderings).[65] Hayyim Vital, Isaac Luria's chief disciple, had a form of positive possession in addition to the practice of *yihudim*, taught to him by Luria. Vital engaged in the recitation of the Mishnah as a form of possession by the souls of ancient sages. He learned this from Joseph Karo but had his own variation of the procedure. Karo would recite significant amounts of Mishnah from memory to induce the appearance of his *maggid*. Vital's variation was to recite the same passage over and over, in order to receive a visitation from the sage mentioned in the passage he was reciting.[66] Another Safed figure associated with the Mishnah was Joseph Ashkenazi, who was known as "the *Tanna* of Safed" for his constant recitation of the Mishnah.[67] Of all of these forms of positive possession, the best known were the *yihudim*, associated with Isaac Luria.

Isaac Luria and *Yihudim*

In contrast to Rabbis Joseph Taitazak and Joseph Karo, the fame of Rabbi Isaac Luria rests completely on his charismatic authority.[68] He was the first significant Jewish religious figure who had a major influence on Jewish religious life and practice without having attained distinction as a halakhic authority or Talmudic commentator, through the publication of halakhic or rabbinic works that became authoritative. Isaac Luria was born in Jerusalem but moved to Cairo at a young age when his father died. His mother returned with him to her family. Isaac Luria received an excellent rabbinic education in Egypt before he came to Safed and was a student of Rabbi David ibn Zimra, a major halakhic authority and kabbalist, and Rabbi Bezalel Ashkenazi, author of the important halakhic work *Shita Mekubezet*. Luria was even a signatory to several halakhic decisions of his teacher, Rabbi Bezalel Ashkenazi.[69] Yet, halakhic or Talmudic expertise played no role in Luria's later fame.

Luria became a public figure several months after his arrival in Safed, in the spring of 1570. He had joined the circle of Rabbi Moses Cordovero, who was the most important kabbalist teaching in Safed at the time. Cordovero fell ill in the summer of 1570. Shortly before his death, his disciples asked for a sign that would help them discern who would be worthy to be Cordovero's successor. He responded that whoever saw the pillar of fire over his grave was the one destined to be his successor. At the funeral, Isaac Luria stated that the grave was being dug in the wrong place since there was a flame over another place in the cemetery.[70] This event was considered the moment when Luria first publicly displayed his spiritual attributes that made him qualified to be a spiritual leader.

There was a fundamental difference between the religious authority of Cordovero and Luria. Cordovero's authority derived from his status as an authoritative interpreter and commentator on the Zoharic kabbalistic tradition. He was considered its last and greatest interpreter before the innovations of Lurianic kabbalah. Thus, his authority derived from his being a link in the chain of tradition, in this case the kabbalistic tradition. Luria, in contrast, was the originator of a new kabbalistic tradition that derived in part from the Zoharic tradition, but that moved in a new direction. In addition to Luria's theoretical innovations, he was the most important source of authority for new kabbalistic rituals and traditions that transformed the practice of Judaism. Many of these traditions, like Tikkun Leyl Shavuot, had been mentioned in the *Zohar*, but there is no evidence of any group actively engaging in these rituals before the sixteenth century. Some other traditions, like Kabbalat Shabbat, were created by Safed kabbalists before the arrival of Luria, but later, it was under the umbrella of Isaac Luria and his charismatic authority that they were accepted by communities throughout the Jewish world. This raises the question, what was the source of Luria's religious authority that convinced his colleagues and disciples in Safed to accept his authority and from there to the whole Jewish world over the course of years?

Religious authority through divine revelation continued through the Middle Ages in a variety of forms.[71] One of the more popular forms was the revelation of Elijah the prophet. There was a venerable tradition that Elijah never died and continued to appear to worthy individuals.[72] There are traditions of Elijah's appearance to Rabbi Isaac Luria. According to Shloimel Dresnitz's hagiography, Luria spent six years in solitary study of the kabbalistic mysteries on a small island in the Nile, returning to his home only on Sabbaths and festivals. During these years, Elijah was a frequent visitor to Luria and taught him kabbalistic secrets. It was also Elijah who told Luria that the time had come for him to move to Safed and teach kabbalah.[73] Elijah continued to appear to Luria after his move to Safed, according to a variety of sources.[74] However, revelations from Elijah were not the primary source of Luria's religious authority in Safed. Rather, Luria's authority was based on a phenomenon unique to Safed and its environs, direct contact with the soul of Rabbi Simeon bar Yohai, the purported author of the *Zohar*, whose grave was in Meron, near Safed.

Luria communed with Rabbi Simeon bar Yohai, who was seen as his heavenly mentor and spiritual guide through a spiritual process called *yihudim* (unifications),[75] which was a version of the medieval kabbalistic concept of *ibbur*. The most important difference was that a *yihud* was a union and impregnation that could be invoked by the kabbalist through a series of prayers and mystical incantations, whereas *ibbur* was a process that was only initiated from heaven and was not in the control of the human being who was impregnated. A *yihud* could take place at the grave of the deceased saint with whom one wished to communicate, or when this was not practical, in one's home. Of the two, the communion at the gravesite was more desirable and effective. R. Shloimel Dresnitz, author of the first hagiography of Rabbi Isaac Luria, quoted several descriptions of Luria's practice of *yihudim*, by disciples who had accompanied him on his visits to Meron to prostrate himself on the grave of Rabbi Simeon bar Yohai, and invite the soul of the deceased to come down from heaven and unite with his soul in his body. When this union was accomplished, Luria could communicate with Rabbi Simeon's soul and acquire information about future events or obtain a better understanding of a text that was not clear. Following are two descriptions of *yihudim* by Luria when he was accompanied by some of his disciples:

> Once the rabbi went to prostrate himself upon the grave of Shemaya and Avtalyon in Gush Halav,[76] at a distance of one *parsa*, for the purpose of inquiring of them the true secrets of the Torah. For such was his custom. Whenever he desired to speak with a prophet or a certain *Tanna*, he would travel to his grave and lay himself down upon it with outstretched arms and feet, *"putting his mouth upon his mouth . . ."* [2 Kings 4:34], as Elisha did with Habakkuk.[77] He would concentrate upon a *yihud*, and elevate the *nefesh, ruah,* and *neshamah*[78] of this *zaddiq*. . . . He would bind his own *nefesh, ruah,* and *neshamah* to those of the *zaddiq*, and bring about supernal unification. By means of the *yihud*, the soul of this *zaddiq* would be invested with a new light, greater than that which he had previously [during his lifetime]. In this way, the dry bones that lie in the grave revived: the *nefesh, ruah,* and *neshamah* of that *zaddiq* descended to his bones, bringing him to actual life, [and] speaking with him [i.e., Luria] as a man speaks to his neighbor, revealing to him all the secrets of the Torah concerning which he asks of him. All of these *yihudim* are in my possession, written down, praised be God. For the rabbi transmitted them to his disciples, all ten of whom successfully practiced them. As a consequence, the *zaddiqim* [with whom they commune] spoke to them, answering all their questions. However, they possessed the strength to do this only during the rabbi's lifetime. After his death, their efforts were without

success, with the exception of [those of] our teacher, Rabbi Hayyim [Vital] Calabrese, may God protect and preserve him, who successfully practices them to this day.[79]

Another description of *yihudim* by Luria is found in another of Dresnitz's letters. Hayyim Vital described what he saw when he accompanied Luria on one of his visits to the tomb of Rabbi Simeon bar Yohai.

> He [Luria] used to stretch himself out on the tomb of R. Simeon bar Yohai, and he knew how to cleave Spirit to Spirit, and to concentrate on binding and raising up his soul with that of R. Simeon until he brought about unity above. Afterwards, R. Simeon's soul descended into his body, and R. Simeon would speak with him, revealing to him all that he had learned in the academy on high, as a man speaks with his neighbor.[80]

Despite the optimistic comment at the end of the first passage that Luria's closest disciples could also perform *yihudim* during his lifetime, Hayyim Vital after Luria's death, presents a more sober assessment in his mystical diary, *Sefer Hezyonot* (Book of Visions). Luria reproved Vital because he saw with his powers that Vital was not being diligent in performing the *yihudim* that Luria had taught. In his defense, Vital admitted that he was not able to succeed in having the souls appear to him as they were supposed to.[81] If Luria's *yihudim* were only replicable by others with the active assistance of Luria, then the whole structure rested on the charismatic authority of Luria. After his death, it was only the teachings preserved in the writings of his disciples and the remembrances of his actions that provided the authority of Lurianic kabbalah. It is even more remarkable when one remembers that Luria was in a leadership position in Safed for only two years and two weeks.[82] The inability to replicate Luria's charismatic skills becomes important later when we consider the question of exorcizing a *dybbuk* and how this feat was achieved. It should also be noted that visiting and venerating the graves of holy figures in the Galilee was a widespread practice by many kabbalists in the sixteenth century.[83] At the same time, none of these other practices had the impact or influence of Luria's practice of *yihudim*.

Conclusions

The *dybbuk* first appears in Safed during the short period of Rabbi Isaac Luria's sojourn. Moshe Idel has observed that the concepts of the *maggid* and the *dybbuk* are two sides of the same coin, and it is no accident that both of them first appeared in the same place at the same time.[84] The ideas that come together to form the concept of the *dybbuk* have antecedents in the kabbalistic concepts of *gilgul* and *ibbur*, along with the widely disseminated story of Rabbi Akiva and the Dead Man. This is the first source that posits the idea that the soul of a person survives in the physical world after death and that this is a form of punishment. The concept is picked up in medieval kabbalah, where it has a variety of permutations and the sins that lead to the wandering of the soul begin with sexual sins and slowly the roster of sin is expanded. In the fifteenth century, the concept of *gilgul* becomes the subject of public debate and greater awareness of the concept. All of these pieces came together in Safed and in the person of Isaac Luria, who engaged in *yihudim* to communicate with the soul of Rabbi Simeon bar Yohai and was the only one who was able to exorcise a *dybbuk*, who possessed a person, through the use of *yihudim*. His disciple, Hayyim Vital, was able to exorcise a *dybbuk* with Luria's advice and guidance, but there is no evidence of Vital exorcizing *dybbukim* on his own authority after Luria's death.

Were one to see R. Isaac Luria as he engaged in one of his *yihudim* in Meron, one would see little beyond Luria lying on the grave, praying and perhaps some small bodily movement. On the other hand, the positive and negative public manifestations of *dybbukim* and *maggidim* were public events that the community could see and hear. They helped reinforce Luria's claims to spiritual authority. Having seen a *dybbuk* possess someone or hearing from eyewitnesses about Karo's *maggid* gave greater credence to the idea that Luria could meditate on the grave of a great Talmudic figure like Rabbi Shimon bar Yohai. He could also come back with new interpretations and teachings that derived from a heavenly source that vouched for the authenticity and authority of the new teachings and rituals. This also vouchsafed for the religious authority of the kabbalists who were initiating and teaching these new teachings and rituals.

Chapter 2

Dybbuk Possession in Safed in the Sixteenth Century

The *dybbuk* stories that originate in Safed will be considered in two parts. The first part are stories from primary sources that discuss exorcisms in Safed. The second part will discuss the publication and public dissemination of Safed exorcism stories that were published in the seventeenth century. The earliest story is an unusual story of an exorcism by Rabbi Joseph Karo that is preserved in Rabbi Judah Halliwah's "Zofnat Paneah," which remains in manuscript. The second group of stories are derived from Rabbi Hayyim Vital's mystical autobiography/diary, *The Book of Visions* (*Sefer Hezyonot*). There is also an incident that occurred in Safed during Luria's lifetime that involved both Rabbi Isaac Luria and Vital but was not published until the seventeenth century. It relates the possession of the nephew of Rabbi Joshua bin Nun, an important figure in Safed during this period. There is another Safed exorcism story that does not involve either Luria or Vital. It is an exorcism by Elijah Falco, an erstwhile disciple of Luria. It plays an influential role in the dissemination and publication of the *dybbuk* stories in the seventeenth century. There are a variety of issues relating to this story that make it more appropriate to be discussed in the context of the publications of *dybbuk* stories in the first half of the seventeenth century.

The *Dybbuk* Exorcised by Rabbi Joseph Karo

The concept of *gilgul* was a topic of discussion among the kabbalists of Safed before the arrival of Isaac Luria in Safed. Several of the important figures in Safed discussed the theory of *gilgul* and offered a variety of reasons for why a soul would transmigrate. Solomon Alkabetz in his commentary on the Book of Ruth offered three reasons for transmigration. The main theme was that this was an opportunity to finish an unfinished task, such as not having children, and not fulfilling the first commandment of "be fruitful and multiply." Another motif was the atonement for a sin or sins committed in a previous lifetime. These discussions were mostly abstract and theoretical. Certain biblical stories, like that of Job, were cited as illustrations. Job was righteous, but his soul had not been righteous in a previous lifetime, and that is why he was being punished. As a result, both Job and his friends were justified. Job was indeed righteous in this lifetime, but he was being punished for transgressions in a previous lifetime.[1] However, these discussions were primarily in the realm of theory, and there were no contemporary examples of an actual soul becoming a *dybbuk* before the arrival of Isaac Luria, with the one exception.

As mentioned above, the first *dybbuk* text from Safed is from Rabbi Judah Halliwah's work, "Zofnat Pa'aneah," which remains in manuscript. R. Judah was a kabbalist active in Safed in the middle of the sixteenth century.[2] This story of an exorcism by Rabbi Joseph Karo that took place in Safed in 1545 was first published in an article by Moshe Idel.[3]

Karo was not known as an exorcist or miracle worker from other sources, and more research is needed before conclusions can be reached about this event. While some of the details of this story are compared to those found in Hayyim Vital's *Sefer Hezyonot*, there are significant differences. Two unusual elements in this story are that Karo threatened the Spirit with torture and that the Spirit was seeking revenge against the person who was being possessed for prior acts against the Spirit. The motif of physical coercion is reminiscent of the pre-Safed discussions of the exorcism of demons and evil spirits. It is also a motif in the Falco Letter, which will be discussed below. It was very different from the methods utilized by Isaac Luria. The motif seeking revenge is similar to the story of the nephew of Joshua bin Nun found in Shlomo ben Gabbi, *Sefer Meirat Eyna'im*, discussed below. Is this story evidence for some charismatic powers that Karo possessed as they are in Vital's stories about Isaac Luria?

The "exorcism" is more reminiscent of an expulsion of a demon or evil spirit found in earlier literature, and unlike the exorcisms of Rabbi Isaac Luria and Vital. The story occurred in 1545, long before Luria's arrival in Safed. A Spirit entered a young man who had an epileptic fit and spoke great things. Karo's method of learning about the spirit and eventually healing the youth is related to the earlier tradition of exorcizing demons and evil spirits discussed above and is not related to Luria and Vital and their methods of exorcism. It may well be an example that lends credence to the idea to be considered below that the exorcisms of *dybbukim* by Luria and Vital are outliers in the broader history of possession and exorcism in the Jewish tradition.[4]

Exorcisms in the *Book of Visions*

A primary source for possession stories from the sixteenth century is Hayyim Vital's mystical diary, *Sefer Hezyonot* (Book of Visions). The history of the manuscript of the *Sefer Hezyonot* (Book of Visions) and its eventual publication is complicated and worth recounting. This diary was preserved in one manuscript that has been verified by leading experts to have been written by Hayyim Vital himself. Moshe Vital, Hayyim Vital's grandson, found the manuscript among a batch of his grandfather's papers and prepared an abbreviated version containing mostly biographical information. Several manuscript copies of this abbreviated text exist. It was first printed in Ostraha in 1826 and reprinted numerous times under the title *Praises of Rabbi Hayyim Vital* (*Shivhei Rabbi Hayyim Vital*).[5] The title was clearly modeled after the earlier hagiography of Rabbi Isaac Luria, *Praises of the AR"I* (*Shivhei ha-AR"I*). The great scholar and bibliophile Rabbi Hayyim Joseph Azulay mentions having seen a copy of Vital's diary that he named *Sefer Hezyonot* (Book of Visions), in his classic bibliographical work, *Shem ha-Gedolim*.[6] The abbreviated text was the only version of this work known before the discovery of the complete manuscript of the *Sefer Hezyonot* (Book of Visions) by Aaron Zeev Aescoli.[7]

The first edition of the complete *Sefer ha-Hezyonot* was published in 1954 by several of Aescoli's colleagues, after Aescoli's untimely death.[8] Shortly after the publication of the book, several influential rabbis declared that this book could not be the work of a holy and pious rabbi like Hayyim Vital because of certain statements and several stories in it that could not have been written by such a holy person. It was reminiscent of the opposition to the authenticity of Rabbi Joseph Karo's *Maggid Mesharim*, discussed above.[9] In response, the publisher withdrew all copies that not yet been distributed, and the book became a rarity. I published an English translation of the *Sefer ha-Hezyonot* in 1999, using the Aescoli edition as the basis for the translation.[10] I then reedited the Hebrew text using a copy of the original photocopy of the manuscript used by Aescoli in consultation with Aescoli's edition.[11] This edition was published by the Ben Zvi Institute in Jerusalem.[12]

The differences between the Aescoli edition and my edition are several. Aescoli's edition contains five parts, while my edition does not contain the fifth and last part. The reason for this is that when the photocopy of the original manuscript was examined, it was discovered that the fifth part was written in different handwriting, in the style of Italy in the seventeenth century. After discussion and consultations with the leading experts in the field, it was decided that this section should be deleted from the new edition, leaving only those parts that were in Vital's own handwriting. My edition adds an introduction, and the annotations were expanded beyond those in Aescoli's edition.

There are only three stories about *dybbukim* and exorcisms in the *Book of Visions*. Two of them are fragmentary accounts that involve Vital as exorcist, and the third, most complicated one, involves Vital as the one being possessed. What stands out is the relative lack of interest by Vital in the *dybbuk* or the exorcism. In the two cases where Vital is the exorcist, the aspect of interest is not the *dybbuk* or the exorcism but ancillary aspects that illustrate the holiness of Vital as seen by others. He has no interest in the subject of exorcism beyond the aspect that aggrandizes him and his holiness. Another aspect of note is that aside from the exorcism of the *dybbuk* from Vital himself, Isaac Luria does not have much interest in exorcising a *dybbuk*. In the case found in the *Book of Visions*, Luria is busy and sends Vital to solve the problem. Similarly, in a story first published in the seventeenth century where Luria is mentioned, he demurs from taking an active role. There are no obvious reasons for these issues.

Exorcisms by Hayyim Vital in the *Book of Visions*

The Widow in Safed (*Book of Visions* 1.25 [73])

At the end of the first part of his mystical diary, Hayyim Vital has several paragraphs that describe signs seen by other people that testified to

Vital's greatness.[13] Among them are descriptions of haloes of light or a pillar of fire seen around or above Vital. The first of these visions of light relates to Vital's attempt to exorcise a *dybbuk*. It is a brief account. Vital says that his teacher, Rabbi Isaac Luria, taught him how to exorcise evil Spirits with a *yihud* (unification). He describes how he came to the home of the woman who had been possessed. When he sat down near her, the *dybbuk* turned away from him. Vital was so angered by this lack of respect that he slapped "his" face. The evil Spirit protested and asked why Vital had done this and explained that he meant no disrespect. Rather, Vital's face burned like a flame and the *dybbuk* feared that Vital's great holiness would burn his soul.

What is fascinating about this little story is that it is all about the evil Spirit recognizing the greatness and holiness of Vital. Vital does not even bother to mention what happened with the exorcism. Did he succeed in exorcising the *dybbuk* with the *yihud* that he had been taught? We know from other sources that when Isaac Luria tried to teach his students how to do *yihudim* to contact the souls of rabbinic and mystical worthies buried in the vicinity of Safed and Meron, he met with limited success. Vital himself mentions his difficulties achieving the state of *yihud* when he attempted it.[14]

There are two important additions to this story found in other sources that expand and illuminate it. Shloimel Dresnitz was a kabbalist who came from Europe to learn about Isaac Luria and the kabbalistic renaissance in Safed. He arrived almost thirty years after Luria's death and the deaths or departures of many in Luria's circle. He wrote four letters to a friend in Europe describing what he had seen and heard in Safed.[15] Appended to the end of the third letter he wrote was a description of a *dybbuk* exorcism that is based on this incident mentioned by Vital. Dresnitz's description of this possession and exorcism is much longer and detailed than what we find in Vital's account. This text was first published in 1629 and will be discussed below in the next chapter.

Vital reports in the story of the widow that Rabbi Isaac Luria taught him a *yihud* that would enable him to overcome and exorcise the *dybbuk* who had possessed the widow, but he does not provide any details. However, this information is found in another of Vital's writings, *Sha'ar Ruah ha-Kodesh* (Gate of the Holy Spirit), which is devoted to attaining a variety of elevated spiritual states. The *yihud* for exorcising a *dybbuk* is included among the *yihudim* for various purposes found in this volume.[16] Several things are important about this *yihud*. First and foremost, it shows that exorcising a *dybbuk* is a complicated and spiritually dangerous task that should only be undertaken by a person of the highest spiritual attainment and an expert in the intricacies of kabbalah. Second, when one compares it to the later descriptions of exorcisms, the differences are great. This is also true when one compares it to the two most important texts of the seventeenth century that describe exorcisms and are the models for subsequent descriptions of *dybbuk* exorcisms. These two are the story of an exorcism described in the letter of Shloimel Dresnitz, and the other foundational document is a description by Elijah Falco, who had studied with Isaac Luria but was thrown out of Luria's circle for reasons that are unclear. This letter has come to be known as the Falco Letter. The significance of these differences will be discussed in the next chapter.

The Daughter of Daniel Romano (*Book of Visions* 2.35 [97])

The second story that Vital describes in the *Book of Visions* is even more prosaic. It takes place many years after Vital and left Safed and was living in Damascus. He reports that he had a dream in which a wealthy man who had died in Damascus a year before came to him in a dream and asked that Vital save his soul. The person said that Vital was the only one in the generation who was able to save him. The next morning, Daniel Romano came to Vital with his daughter, who was possessed. Vital reports that he healed her, and there is no further report. Again, the point of the story is that someone recognized Vital's greatness. That it was a *dybbuk* exorcism is an afterthought.

It is noteworthy that there would be no *dybbuk* stories if all we had were the stories that are found in Vital's *Book of Visions*. At best, these stories would merit a footnote or two in the analysis of Luria's practice of *yihudim*. It is also interesting that Isaac Luria rarely was an active participant in the exorcism stories found in Vital's writings and also in the later traditions that will be discussed in the next chapter. There two exceptions, and in both cases the circumstances are unusual. The first case is his active participation in the exorcism of a *dybbuk* from his disciple, Hayyim Vital. The second one is the possession of the nephew of Rabbi Joshua bin Nun. Rabbi Joshua bin Nun was one of the wealthiest people in Safed and was a major financial supporter of the scholars and yeshivas of Safed. This may well explain the participation of Rabbi Isaac Luria in his nephew's situation.

The Possession of Hayyim Vital

The most unusual story of *dybbuk* possession in Safed is the possession of Hayyim Vital himself.[17] There is no direct account of this incident; it must be pieced together from a series of fragments inside the larger story of events that transpired over a period of months in the spring and summer of 1609 in Damascus. The image that Hayyim Vital presents of himself in the *Book of Visions* is of a figure who was born to accomplish great things and even one who had a messianic mission.[18] Vital tried to lead the community of Luria's disciples in Safed after his teacher's death, with little success.[19] He left Safed, spent some time in Jerusalem, and spent the last twenty years of his life in Damascus, dying there at the age of seventy-seven in 1620. His time in Damascus was a period of great difficulty, materially and spiritually. He saw his primary mission as preaching repentance to the Jews in Damascus, and through this he would fulfill the messianic expectations that had been a part of his time in Safed with his teacher, R. Isaac Luria. A theme that runs through his diary is the difficulty of bringing his message of repentance to the Jews of Damascus and the enmity of the other rabbis in the city. The year 1609 was particularly difficult for Vital. He was meeting with greater than normal resistance to his preaching and efforts to bring the messianic age closer. As a result, he became depressed and despaired of success in his mission.[20] During the Intermediate days of Passover, he sent a disciple to visit a magician to learn what he was doing wrong and what he should do to be more successful in his spiritual endeavors. Seeking the advice and counsel of a variety of seers and visionaries, male and female, Jewish and non-Jewish, was not unusual for Vital. Vital describes a few such encounters throughout his *Book of Visions*.

R. Jacob Segura, his disciple, went to the house of a magician who was expert in geomancy and seeing demons. He first cast the sand lots with a spell as was customary. He asked: "Who is R. Hayyim Vital the kabbalist and for what purpose was he created?" They answered him: "You are not asking about yourself, but about someone else. He is a very exalted person, and every day he meditates privately and grieves over one matter that he longs for."[21]

The next day, the magician came to Vital's house to meet him, having heard of his greatness from the various heavenly and demonic beings. The big question that Vital had was, "Why has my teacher *z"l* not been revealed to me in a dream for a long time, as he had previously?"

The answer that he received was that his teacher, R. Isaac Luria, was upset with him because he was not doing his utmost to cause people to repent. "You have already been informed that you only came into the world to cause the people to repent. Previously, you responded, but now you desist, therefore I also desisted from coming to you."[22] Vital was still not satisfied with the responses he had received. On the one hand, he had been assured of his greatness, but at the same time, he was castigated for not fulfilling his mission, which was to finish the task begun by his teacher, to bring the Messiah.

That summer, on the 29th of Tammuz, "A great thing occurred in Damascus," as Vital puts it. The daughter of Raphael Anav was possessed by a Spirit, the sage Piso, who had been sent from heaven to bring several messages to the Jews of Damascus, and more specifically to Hayyim Vital.[23] The tenor of the messages that were directed to Vital were similar to what he had heard from the previous séances with other magicians and seers. The sage Piso had a message for Vital, but Vital did not come to the house of Raphael Anav to hear the message, and Piso left after the Sabbath. Raphael Anav's daughter had a series of visions and visitations from an angel after the departure of the sage Piso. As before, Vital was very concerned that he still was not receiving communications from his teacher, R. Isaac Luria. He had the opportunity to ask the angel through her why he still had no communication with his teacher.

> The tenth of *Ab*. I [Vital] asked her via her father: Why does the *zaddiq* known to me refuse to speak to me? What is his name and is there any hope that he will return? She responded that on the night of the eleventh of *Ab* she saw my teacher *z"l* and he said to her: Tell him in my name, that he should not ask these questions so many times. I cannot answer him, except for these three words: "Happy are the dead in your house."[24] He will understand the meaning of these words himself.
>
> The night of the twelfth of *Ab*. In a dream, she saw my teacher *z"l* in a cave and he said to her: What did R. Hayyim reply to you? She said to him: He told me that he did not understand the three words. He said to her: Such an easy thing. Has his intellect been so retarded that he did not understand? Where is the wisdom that I taught him?

> Remind him of the evil Spirit [*ruah ha-ra'ah*] that I expelled from him. It has been four years that he has not seen me in a dream. Now I planned to return to him, but since he does not understand my response, I do not want to return to him.
>
> In my humble opinion, the meaning of the above-mentioned evil Spirit concerns the resurrection of the dead. He revived me on our journey to Kfar Akhbara because of the Spirit who was in the grave of the gentile injured me, or perhaps it is related to what twisted my mouth with the first Unification that I taught myself.[25]

In his response to Vital, his teacher alluded to two incidents that happened while Isaac Luria was still alive where Vital did not listen to Luria's instructions. It was this disobedience that caused him not to visit Vital in his dreams for more than four years. The second incident was a minor infraction where Vital tried to perform a unification, and it harmed him in a minor way that Luria was able to correct.[26] The first incident mentioned had some connection to an evil Spirit (*ruah ha-ra'ah*) that possessed Vital, and apparently Vital had forgotten about that incident. He does not even understand why Luria is upset even when Luria gives him a hint. The story that Luria was alluding to is not found in the *Book of Visions*, but is found in a different work, the *Sha'ar ha-Gilgulim*. Vital describes the following incident, which I believe is the event alluded to by Luria.

> In the year 5332 [1572], we went out in the fields, and we passed the ancient grave of a gentile [*goy*] that was more than a thousand years old. He saw my Animus [*Nefesh*] from his tombstone and he tried to harm me and kill me. There were many angels and innumerable Souls [*Neshamot*] of *zaddiqim* arrayed to my right and left, and he was powerless to harm me. My teacher commanded me that when I return, I should not do so on that road. Afterwards, the Animus [*Nefesh*] of that gentile followed me from a distance. There in the field I became angry with Rabbi Judah Mishan[27] and the Animus of the gentile began to attach itself to me and cause me to sin even more and I did not want to listen to the teachings

of my teacher, z"l. He began to cry and said: all the Souls and angels have left him because of the anger and as a result that Animus rules over him. What shall I do? I wish that he would harm him and let him remain living; then I will be able to heal him. However, I fear that he will kill him and everything that I think will repair the world will not be accomplished by him, as is known to me. I could not tell, since I had not been given permission, whether I have struggled for nothing, and the world would be destroyed. He did not eat the whole night out of anguish and worry. I returned on that road alone. When I reached his grave, a wind lifted me and I saw myself in the air, running twenty stories above the ground until I reached a land at nightfall and was left there. I slept soundly until morning. I wanted to get up, but all of my limbs were very weak and painful, but I slowly reached the door of my teacher, z"l. When I arrived, I was barely alive, like Jonah, and my teacher laid me on his bed, closed the door, and prayed. Afterwards, he entered the house alone, walked around the house, returned to the bed, and stretched himself over me.[28] He did this until noon, when I was almost dead, and at noon I saw myself that my Soul was slowly returning to me until I opened my eyes, got up, and recited the blessing "*He who resurrects the dead.*" All this is absolutely and undoubtedly true.[29]

There are many interesting aspects to this story, but the one that interests us most here is the identity of this evil Spirit (*ruah ha-ra'ah*) who was so powerful that he was able to overcome and possess Hayyim Vital and come close to withstanding the best efforts of Isaac Luria to exorcise him. Vital calls him a gentile (*goy*), in other words, a non-Jew. The problem is that according to kabbalistic concepts of the soul, only a Jew has a Spirit (*Ruah*) that can possess another Jew.[30] Further, Luria uses the term evil Spirit (*ruah ha-ra'ah*), which is the term used for a *dybbuk* in all the Safed possession stories. Who was this spirit of a Jew who was so powerful that he could overcome a great kabbalist like Vital and at the same time so evil that he would want to kill Vital and by doing so, put an end to his messianic mission to bring repentance and redemption to the Jews? The answer is found in the *Hakdamah* 37, the one before this one, which describes how Luria wandered around the environs surrounding Safed with his disciples and identified the graves of a wide variety of figures, including Talmudic figures and most of the individuals mentioned in the *Zohar*. Surprisingly, one of the graves that Luria "identified" is that of Jesus of Nazareth. We find in the *Sha'ar ha-Gilgulim*:

> To the north of Safed, may it be rebuilt and reestablished in our day, going from Safed in a northern direction to the village of Ein Zeitun [the spring of olives], there is a carob tree by the road. That is the grave of Jesus the Nazarene, may his name and memory be blotted out. There is a crossroads there. To the right you continue to Ein Zeitun, and to the left it goes to the Kharal, as mentioned.[31] In the middle of these two paths there is a large valley of olive trees.[32]

The idea that Jesus was buried in the Galilee may sound strange at first. However, as Elhanan Reiner has shown in an important study, there is a long tradition about important figures named Joshua and their connection to the Galilee.[33] The indication from the evidence cited above seems to be the following: the Galilean traditions about Joshua son of Nun, Joshua son of Jehozadak the priest, the priestly course of Joshua, and, in particular, the traditions about Joshua son of Perahiah and Jesus Christ[34] represent different treatments of a general tradition about the name Joshua-Jeshua-Jesus, perhaps as a name with magical qualities or as a general myth about a redeemer or messiah of that name who is clearly associated with the Galilean geographical context here considered.[35] Ze'ev Vilnay, in his authoritative guidebook to the land of Israel, reports an interesting legend about a certain spot in the vicinity of Ein Zeitun that appears to be the abode of a powerful demonic figure:

> The road from Ein Zeitun to Meron. To the intermittent spring . . . the road turns left to the intermittent spring, called in Arabic the spring of the demon. Arab legend tells that a demon lives in the depths of this spring, who stops the waters that flow from this spring, from time to time. The Muslim a-Dimaski, who was the ruler of Safed, talks about this spring in 1310. People would come to drink the water and wash in the spring. Suddenly, the water flow stopped, and the spring dried up, as if it had never had water. The people then called

out "Holy Sheik!³⁶ We are thirsty"—and the water appeared. After some time, the water stopped again, and they called out again, and the water flowed again.³⁷

To summarize the evidence that has been presented: Vital was possessed by a powerful evil Spirit when his spiritual defenses were lowered in a moment when he had been angry at Rabbi Judah Mishan, as they were passing near the grave of Jesus. Anger was one of Vital's weaknesses because he came from the root soul of Cain. It is noteworthy that immediately following the story of his possession, there is a discussion about Cain and the negative impact of anger.³⁸ What other Jew is buried in the vicinity of Ein Zeitun, according to the teachings of R. Isaac Luria, who is so powerful and so evil that he could bring Hayyim Vital to death's door, and by doing so destroy Luria's hopes to bring the Messiah with the assistance of Hayyim Vital? Within the universe of Lurianic kabbalah and the stories found in Vital's mystical diary, the *Book of Visions*, it can only be Jesus of Nazareth who was the evil Spirit that possessed Hayyim Vital. In the universe of Safed kabbalists, Jesus may have been a heretic as described in the Talmudic stories where he is mentioned, but this does not diminish his status as a Jew.³⁹

The Possession of the Nephew of Rabbi Joshua bin Nun

Rabbi Joshua bin Nun was a well-known figure in Safed. He is particularly known regarding two events. In 1575, after the death of Rabbi Isaac Luria, Vital made his disciples sign a document obligating them to share their knowledge of Luria's teaching only with Vital and no others. Vital wanted to be the authorized interpreter of Luria's teachings. Twelve people signed the document. Nine of them were direct disciples of Luria. Rabbi Joshua bin Nun was one of the latter three.⁴⁰ The second story is found in one of Shloimel Dresnitz's letters. Dresnitz tells how during a time when Vital was seriously ill, Bin Nun who was very wealthy bribed Vital's brother and hired scribes who transcribed six hundred pages of Vital's writings in a three-day period when Vital was in a coma.⁴¹

The details of the story differ in significant ways from the more standard *dybbuk* story. The story does not start with the appearance of the *dybbuk*, but rather the young man in question had been ill for many years, and no medical care helped. The possibility of epilepsy is mentioned in the story as a cause of the illness. Already in the ancient world, a common explanation for epilepsy was possession by a demon or evil Spirit. This explains why the family in desperation turned to Rabbi Isaac Luria in search of a spiritual cause for the illness. He examined the young man and decided that he was possessed by a *dybbuk*. Luria compelled the *dybbuk* to explain why he was possessing the young man. At this point, the story becomes very similar to the possession story of Rabbi Joseph Karo with the *dybbuk* seeking revenge for an incident where they had interacted in a previous life, and the *dybbuk* had been harmed by the soul of the young man. These similarities raise questions about the veracity of the details. Could it be a conflation of an actual incident to which was attached the Karo story to explain why the young man died despite the efforts of the great kabbalist, Isaac Luria. Bin Nun was not only a scholar but very wealthy and a financial supporter of many of the yeshivot in Safed, and yet Luria could not save his nephew. A supernatural reason could be the only answer.

This story took place in Safed and mentioned people known in Safed, but the story was not published until the middle of the seventeenth century and is found in two separate accounts that are roughly contemporary. The broad outline of both versions is similar, but there are interesting differences in the details.

Conclusions

The primary conclusion that can be drawn from the Safed *dybbuk* stories is that *dybbuk* possession was a reality in Safed, but it was a relatively rare phenomenon. We only have a handful of stories about *dybbuk* possession. The first story, involving the greatest halakhic scholar of the age, Rabbi Joseph Karo, is highly unusual and needs more study before conclusions can be drawn about it. The first desideratum is a more thorough analysis of the text where this story occurs, *Sefer ha-Meshiv*. The larger context may shed more light on the issues surrounding the story and the activities of Rabbi Karo. The *Maggid Mesharim* demonstrates that there was a mystical side to Karo, and the idea that he would exorcize a *dybbuk* is well within the realm of possibility. However, many questions remain to be answered. Was this the only incident of this kind in his career? What was the significance of this story? Since it seems to have been the first event of its kind, the question of why then and there is of great importance in understanding the origins of this concept. Until more information is discovered, it is difficult to draw any conclusions about this incident. Was it a unique event, or was it a role model for the later incidents that are found in Vital's *Sefer Hezyonot*? There is a twenty-five-year gap between Karo's incident and Vital's events. Finally, the Karo incident is much closer in style and format to the traditional exorcism accounts that have a long history. Thus, it can be argued that it is another story in a long tradition. It has more in common with the exorcism attributed to Elijah Falco, the erstwhile disciple of Isaac Luria, who also claimed to have exorcized a *dybbuk*. On the other hand, the exorcisms we read about in connection with Luria and Vital have a different methodology and motivation.

The stories found in Vital's *Sefer Hezyonot* primarily revolve around Vital and his own experiences. Therefore, it is not surprising that Vital's descriptions of these events revolve around his participation in those things that redound to his glory. An interesting example is the very detailed secondhand account that describes an exorcism that is mentioned by Vital. What Vital mentions in passing is described in great and extended detail by an outside observer. Shloimel Dresnitz's account has many vivid details about the story of Vital's exorcism of the widow in Safed.[42] Vital's own possession is a fascinating incident, which Vital does not discuss, but must be pieced together from fragments that he mentions in passing to explain other events that are more important to him and his crafting of his persona. Finally, there is another aspect of the possession stories in the *Sefer Hezyonot* that deserves consideration. That is the almost complete absence of Rabbi Isaac Luria. Aside from his involvement in the exorcism of Vital by Luria, which is not surprising since no one else could do it, Luria is mentioned twice in connection with an exorcism. The first is the story of the widow, where Luria teaches Vital the *yihud* and tells him to go and exorcise the *dybbuk*. What does this say about Luria and his attitude to *dybbuk* possession? One can interpret this in two ways; either it was part of Vital's apprenticeship, or Luria did not consider it important enough for him to disrupt his study or teaching to deal with it. In the story where Luria is asked to exorcise someone associated with a very important family in Safed, the nephew of Joshua bin Nun, the key point is that there too he demurs from becoming involved in the problem of exorcizing a *dybbuk*. It is also interesting that this story was told secondhand and is recounted in much greater detail than the exorcism accounts found in Vital's *Sefer Hezyonot*.

The key conclusion from this study of the *dybbuk* stories in Safed is that the origins of the *dybbuk* phenomenon are to be found in Safed in the sixteenth century. At the same time, it would appear that some of these stories were not published until much later. Vital's *Sefer Hezyonot* was not fully published until 1954, and the earlier abridged version did not include the *dybbuk* stories. At the same time, some *dybbuk* stories were transmitted orally before they were committed to writings. Several of them formed the foundations for the first published accounts in the seventeenth century, and it is these accounts that are the basis of the *dybbuk* stories that were disseminated in the following centuries. The next chapter will discuss and analyze the *dybbuk* stories that were the foundation of the later traditions.

There are two Italian exorcism stories, one from the sixteenth century and one from the seventeenth century, that are mentioned for the sake of completeness, but in fact have nothing in common with the Safed exorcism tradition.[43] The first story is found in *Shalshelet ha-Kabbalah* by Gedaliah ibn Yahia, first published in Venice in 1587. The story has nothing to do with the Safed *dybbuk* tradition but has many elements common to Christian and Jewish Italian popular culture and is influenced by Christian ghost stories, as mentioned above. A recent study by Roni Weinstein has documented the closeness of the Jewish and Catholic communities during this period with regard to the influence of magic on popular culture in Italy.[44] The second incident is a passage in a letter by Rabbi Moses Zacuto in 1672. It is a description of how to react if one is confronted with a woman who is possessed. This story is in many ways a harbinger of what comes later. The rabbis did not know how to exorcize the *dybbuk* using the Lurianic methods, which were unknown to them, so they resorted to the traditional methods of exorcizing a demon or evil Spirit that were well known and practiced since the Talmudic period. The second half of the seventeenth century was the beginning of a new tradition of *dybbuk* exorcisms by *ba'alei shem*, who utilized the traditional methods of exorcism, as will be discussed below. The Zacuto story is an early version of this later tradition that is a revival of the older methods of dealing with demons and evil Spirits.[45]

Chapter 3

The Published *Dybbuk* Accounts in the First Half of the Seventeenth Century

The first published accounts of *dybbuk* possession and exorcism appeared in the first half of the seventeenth century. There are two very different texts that are basic for the dissemination of the *dybbuk* legend in broader Jewish society. These two stories are the Shloimel Dresnitz Letter and the Elijah Falco Letter. Their origins and the exorcisms they describe are very different in form and content, and each will be discussed as a separate entity. Each of these two core texts was published in more than one version. These versions and their significance will be discussed in the respective sections. The earliest published account of a *dybbuk* possession was hidden in a large collection of 254 stories about Talmudic and medieval rabbinic stories, the *Mayse Bukh*, first published in Basel in 1602. This brief story escaped notice for the most part since many of the stories in this collection also had a magical or supernatural aspect. It was an abbreviated version of a story in two versions that has come to be known as the Falco Letter. The text in the *Mayse Bukh* is the second and shorter of the two versions. The first and longer text was not published in a full version until 1651. This text will be discussed below in the context of the Falco Letter.

The Dresnitz Letter

Ta'alumot Hokhmah was a collection of kabbalistic treatises, published in Basel from 1629 through 1631, by Samuel Ashkenazi, a disciple of the peripatetic scholar Rabbi Joseph Solomon Delmedigo of Candia who had collected the included documents in the course of his travels.[1] This kabbalistic miscellany included three letters written by Rabbi Shloimel Dresnitz, a scholar from Moravia who had journeyed to Safed at the beginning of the seventeenth century to learn more about Rabbi Isaac Luria and Lurianic kabbalah. Exactly how these letters came to be published in this collection are not clear. Delmedigo spent time in several cities in Eastern Europe, and it is possible that he came across the letters during his travels. A fourth letter written by Dresnitz remained in manuscript and was not published until the twentieth century.[2] Everything that we know about Rabbi Shloimel Dresnitz comes from his own writings, and his biography is reconstructed from references in his writing.[3] He was born in Lundenberg and later moved to Dresnitz (Strassnitz), both in Moravia. At the age of twenty-two, he had a spiritual awakening and began to intensively study kabbalistic and ethical works, and in 1602, he decided to move to Safed to continue his kabbalistic studies. After his arrival in Safed, Rabbi Issachar Baer of Kremnitz asked his friend Rabbi Shloimel to see if he could obtain an approbation for a kabbalistic text that he wanted to publish. The approbation was not forthcoming because of a prohibition against disseminating Lurianic teachings outside the land of Israel. Rabbi Shloimel wrote a series of four long letters to his friend, Rabbi Issachar Baer, recounting all the wondrous things he had heard about Rabbi Isaac Luria, the fountainhead of Kabbalah in Safed, and other stories he heard from his teachers. The subsequent history of these letters is somewhat murky.[4]

Another version of some of these letters was published by Naphtali Bacharach, a kabbalist from Frankfurt am Main who published an important work of Lurianic teachings, entitled *Emek ha-Melekh*, in Amsterdam in 1648.[5] Bacharach opened his work with a collection of hagiographic stories about Luria and his disciples. The Dresnitz Letters were included in this section. According to Gershom Scholem,[6] Bacharach claimed that Delmedigo had been his student, and many things that Delmedigo published in his books were stolen from manuscripts that Bacharach had brought back from Israel.[7] Regardless of the merits of this controversy, the letters in Delmedigo's work are the standard source for these used by later authors. These letters are also the basis for the hagiographical work *In Praise of the AR"I* (*Shivhei ha-AR"I*), which was first published in Shklov in 1795 and became the standard hagiographical account of Rabbi Isaac Luria's life and deeds.[8]

Appended to the end of the third letter in *Ta'alumot Hokhmah* was a story about the exorcism of a *dybbuk* that had entered a widow in Safed. The core of this story is found in Hayyim Vital's mystical diary,

Sefer Hezyonot.[9] Vital's version is brief and does not give many details. The version that Dresnitz reported was much richer in detail. An obvious question that must be dealt with is to what extent the expansions of the story in Dresnitz's account are factual details gleaned from his informants who had been alive during the events described and to what extent are some of the descriptions taken from literary sources, either by Dresnitz or his informants. Bacharach also published a version of Dresnitz's story in his *Emek ha-Melekh*. Menasseh ben Israel reprinted Bacharach's version of the story in his book, *Nishmat Hayyim*, published in Amsterdam in 1652. This work was an attempt to prove the existence of the soul, and the Vital story and the Falco Letter are both found in this book. We know that Ben Israel copied the story from Bacharach because of a small mistake. There is a figure in the story whose name is given as Rabbi Joseph Arzin in the Bacharach and Ben Israel texts, while in Delmedigo and Sambari's *Sefer Divrei Yosef*,[10] the name is Rabbi Joseph Ashkenazi. The similarity is indicative that Bacharach is the source for Ben Israel.[11] I have not translated both of these texts in the appendix because these two versions of the story are sufficiently similar to the version in *Ta'alumot Hokhmah* that they do not add any additional information to the broader discussion of the subject.

An interesting conundrum is that there is a second version of the Dresnitz story that is independent of Dresnitz's account, and it is similar in enough important details to confirm that they are both based on the same incident. The second independent account is by Joseph Sambari, author of the chronicle *Divrei Yosef*, which will be discussed below.

Another interesting aspect of these accounts are the literary allusions drawn from earlier rabbinic and kabbalistic sources that described Gehenna and its torments. There are also echoes of the story of Rabbi Akiva and the Dead Man that is the original source for the *dybbuk* story as discussed above. A detailed analysis of these elements of the stories is a desideratum but is beyond the parameters of this study.

The Falco Letter

The other major source in the first part of the seventeenth century that influences later *dybbuk* stories is known as the Falco Letter. Its author, Elijah Falco[12] was a disciple of Rabbi Isaac Luria in Safed. The primary source of information we have about Falco is a passage in Hayyim Vital's *Book of Visions*:

> My teacher z"l told me that not all of our colleagues will be permanently established and a few of them still need to be clarified and changed and others will be put in their place, as I will explain, with God's help. I will now write about the colleagues who study with us, though I do not know which ones will have others exchanged in their place.
>
> The second group who are after midnight includes: the young Hayyim, Rabbi Jonathan Sagis z"l, Rabbi Joseph Arzin z"l, Rabbi Isaac Cohen z"l, Rabbi Gedaliah ha-Levi, Rabbi Samuel Uceda, Rabbi Judah Mashan, Rabbi Abraham Gabriel, Rabbi Shabbetai Menasseh, Rabbi Joseph ibn Tabul, and Rabbi Elia Falco z"l.[13] . . .
>
> My teacher z"l told me on that day that R. Elia Falco z"l was average, and this is the secret of what the sages said about the verse, "*All the host of heaven standing in attendance, etc. Who will entice Ahab, etc.*" [I Kings 22:19–20]. The Talmudic sages said, "*Ahab was indecisive.*"[14] Because of this he could not be punished until he turned to the evil side, since while he was indecisive, he could not be punished. Similarly, from Ahab to R. Elia Falco, both of whom were from the same source, they always remained in between and indecisive. This is the reason that my teacher z"l wanted to dismiss him from our fraternity. He did not remove him because he was indecisive, until there occurred the great vexation with Rabbi Joseph Arzin, may God protect him, and then he began to turn to the evil side. However, despite this, the minority of good still remained and then he was dismissed from our fraternity. Concerning Rabbi Joseph Arzin, he told me that if his father would have come to Safed in that year, he too would be damaged. Aside from this, on the day he expelled Rabbi Elia Falco, he certainly wanted to expel him also.[15]

This is the primary reference to Elijah Falco in the Lurianic corpus. It tells us that he was a disciple of Rabbi Isaac Luria, who was in the same group of disciples as Hayyim Vital. Luria taught four groups of disciples, and the teachings appear to have been tailored to the spiritual status of the disciples. We know this from surviving copies of teachings copied by students in the different groups. It would appear that Falco did something that angered Rabbi Isaac Luria, and he was expelled from the group of disciples. The only other thing that we know about Falco is that he was associated with a letter that circulated that described two incidents of *dybbuk* possession. He was the central figure in the first exorcism, which was described in great detail in this letter. There is a second exorcism, where the participants are anonymous. In both cases, the exorcism ended with the death of the person being possessed. The cause of death in both cases was the exiting of the respective Spirits possessing them, which choked them as they exited from their bodies via their throats. We can only speculate if this incident was the cause of Luria's displeasure.

There are several possible explanations for Luria's displeasure with Falco and his attempt at exorcizing a *dybbuk* if this is the case. First would be his method of exorcism. Falco's method of exorcizing the *dybbuk* in his account is not the use of Lurianic *yihudim* that are described in the writings of Hayyim Vital.[16] Rather, he seems to have reverted to the older methods used to exorcize demons and evil spirits that go back to the ancient world, which were in the category of practical kabbalah and magic. Yuval Harari, in his important study of practical kabbalah and magic, observes that in sixteenth century Safed, there was reluctance by the major figures like Rabbi Moses Cordovero and Rabbi Isaac Luria with regard to the use of practical kabbalah and magic.[17] Hayyim Vital mentions in his *Sha'ar Ruah ha-Kodesh* that he asked his teacher, Rabbi Isaac Luria, about the use of practical kabbalah. Vital writes:

> I, the writer Hayyim, asked my teacher, of blessed memory, about the use of practical Kabbalah, which is forbidden in all the books of the later kabbalists. How, then, did R. Ishmael and R. Akiva, may they rest in peace, [as is written] in chapters of the *Hekhalot*, use the awesome names for remembering and opening the heart [meaning to improve the ability to learn, understand, and remember]. And he answered that, in their time, the ashes of the red heifer had been attainable, and they could be completely purified of every uncleanness, but we are all defiled by the dead and we do not have the ashes of the red heifer to purify ourselves from the defilement of the dead . . . so we do not have permission in our time to use the holy names and the punishment to their user is great . . . Another time, my teacher, of blessed memory, replied . . . in a different way, as follows: Be aware that all

the names and the amulets now written in books are mistaken, and even the names and the amulets that have been tried and approved by an expert have many errors in them, and that is why it is forbidden to use them. Indeed, if we knew the names with their (correct) forms and truth, we would also be allowed to use them.[18]

An additional possibility or complicating factor could be that Luria was unhappy when he learned that Falco had publicized these events. Luria and Hayyim Vital after him were very careful not to publicize their kabbalistic teachings and went to great lengths to keep these teaching secret and their knowledge restricted to a very small select elite. Falco appears to have sent out a circular letter describing his exorcism. We do not know exactly when or how he disseminated it.

There are a number of sources that describe how the information concerning Falco's exorcisms was disseminated beyond Safed. There are two sixteenth-century sources that describe a letter signed by sages in Safed that talked about possessions and exorcism in Safed. Gedaliah ibn Yahya in his *Shalshelet ha-Kabbalah* has a chapter entitled "Discourse on the Magical Arts," where he describes an incident of possession in Ferrara in 1575. At the end of this discussion, he mentions that he saw a letter signed by sages in Safed that described events that happened there.[19] The likeliest assumption is that this was the letter about Falco's exorcisms. However, he only mentions the existence of the letter but does not describe its contents. The second sixteenth-century source is found in Rabbi Eliezer Ashkenazi's *Ma'asei Adonai*, published in Venice in 1583. Ashkenazi mentioned that he had heard reports about people being possessed by Spirits who spoke through the person who was possessed. He also mentioned that he has seen a letter that came from Safed in 1580 that described a woman who was possessed.[20] Here, too, the description of a letter is not definitive. The earliest document we have that can clearly be linked to Falco's exorcism is the story found in the *Mayse Bukh*, which is discussed below.

A related question concerns the nature of the "letter" that was sent from Safed. Was it a handwritten circular letter or was it a printed broadsheet? Meir Benayahu, in his *Toldot ha-Ari*, suggested that the "letter" was published as a broadsheet that circulated widely.[21] His primary evidence for this assumption is a statement by Menasseh ben Israel in his *Nishmat Hayyim*. The quotation Benayahu cites as evidence is, "I will put before you the letter (*ha-iggeret*) that was sent from Safed, may it be speedily rebuilt . . . and this is the text as it was published in the past (*miyamim nidpesah*)." It is not clear what he is referring to since his publication of the first *dybbuk* story in Falco's letter was the first known publication of this letter. The second story was published in the *Mayse Bukh* as will be discussed, but this story is secondary, and Ben Israel published both stories. If there was a published broadsheet, there is no other evidence for it, and no copy is known to exist. Joseph Sambari, who published these texts in his *Divrei Yosef*, states that he copied his account of these events from Falco's own manuscript.[22] Both Gedaliah ibn Yahya and Eliezer Ashkenazi also write about this text as a letter. Without the appearance of new evidence, we must assume that Falco's letter was circulated as a handwritten letter that may have been copied and circulated in that way.

The *Mayse Bukh* Story[23]

The first *dybbuk* story was published in the *Mayse Bukh*, published in Basel in 1602. It is the best known and most popular Yiddish collection of hagiographic stories about Talmudic and medieval rabbis, along with a number of stories taken from earlier collections of hagiographic tales. Since its first publication, it has been reprinted in Yiddish twenty times and translated into English, French, and German.[24] The editor and publisher, Jacob ben Abraham of Mezhirech, was very learned and contributed to the publication of ten other Hebrew and Yiddish books at the press of Konrad Waldkirch in Basel between 1600 and 1611.[25] He collected stories from a variety of sources, both printed and manuscript. The stories were divided into three sections. The first, stories 1–157, are from Talmudic and midrashic sources. The second cycle of stories, 158–182, is about Rabbi Judah ha-Hasid and the *Hasidei Ashkenaz*. The last section is a miscellany of stories taken from a variety of medieval Jewish sources.[26]

The story about the "The Evil Spirit"[27] is story 152, which places it near the end of the section of rabbinic stories. Gaster could not find a rabbinic source for this story, so he consulted Prof. Louis Ginzberg, the great Talmudist and leading authority on rabbinic aggadah. Gaster quotes Ginzberg's response: "This is to my knowledge," writes Dr. Ginzberg, "the earliest story about a *dibbuk*, which is first met in the writings about Luria and his pupils. The nearest to that given in M.B. [*Mayse Bukh*] is the one told about Luria and Vital in the different versions of *Shivhei ha-Ari*, which however, were published later than the M.B."[28]

Prof. Ginzberg's accurate intuition raises two questions: Why did he put this story in the section on rabbinic stories, and where did he find this story? He probably put the story in the rabbinic section since there are stories about "evil spirits" in rabbinic literature, but they were not found as often in medieval stories. As Prof. Ginzberg noted, stories about Luria were not yet being circulated, and it is likely that the story came to him from a secondhand source. The reference to Constantinople that appears in the versions of the Falco Letter published later does not appear in the *Mayse Bukh* version. Thus, there is no information that would have alerted him that this was a medieval story and not a rabbinic story. Story 157 in the *Mayse Bukh* rabbinic story section also has an unusual provenance. It was first published in the *Brantshpigl*, and one must assume that he also puts it in the rabbinic section simply because it sounds "rabbinic."[29] The *Brantshpigl*, by Moshe Henoch's Altschul, was also published in Basel in 1602, the same press and same year as the *Mayse Bukh*. This coincidence is further evidence of the editor's thought process.

Jacob ben Abraham collected the source material for the *Mayse Bukh* from a wide variety of sources,[30] but the specific source for the *dybbuk* story can be identified as being part of the Falco Letter. The question is how did the Falco Letter get from Safed to Jacob ben Abraham in Europe? The likeliest intermediary is Rabbi Eliezer Ashkenazi, author of *Ma'asei Adonai*, where he mentions that he saw a letter that mentioned the possession of a woman by a *dybbuk*. The Falco Letter contained two *dybbuk* stories, the first about a woman and the second about a young boy, that is the subject of the story in the *Mayse Bukh*. Ashkenazi lived in Egypt from where he was in contact with scholars in Safed, including Rabbi Joseph Karo. After he was compelled to leave Egypt, he spent some time in Venice in 1563 before leaving for Prague. He eventually accepted rabbinic positions in a number of Polish cities and died in Cracow in 1586.[31] As discussed above, Ashkenazi mentioned having received the Falco Letter or information about its contents in 1580, when he was already living in Poland. Though there is no direct known connection between Jacob ben Abraham and Rabbi Eliezer Ashkenazi, though they were contemporaries, and they may have met. Another possibility is that Jacob could have heard about this story in the course of his collecting materials for his collection of stories from an intermediary source. This might explain the discrepancies between the story in the *Mayse Bukh* and the version of this story found in the later sources. Another possibility is that Jacob ben Abraham rewrote the text he saw and deleted some details. There is evidence in the *Mayse Bukh* that other stories were summarized or abbreviated when they were compared to their original sources.[32] This would be a plausible explanation for the discrepancies in the two versions.

Among the significant differences in detail are that the version in the *Mayse Bukh* does not mention that the spirit's sin took place in Constantinople or several discussions between the spirit and the sages. The *Mayse Bukh* adds several details not found in Falco's letter. The sin is identified by one of the onlookers as sodomy and uses the term "evil Spirit" where Falco uses the more neutral term, "Spirit" without the pejorative adjective. The most significant difference between the two versions is how the story ends. In the Falco Letter, the exorcism is unsuccessful, and the young man who was possessed died within eight days after the exorcism. In the *Mayse Bukh* version, the exorcism is successful, and the Spirit leaves the youth and flies away. Fragmentary information and the need to complete a narrative would explain many of the discrepancies. The most significant discrepancy, changing the failure and death to a successful conclusion, is in accord with the general tone of the *Mayse Bukh*. As Moses Gaster noted, the *Mayse Bukh* is a work of moral and ethical instruction that glorifies the Talmudic and medieval rabbis who are the heroes of the stories. The failure to save the possessed youth and his death would be out of character with the positive tone of the stories in the *Mayse Bukh* and other works of this genre.[33]

Nishmat Hayyim

Menasseh ben Israel's *Nishmat Hayyim* is the first published work that contains the full text of the Falco Letter, that is, the two exorcism stories that comprise the Falco Letter. The first story is an exorcism presided over by Elijah Falco with the help of several others in Safed. The second exorcism is a version of the story first found in the *Mayse Bukh*, with some changes. The *Nishmat Hayyim* is also the first published work that contains both exorcism stories, from the Dresnitz Letter and the Falco Letter. Menasseh Ben Israel's connection to Delmedigo is very clear. Delmedigo's book, *Elim*, was published by Menasseh ben Israel in Amsterdam in 1629. Thus, it is reasonable to assume that Menasseh ben Israel was familiar with Delmedigo and his other writings. It is likely that his text of the Dresnitz Letter came from Delmedigo's *Ta'alumot Hokhmah*. How Menasseh came into possession of the Falco Letter remains a mystery along with much else relating to the transmission history of this text before its publication by Menasseh Ben Israel. Both the Dresnitz and Falco Letters are directly related to the theme of *Nishmat Hayyim* and explain his interest in them.

Menasseh ben Israel wrote *Nishmat Hayyim* as part of his work on explaining biblical theology. Joseph Dan observes:

> The most important idea to be expressed in this work is that the Bible *does* include references to the eternity of the soul, a celebrated exegetical problem from Midrashic literature and throughout the Middle Ages. Like many other works by the same author, *Nishmat Hayyim* presents an exegesis of relevant Biblical passages to prove that the Bible regards the soul as eternal, to receive its due after the body's death and to be resurrected in the messianic future. . . . Most of the book is dedicated to a detailed analysis of the nature of the soul and its relationship to the body. In the course of this analysis, Ben Israel presents a most impressive anthology of views concerning the soul; it is an anthology of encyclopedic dimensions—seldom if ever surpassed in erudition in the history of Jewish culture.[34]

The *dybbuk* was not a central concern in *Nishmat Hayyim*; it was just another piece of evidence in Menasseh ben Israel's quest to demonstrate the eternality of the soul.

Divrei Yosef

The second important source that includes both the Dresnitz Letter and the Falco Letter is Joseph Sambari's chronicle *Divrei Yosef*. Sambari's chronicle, written in Cairo, covered the history of Jews in the Islamicate world from the beginning of Islam until his own period. He finished the work in January 1673, but the complete text was not published until 1994.[35] However, excerpts from this work were quoted in a variety of sources in the centuries since its completion.[36] Sambari was very interested in the kabbalists of Safed and collected many traditions about Isaac Luria and his disciples in his chronicle, including the exorcism stories relating to Rabbi Hayyim Vital and Elijah Falco. Included in Sambari's work are many earlier documents, and among them is the *Toldot ha-Ari* (History of the AR"I). Meir Benayahu published this document in his *Toldot ha-Ari* and claimed that this text was the earliest hagiographic account of Rabbi Isaac Luria and preceded Dresnitz's account. He also argued that the Dresnitz Letters were based on the *Toldot ha-Ari* manuscript.[37] Gershom Scholem and other scholars examined Benayahu's claims, rejected them, and decided that Dresnitz's account was the earliest one. The most comprehensive study of the relationship between Dresnitz's letters and *Toldot ha-Ari* is by David Tamar, who agreed with Scholem and others, against the opinion of Benayahu.[38] Joseph Dan described the important differences between Dresnitz's letters and the *Toldot ha-Ari* that explain why the consensus of scholarly opinion gives priority to Dresnitz's letters over *Toldot ha-Ari*. He writes:

> *Toldot ha-Ari* is a more fantastical, romantic, and imaginative work than *Shivḥei ha-Ari*. It includes, for example, a version of "The Story of the Jerusalemite," a 13th century tale about the marriage between a man and a demon, adapted to serve as a vehicle to demonstrate Luria's greatness. The famous story of the *dybbuk* (a spirit which entered a girl's body) which appears in *Shivhei ha-Ari* as an addendum, and is not among Shloimel's original letters, is an integral part of *Toldot ha-Ari*. The supernatural tales found in *Toldot ha-Ari* are also not in *Shivhei ha-Ari*. In *Toldot ha-Ari*, Luria is sometimes portrayed as a famous rabbi and judge, respected in Safed and all over the Jewish East. This is not a historical fact, and nothing of the sort is mentioned in Shloimel's letters. It may therefore be inferred that *Shivhei ha-Ari* is a compilation of intimate accounts told by Luria's pupils, whereas *Toldot ha-Ari* is a collection of fantastical and imaginary hagiographies which were associated with Luria by later admirers, after his fame had spread all over the Jewish world. At the same time, there is

little doubt that *Toldot ha-Ari* also includes some true stories about Luria which Shloimel either did not know or did not include in his extant letters. It must therefore be considered also as a source on Luria's life and works.[39]

Though Benayahu's arguments were rejected by the scholarly consensus, Scholem admitted that there were a number of manuscripts with Lurianic hagiography circulating in the seventeenth century. The existence of these manuscripts also explains the difference in details of the various versions of these stories. Sambari is certainly one of the manuscripts that Scholem had in mind.

The story in Sambari, in contrast to the accounts of Bacharach and Ben Israel, is not a copy of the Dresnitz Letter. There is no doubt that the two versions describe the same event. At the same time, there are enough differences in style and form in the Sambari version that show it is not based on Dresnitz but is an independent version. The Dresnitz Letter is a coherent narrative written as a story, with an introduction, body, and conclusions. The Sambari version leaves out the framing section at the beginning of Dresnitz, and the sequence of events is different. For example, the key question of what allowed the *dybbuk* to enter the woman's body is found at the beginning of Sambari, while in Dresnitz, it is found almost at the end of the story. There are also details that are found in one version and are missing in the other. The *dybbuk* is able to come back to the house after the exorcism and attempts to possess the woman again in the Dresnitz version. The family goes back to Rabbi Isaac Luria, and he sends Vital to the house to check the *mezuzot*. He discovers that the door is missing a *mezuzah*, and when a proper *mezuzah* is inserted, the *dybbuk* leaves and never comes back. This is how the Dresnitz story ends.

The Sambari version ends very differently. There is a long narrative in which Vital's teacher, Rabbi Isaac Luria, warns him that the demons and evil spirits are angry with Vital because he exorcized the *dybbuk*. He tells Vital not to go out alone at night or when it is foggy as this is a time of danger when malevolent spirits are about. Vital ignored his advice, and not long after, he was harmed and had to be healed by his teacher. This epilogue is not found in the Dresnitz Letter. Sambari may or may not have known about the Dresnitz Letter. However, living in Cairo and doing extensive research on the history of Jews in the Islamicate world, he certainly would have found primary sources about Safed in the time of Isaac Luria. It is quite possible that he found different traditions concerning this episode, and he incorporated them in his narrative. It is impossible to judge whether the Dresnitz version or the Sambari version is the more authentic. Ultimately this is not of crucial importance as the main elements of the story are in agreement.

In contrast, the text of the Falco Letter that is found in both *Nishmat Hayyim* and *Divrei Yosef* is substantially similar. The slight changes that are found in these two versions could easily be attributed to scribal errors. This similarity leads to the conclusion that the source of the Falco Letter was a written text of some sort, perhaps a circular letter that was copied and disseminated, as opposed to oral or archival traditions that differed in detail from version to version as in the case of the story found in the Dresnitz Letter and Sambari.

Differences between the Dresnitz and Falco Letters

At first glance, the Dresnitz and Falco accounts seem to be discussing the same event. Some of the details are in accord, but when one carefully compares the two accounts, there are great differences. The Dresnitz account seems to be a fairly straightforward account that elaborates on the brief version found in the *Book of Visions*. The people involved in the case and the methods of approaching and exorcizing the *dybbuk* are in accord with the Lurianic materials relating to the subject. However, when one asks the same questions of the Falco version, we find little that makes sense in the context of Safed. The only known figures from Safed mentioned in this story are Falco and Solomon Alkabetz, who plays no role beyond having his name mentioned. The story has no context like the Dresnitz Letter. It seems to be a self-consciously created document meant to stand alone. It has an introduction that tries to make it a morality tale. The action begins with a crowd gathering to witness a spectacle. Unknown persons who supposedly knew about adjurations decide to intimidate the *dybbuk* by passing smoke and sulfur under the nostrils of the possessed. This is the standard method found in the long history of the exorcism of demons and evil spirits, beginning with the exorcism first described by Josephus and continued through the Middle Ages in both Jewish and Christian communities. We have also seen that Rabbi Isaac Luria was strongly opposed to these methods of exorcism. In contrast to Falco, Vital worked under the direction of Luria and exorcized the *dybbuk* using *yihudim* and not with the methods that had been the traditional ones for exorcizing demons and evil Spirits but rejected by Luria.

It can be argued that what Falco did is an act of rebellion against the authority of his teacher, Rabbi Isaac Luria, if these events actually happened. When the *dybbuk* is asked whom he would like to have as his exorcist, he names Falco. There is no other exorcism story where the *dybbuk* has his choice of exorcist. Why is Falco so special? We are not told. In summary, there are enough similarities between the Falco and Dresnitz accounts to suggest that the basis of the two is the same event. At the same time, the Falco version does not make logical sense in terms of who Falco was that he should be called upon to perform such an important ceremony, and enough details surrounding the story do not make sense in the context of what we know about Safed. Perhaps the most glaring discrepancy between the Dresnitz account and the two events in the Falco Letter is that in the Dresnitz version, the possessed person survives the exorcism, while in the Falco stories, the person being exorcized died at the end of the exorcism. Despite this, when one looks at later accounts of exorcisms, the Falco story was more influential than the Dresnitz story. The Falco account is based more on knowing adjurations and writing amulets and rituals that we associate with the well-known historical practice of exorcism. In contrast, the exorcism in the Dresnitz story is based on the unique charisma and kabbalistic knowledge of Isaac Luria, which was not known until some volumes of Vital's were published in the nineteenth century.[40] In the exorcisms of later centuries, *ba'alei shem*, who were healers, amulet writers, and members of the secondary elite, were the exorcists and not famous rabbis or kabbalists. Elijah Falco was the likelier prototype for the *ba'alei shem* who became exorcists than was Hayyim Vital.

Samuel Vital and the *Dybbuk* in Cairo (1666)

Before turning to the next chapter of the history of the *dybbuk*, the exorcisms performed by *ba'alei shem* in Central and Eastern Europe utilizing the traditional, pre-Lurianic methods of exorcising Spirits and demons, there is one *dybbuk* story in the second half of the seventeenth century that harkens back to the Safed exorcisms of Rabbi Hayyim Vital. The story took place in Cairo, in 1666, and the exorcist was Rabbi Samuel

Vital, the son of Rabbi Hayyim Vital and the editor of one version of his writings. It is also a firsthand description of exorcizing a *dybbuk* using the methods taught by Rabbi Isaac Luria without the presence of Luria. Another unusual aspect of this story is that the *dybbuk* wanted to be exorcized and sent to his punishment and eventual reform, unlike the later stories where the *dybbuk* fights the exorcism.

Vital describes how a young woman was possessed, and her father came to him for help. He visited her but was uncertain if she was possessed by a demonic Spirit or a *dybbuk*. While they were discussing this, the Spirit shouted out that he was a gentile,[41] and the Spirit reached out and injured Vital's thigh. Vital had to go home, but he advised that a gentile judge be called to deal with the Spirit. This was not unusual in the Muslim environment, and there are several occasions described in his father's *Book of Visions* where he consulted Muslim healers and visionaries.[42] The Muslim judge came and was able to expel and neutralize the gentile Spirit.

Shortly after the Spirit was removed and neutralized, another voice was heard from the girl. It was a Jewish *dybbuk* who asked that Rabbi Samuel be brought so that he could exorcize the *dybbuk*. Unlike other *dybbuk* stories where the *dybbuk* does not want to be exorcized and fights with everything at his disposal, this *dybbuk* was asking to be exorcized and sent to Gehenna so that he might begin the *tikkun* of his soul. Rabi Samuel was reluctant to come after his earlier experience, but the *dybbuk* convinced him that the earlier aggressive behavior was not his fault but was caused by the other Spirit. The *dybbuk* convinced Vital of his sincerity and desire to begin the process for the *tikkun* of his soul. The most interesting part of this incident is Vital's detailed description of the exorcism process he employed, which was based on his father's writings, which were in his possession. His account is found at the end of Hayyim Vital's *Sha'ar ha-Gilgulim*, which was first published in Jerusalem in 1863. As a result, it did not influence the history of the *dybbuk* phenomenon before the twentieth century.

Chapter 4

The *Dybbuk* in the Second Half of the Seventeenth Century
The Age of the *Ba'alei Shem*

Introduction

The concept of the *dybbuk* and the methodology of exorcising the *dybbuk* moved into a different direction from the Lurianic methodology at the end of the seventeenth century. The exorcism of the *dybbuk* was no longer the realm of the kabbalist but became the province of the *ba'al shem*. The *dybbuk* first appeared in Safed during Rabbi Isaac Luria's period. The exorcism of the *dybbuk* was accomplished by Luria or his disciple, Rabbi Hayyim Vital, through the use of kabbalistic meditations known as *yihudim*. The incident involving Rabbi Elijah Falco, Luria's disgraced disciple, is problematic as described above, but has an important influence on the *ba'alei shem* and their exorcisms at the end of the seventeenth century. The stories about *dybbuk* possession of the seventeenth century looked back to Safed and the charisma of Isaac Luria. The stories included in the seventeenth-century texts are either hagiographical accounts relating to Rabbi Isaac Luria or reports of the Falco Letter. Menasseh ben Israel and, somewhat later, Joseph Sambari reported both the stories related to Luria and the Falco Letters. It is noteworthy that there were no other verifiable accounts of *dybbuk* possession or exorcism until the last decade of the seventeenth century.[1]

The new *dybbuk* possession stories that emerged at the end of the seventeenth century differed in every important aspect from the Safed stories that introduced the concept of *dybbuk* possession. The locus shifted to Central and Eastern Europe, the exorcist was no longer a kabbalist, but rather a *ba'al shem*, and his exorcism methodology was not kabbalistic *yihudim* but magical exorcism practices that were first described by Josephus for the exorcism of demons and evil spirits. Descriptions of the exorcism of demons and evil spirits can be found in many ancient and medieval Jewish sources, and the methods of exorcism practiced by most of the exorcists were similar to those first described by Josephus. This chapter will focus on three exorcism stories published in the last decade of the seventeenth century. Two of them take place in Prague and Nikolsburg, respectively.[2] The exorcists and other prominent figures mentioned in these stories are well documented historical figures. The accounts of the events were published shortly after the events by the people involved, so there is no reason to doubt that we are dealing with actual events. The third story was published anonymously, without any indication of author or place and date of publication. The analysis of paper and fonts indicates a publication date of the late seventeenth century. It is a fictional account that is most likely a parody, mocking the two historical accounts, and was published shortly after them.

The central figure in the most important story, the Nikolsburg *dybbuk* account, was Rabbi Moshe Graf, also known as Rabbi Moshe Prager. He was consistently referred to as a *ba'al shem*, but what is a *ba'al shem*?[3] In the nineteenth century and beyond, a variety of authors and scholars made the term *ba'al shem* synonymous with a charlatan, a fraud, a swindler, and one who preys on gullible, pious people. There were two forms of impetus for this deliberate falsehood, beyond ignorance. One group were those who intended to denigrate Hasidism and its founder, Rabbi Israel Ba'al Shem Tov. The second group included those who wished to portray popular Jewish religious culture as ignorant and backward. Sometimes the two motivations overlapped. The guilty included modernizers of various political and religious persuasions along with those who had their differences with Hasidism. The term must be evaluated objectively, and a proper understanding of the term must be established.[4]

The idea that diseases and other human maladies, particularly diseases displaying unusual behavior, epilepsy being the classic example, and some forms of mental illness, were caused by malevolent beings, such as demons and evil spirits, is a venerable and ancient concept. A classic remedy to defeat these beings was through the theurgic powers attached to divine names. There were people who had the arcane knowledge and charisma to properly deploy the magical power of divine and angelic names. They came to be called *ba'alei shem* (masters of the Name) in the early Middle Ages. In the Early Modern period, certain rabbis in Europe attained fame for their particular abilities to utilize the divine Names through writing amulets or other means, to heal people. Their fame was spread by their own publications and stories of their magical deeds that were published by others. When kabbalistic texts began to be published in the sixteenth century, the handbooks of remedies, amulets, and similar practices came to be called "practical kabbalah" in contrast to the kabbalistic writings and teachings that were more spiritual and theoretical.[5]

The name *ba'al shem* was a title for rabbis in Central and Eastern Europe who were known as experts in the healing and magical arts, beginning in the thirteenth century. Karl Grözinger, in his study of *ba'alei shem* in Germany, was able to identify thirty-seven rabbis who were identified as *ba'alei shem* in literary sources. The last rabbi to be given the title of *ba'al shem* was Rabbi Seckel Wormser of Michelstadt (Hessen, Germany) who died in 1847.[6] His grave is still a place of pilgrimage. There were also famous rabbis who functioned as *ba'alei shem* without having the title. The most famous rabbi who was associated with amulets and healing through them was Rabbi Jonathan Eybeschutz, one of the most important rabbis in the eighteenth century. He was the rabbi of important communities, a major author and halakhic authority. At the same time, he had a reputation as an expert in writing amulets for various purposes. A famous controversy broke out between him and Rabbi Jacob Emden over a protective amulet that Rabbi Eybeschutz had written for someone. The controversy was ignited by Rabbi Emden, who claimed that the contents of the amulet showed that Rabbi Eybeschutz was a secret believer in the false messiah, Shabbetai Zvi. The arguments pro and con about this accusation and Eybeschutz's relation to Sabbateanism continue to the present. The least controversial aspect of the whole affair was the idea that a Rabbi of Eybeschutz's importance and fame would write an amulet for someone. This was considered a completely acceptable and appropriate activity for a rabbi who was familiar with this subject. Though *ba'alei shem* are associated in the modern period with the exorcism of *dybbukim*, their primary function in the period that they flourished was as healers of physical and other problems. During this period, university-trained physicians were few and far between in most Jewish communities, and *ba'alei shem* filled the role of healers through the use of amulets, herbs, and other folk remedies.[7] *Dybbukim* were a small and not particularly important part of their function in the Jewish community. Common to all the *ba'al shem* was their standing as respected rabbinic figures, communal leaders and, in many cases, authors of books, some of which continue to be studied. It was a title of respect and honor for the rabbis who were worthy to be given this title by their contemporaries.[8]

The first exorcism in Central and Eastern Europe occurred in Prague in 1690. There is a brief account that is almost naive in its simplicity and brevity. The central figure was Rabbi Hirsch Segal, who was the rabbinic judge in Nikolsburg during the more famous story that occurred there in 1695. This story survives because Rabbi Segal told it to his friend Rabbi Akiva Baer, who was the author of the first Yiddish collection of kabbalistic hagiography, *Ma'asei Adonai*.[9] Rabbi Akiva Baer was also acquainted with Rabbi Moshe Prager, who was the central figure in the second and more famous story of a *dybbuk* exorcism that occurred in Nikolsburg in 1695. Rabbi Hirsch Segal was also a participant in the 1695 story.[10] The story of the Nikolsburg exorcism was the subject of two accounts. The exorcist, Rabbi Moshe Graf, who was also called Moshe Prager, was the author of several books. There is even an incident in the story where the *dybbuk* mocks him, saying that he has gone away to arrange for the publication of a book. Prager published a relatively short account of this story in his Hebrew book, *Sefer Zerah Kodesh Mazevatah* published in Fürth in 1696.[11] There is another much more detailed version of this story in Yiddish that was also published in Fürth in 1696. Unlike the Hebrew version, only one copy of the Yiddish text has survived.[12] The texts of these two stories in their original languages are found in Sara Zfatman, *Leave Impure One: The Exorcism of Spirits in Early Modern Jewish Ashkenaz*, which is a major monograph about these two stories. In this study, I have translated the two Yiddish texts, the Prague exorcism by Rabbi Hirsch Segal and the Nikolsburg exorcism by Rabbi Moshe Prager into English to make them available to a broader audience. There is little for me to add to Zfatman's important study of these events other than the translations of the texts. For the purposes of this study, the key aspect of these exorcism stories that is noteworthy is the return to the pre-Lurianic modes of exorcism of evil spirits, which was now being applied to the *dybbuk*. From our perspective, the *dybbuk* was something very different from the evil spirits and demons had afflicted Jews for almost two millennia. In this context, it should also be noted that the "*dybbuk*" was still named as an "evil Spirit," and the community and the exorcist did not make a distinction. This might explain why the old modes of exorcism were still employed. The Falco exorcism that was widely known also played a role because his methodology sounded familiar and accessible, in contrast to the Lurianic *yihudim*, which were not understood or publicly available. The Lurianic texts circulated in manuscript form among small groups of scholars, but there is no evidence that the Lurianic writings were associated with *dybbuk* possession during this period.

Story of the Spirit in Koretz, the third *dybbuk* story to be considered in this section, is a sixteen-page pamphlet published without indication of author, place, or date of publication.[13] Sara Zfatman has suggested that based on the physical evidence of paper and fonts the date and place of publication are probably the second half of the seventeenth century and Prague. However, based on my examination of the text and its context, I would suggest this text was published after the Prague and Nikolsburg and is a parody of these earlier verified texts.

The *Story of the Spirit in Koretz* appears to be another account of a *dybbuk* exorcism. However, upon closer examination, it becomes clear that there are many differences between earlier accounts and this text. Earlier accounts are embedded in larger texts, where the exorcism serves some larger purpose or demonstrates some ideas, as we find in the Safed stories. Previous exorcism reports are historically verifiable in that the names of the exorcist are known, and other details can be verified, such as the author of the source where the account is reported. In this case we are presented with an anonymous sixteen-page pamphlet without any indication of author or publisher, or place of publication. Yiddish pamphlets of this type were common in this period and contained a wide variety of materials. Many of them were paraphrases of rabbinic, aggadic, and even kabbalistic materials. However, the story of the *dybbuk* in Koretz has no evidence of being an adaptation of a previous historical event, if we assume it was published prior to the Nikolsburg story. The people mentioned are not historical people, and there is no trace in the literature of a possible source for this story. The purported author was supposedly an anonymous member of the holy group. He speaks in the first person on two occasions, indicating that he was present at the events described. Without the discovery of new historical evidence, Zfatman's conclusion that this story was fictional is accurate. This is very unusual as other hagiographic accounts published long after the events are reputed to have occurred are usually attributed to some great worthy in the past. Thus, it makes sense only if we assume that it is a response by someone who wished to mock the Nikolsburg exorcism.

One unique aspect of this *dybbuk* story is the behavior of the young woman who was possessed. In all the other *dybbuk* accounts, the person being possessed remains completely unconscious and passive during the whole exorcism. The only voice that was heard was that of the *dybbuk*. When the *dybbuk* left the person being possessed and if they survived, they were usually unaware of what had transpired. In the unique case of the Koretz *dybbuk*, the young woman is active, and the voice is heard several times. She sings a *piyyut* called "*Adir Iyom ve-Norah*" and then utters a prayer in *tehinnah* form asking God why she is suffering this way. Another interesting oddity is that one of the rabbis who attempts to exorcise the *dybbuk* unsuccessfully is the rabbi of Mirapol. These two unusual things lead to thoughts of S. Anski and his famous play, *Between Two Worlds* (better known as *The Dybbuk*), where the exorcist who fails is the rabbi of Mirapol, and the young woman is conscious and plays an active role in the events that transpire. Whether this is a coincidence or not remains a puzzle. Rabbi Baruch Kot is the one who finally succeeds in exorcizing the *dybbuk*. The word "kot" means dung or excrement in Early Modern Yiddish and also in German.[14] It would be very odd to give this name to the hero of the work, if it were meant to be taken seriously. It makes more sense that this was intended as a parody or mockery. All the previously published *dybbuk* accounts, before Prague and Nikolsburg, were based on the Safed accounts, none of which has a story of the possessed person being taken from place to place or failed multiple attempts at exorcism. These characteristics are first found in the Yiddish version of the Nikolsburg exorcism. It is inconceivable that the author of this work could have created the narrative model of a person possessed who wanders from place to place, and there are multiple failed attempts at exorcism. Logic would dictate that the fictional account is a parody of the published account and thus published after 1696. Whether it was intended as mockery or humorous parody remains a question.

The story is written in an AABB rhyme scheme, which is not followed consistently, making it difficult to break up the text into stanzas. This rhyme scheme is reminiscent of many sixteenth-century Yiddish books, like the *Shmuel Bukh* and others. Perhaps this was an attempt to mimic the style of these older books to give it a patina of antiquity.

Aside from the opening paragraph, the whole text is written as one continuous paragraph. Zfatman has divided it into single sentences. In my translation, I have sometimes combined sentences and created paragraphs as appropriate to make it easier to read. Page numbers of the original text have been inserted in square brackets [ ] to allow easier comparison between the original and this translation. Page numbers refer to the beginning of the page. I have italicized Hebrew terms that are found in the text in a different font. Yiddish texts are printed with the *mashkit* font, sometimes called *weiberteitsch*, while Hebrew words that are not common in Yiddish or are verses or technical terms are printed in the fonts normally used for Hebrew.

My translation is based on the transcription of the Yiddish text published by Sarah Zfatman-Biller in "Tale of an Exorcism in Koretz: A New Stage in the Development of a Folk-Literary Genre" (Hebrew).[15] This translation relies on Zfatman's annotations, but I only annotate biblical, rabbinic, and other sources that are relevant for the understanding of the text by the nonspecialist reader.

In her book, Sara Zfatman discusses two additional *dybbuk* episodes in Central and Eastern Europe during the first half of the eighteenth century, in Detmold and Chmelnik, respectively. They follow the pattern of the Nikolsburg exorcism and do not tell us anything new or significant about the *dybbuk* concept. The next chapter in the history of the *dybbuk* concept moves to Eastern Europe and the emerging Hasidic movement and its founder, Rabbi Israel Baal Shem Tov.

Chapter 5

Rabbi Israel Ba'al Shem Tov and Hasidism

Rabbi Israel Ba'al Shem Tov (Besht) is best known as the founder of Hasidism. The spread and growing influence of the movement among the Jews of Eastern Europe aroused strong emotions, both positive and negative. One focus of the opposition to Hasidism was the personality of its founder and his biography. Questions were raised about his knowledge and the truthfulness of the deeds attributed to him, and some critics in the nineteenth century even went so far as to question his very existence. His profession as a *ba'al shem* was also used as a cudgel to denigrate him and his teachings. The negative stereotype of the *ba'al shem* discussed above was an integral part of the attacks on Rabbi Israel Ba'al Shem Tov and the movement he founded by the various opponents of this movement. Two recent biographies collect and summarize the current state of scholarship, which presents a more interesting and nuanced image of the Ba'al Shem Tov and his activities as a *ba'al shem*.[1]

There is ample evidence that the Besht's primary occupation was that of a *ba'al shem*, and he engaged in all the activities typical of a *ba'al shem*. He appears to have been successful as a *ba'al shem* and could even afford to have a scribe who worked for him to write the amulets, as directed by the Besht.[2] Our concern is more specific, the function and activities of the Besht as an exorcist of *dybbukim*. The primary source for the biography of the Besht is the hagiographical collection of stories entitled, *In Praise of the Ba'al Shem Tov* (*Shivhei ha-Besht*).[3] It was first published in Hebrew, in Kopust, 1814. A Yiddish version was published a year later, in Ostrog and shortly thereafter in Koretz.[4] As with many works in Yiddish, translated from a Hebrew original, the Yiddish was often not an exact translation, but a paraphrase that adds or deletes material. Since the text of the Hebrew edition of *Shivhei ha-Besht* is readily available in English translation,[5] I have chosen to translate the passages that will be discussed from the Yiddish version in order to provide an additional witness to the stories and their reception.

Shivhei ha-Besht was clearly modeled on the hagiographical biography of Rabbi Isaac Luria, *Shivhei ha-AR"I*. The first hagiographical account of Luria's life were the letters sent by Rabbi Shloimel Dresnitz at the beginning of the seventeenth century.[6] These letters were rearranged and published as a separate book with the title *Shivhei ha-AR"I*.[7] An examination of *Shivhei ha-Besht* shows that it is divided into two main parts, like *Shivhei ha-AR"I*. In both cases, the hero's life is divided into two parts, before the revelation of his greatness and after. In the case of the Besht, almost nothing was preserved about his life before his revelation as a *ba'al shem* and holy man at the age of thirty-six. To solve this problem, the editors of *Shivhei ha-Besht* created a series of narratives that paralleled the life of Rabbi Isaac Luria.[8] The key story element for our discussion is why the transition of the Besht took place at the age of thirty-six and how the Besht was revealed.[9] The short answer is that the revelation of Rabbi Isaac Luria as a public spiritual leader also took place at the age of thirty-six. The editors of *Shivhei ha-Besht* could not exactly recreate the circumstances of Luria's revelation, so they chose the exorcism of a *dybbuk* as the setting for his revelation. The exorcism of *dybbukim* was associated with Safed and Luria's activities there.

There are four exorcism stories relating to the Besht mentioned in *Shivhei ha-Besht*. Two of them deal with the exorcism of *dybbukim* and two with the exorcism of demons.[10] The exorcism of demons by *ba'alei shem* has been documented for almost two millennia and is not significant for our discussion. Both of these stories that mention the exorcism of a *dybbuk* mention the importance of the age of thirty-six as the time when the Besht could reveal himself.[11] In the first case (Ben-Amos and Mintz, story 20), a madwoman, as she is called in the text, is possessed by a *dybbuk*. Rabbi Gershon of Kuty, the Besht's brother-in-law, who did not know the greatness of the Besht, took him to see the exorcism. When they entered, the *dybbuk* greeted everyone. The Besht entered last, and people did not pay attention to the *dybbuk*'s words. The *dybbuk* greeted the Besht and told him that the Besht's secret was known to the *dybbuk*. The *dybbuk* knew that the Besht was not allowed to reveal himself publicly until he was thirty-six years old, and that time had not arrived yet. The story ends with the Besht convincing the *dybbuk* to leave quietly, but at the same time, the Besht feels the need to leave the town before his secret is revealed. In the second story (Ben-Amos and Mintz, story 22), it is a madman who was possessed. The Besht is now living in Tlust and has been quietly attracting a few followers. He had begun to display some characteristics of a holy man, and several sick people came to see him, but he refused to see them. One day, a madman was brought to him, and he refused to see him. That night, the Besht had a dream that the next day was his thirty-sixth birthday. In the morning, he woke up, calculated his age, and realized that the dream was true. He cured the madman and began his public career as a *ba'al shem*. For the editor of *Shivhei ha-Besht*, the important part of these *dybbuk* possessions was the parallelism of the career of the Besht and Rabbi Isaac Luria. The possession itself was secondary at best.

Several aspects of these two stories are noteworthy. First and foremost, once the Besht has been established as a *ba'al shem*, there are no further stories about *dybbuk* possessions. Even putting aside the associations with Rabbi Isaac Luria, it shows how rare were the incidents of *dybbuk* possession. Second, it is the first time that *dybbuk* possession was explicitly associated with madness. There is an older tradition of associating *dybbuk* possession with epilepsy or similar illnesses. For example, the stories cited above of Rabbi Isaac Luria and the nephew of Rabbi Joshua bin Nun. This is also the case in the stories in the Prague/Nikolsburg cycle of possession stories. The young man and young woman had been ill for a number of years. The other *dybbuk* stories indicate that the possession is a sudden unexplained event without prior history of illness or mental instability.[12]

Dybbuk possession stories play a role in the later history of Hasidism. The emphasis should be on hagiographical stories since when one examines the context of these stories, they are found in the late hagiographical literature and not in the contemporaneous theoretical literature of Hasidism. The hagiographical literature is problematic as a historical source, so the stories found in this literature must be considered as typological stories that place later hasidic masters in the same situations and following practices associated with the Besht. Thus, the stories about hasidic masters exorcizing *dybbukim* are not reliable witnesses and not relevant to our concerns in this study.[13] There are a number of exorcism stories from the eighteenth century to recent years, but they do not contribute to an understanding of the *dybbuk* concept. Rather, they are a mixed collection of primary and secondary sources in communities that have not been impacted by modernity or reacting to modernity and attempting to preserve premodern traditions. This phenomenon is described in the insightful study of Gideon Bohak.[14] Some of the modern possession stories have been described and studied in an anthropological perspective by Yoram Bilu.[15]

Conclusions

The purpose of this study was to explore the concept of the *dybbuk*, its origins and its history. It is accepted that the *dybbuk* first appeared in Safed in the 1570s. Previous scholarship has not provided adequate answers to many basic questions. The most basic questions are why did it appear in Safed and not before or elsewhere? Is it based on previously existing concepts or is it an entirely new concept without precedent? If, as I have argued, the appearance of the *dybbuk* is the result of a specific set of circumstances, why did it continue to exist long after the circumstances of its creation no longer applied? I have attempted to answer these questions in this study. This concluding chapter will summarize my findings and conclusions in narrative form.

The Prehistory of the *Dybbuk*

The core concept relating to the *dybbuk* is the idea of possession of a person by a malevolent spirit of some sort who causes harm to the person in some manner, and the remedy is exorcism, expelling this malevolent force by a combination of prayers, incantations, adjurations, and other physical means. The person who has the knowledge to perform these required rituals is known as an exorcist. Virtually every traditional belief system has some version of this belief and practice, and what varies are the particulars. For example, Christians would exorcise demons by invoking the name of Jesus. Jews and Muslims might perform a ritual that looks similar to the Christian exorcism, but it would invoke Jewish or Muslim holy names, adjurations, and spiritual authorities. Our concern is Judaism, so the discussion will be confined to the specifics of the

Jewish traditions of possession and exorcism. Detailed discussions and annotation of sources can be found above in the original discussions of the themes that will be summarized here.

The earliest Jewish account of a possession and exorcism is found in the writings of Josephus. He describes in his *Antiquities* how he witnessed the exorcism of an evil spirit from a person, in the presence of the Roman emperor Vespasian. The Talmud and medieval Jewish literature have many stories of demons and spirits and their exorcism by learned rabbis. By the tenth century, a special name began to be used for rabbis who were experts in this art. They were called *ba'al shem* in recognition of the importance of divine names, whether in the writing of amulets or verbal adjurations to exorcise these malevolent spirits. Illness was another realm where *ba'alei shem* played an important role. Where trained physicians were not available or effective, people often turned to *ba'alei shem*. This was particularly true in cases where the patient exhibited strange behavior, diseases like epilepsy or forms of mental illness. The role of *ba'alei shem* continued through Jewish history. The last rabbi who was called a *ba'al shem* died in the middle of the nineteenth century, in Germany.

The *dybbuk*[1] bears external similarities to the evil spirits that were well known and feared. The term "evil Spirit" was even applied to *dybbukim* in Safed and later. It was only in the early eighteenth century that the term *dybbuk* enters the discourse on this subject. Nonetheless, the *dybbuk* has a different origin, purpose, and outcome. The first *dybbuk* did not appear until sixteenth-century Safed, and at that time, only Safed. It was a century after the appearance of the *dybbuk* in Safed that the first credible *dybbuk* event appears that was not directly related to Safed. The *dybbuk* as an idea was not created ex nihilo. It drew upon several concepts and teachings that laid a foundation on which the *dybbuk* concept was built.

The first source that is a foundation is "Rabbi Akiva and the Dead Man," in the minor Talmudic tractate *Kallah Rabbati*. The details of this story present the outline of what came to be called a *dybbuk*. In "Rabbi Akiva and the Dead Man," a person who was a great sinner is being punished in this world because his sins were too great to be punished in Gehenna. Rabbi Akiva meets him, hears his story, and finds a way to have his sins expiated. This story is cited in *Mahzor Vitry* as an influence for the creation of "Mourner's Kaddish. The second source is the concept of *gilgul* (transmigration). The *Zohar* connects *gilgul* with the transgression of the laws of levirate marriage. Later kabbalists connect *gilgul* as a punishment for a variety of other transgressions. In the fifteenth and sixteenth centuries, the concept of *gilgul* enters the public arena in a number of ways. However, the concept remains theoretical and does not have practical consequences.

The *Dybbuk* in Safed

The first possession of a person by a *dybbuk* occurs in Safed in the sixteenth century. The *dybbuk* was the soul of a Jewish male who committed sins so grievous that he was not allowed to enter Gehenna after his death, but was forced to wander the earth, accompanied by angels of wrath whose job was to continually torment the evildoer. Rabbi Hayyim Vital specifically states that a *dybbuk* cannot be a woman or a non-Jew. The only remedy for this evildoer is to find a holy rabbi who has the knowledge and skills to exorcize the *dybbuk* and find an expiation for him that would allow him to enter Gehenna and begin the process of punishment that eventually leads to his expiation and eventual entrance to the Garden of Eden with other Jews.

The second important question is why does the *dybbuk* appear in Safed and not before or elsewhere? The answer is that a unique group of people assembled in Safed and created a hothouse of kabbalistic innovation that ultimately transformed Judaism. An important aspect of the Safed innovations was that they justified their new teachings and practices by appeal to direct revelation through direct contact with the dead Talmudic worthies who were buried in the vicinity of Safed, particularly in the nearby town of Meron. Even before the arrival of Rabbi Isaac Luria, Rabbis Moses Cordovero and Solomon Alkabetz wandered the surrounding countryside and received inspirations and communed with the worthy dead. Rabbi Isaac Luria made regular trips to Meron during his time in Safed to communicate with the spirit of Rabbi Simeon bar Yohai, the purported author of the *Zohar*, the canonical text of the kabbalistic tradition. Luria's primary mode of communication was the *yihud* (unification). Luria would lie on Rabbi Simeon's grave, and with the aid of mystical meditations, he would make contact with the spirit of Rabbi Simeon and have a conversation with him, asking questions and receiving answers and explanations. He would then return to Safed and share his new insights with his disciples and others. His innovative ideas now had the religious authority of Rabbi Simeon and by extension of the Talmudic tradition. However, even his closest disciple, Rabbi Hayyim Vital, when he accompanied Rabbi Luria on one of his visits to the grave of Rabbi Simeon and watched one of these unifications, reported that he only saw and heard one side of the conversation. He saw Rabbi Luria lying on the grave and heard him speaking to Rabbi Simeon but did not see or hear anything from Rabbi Simeon. There was no evidence of the reality of this encounter aside from the word of Rabbi Luria.

The *dybbuk* is a possible solution to the question of the possibility of unifications. Where the *yihud* was a private event that only Rabbi Isaac Luria experienced, the possession and exorcism of the *dybbuk* was a public event, and everyone present could see and hear what was happening. It also verified the validity of the idea of *gilgul* that was a major issue of contention in this period between the kabbalists who believed in its validity and their rationalistic opponents who rejected the concept and its implications. The *dybbuk* was a soul that was being punished because of his sins, and his torments followed the descriptions found in the earlier literature from "Rabbi Akiva and the Dead Man" through a variety of descriptions of the punishments of sinners in the grave and other stories found in medieval sources. The positive side of possession, *maggidim* and *ibbur neshamot*, also manifests itself in Safed, for many of the same reasons.

At the same time, it must be remembered that in the context of Safed, *dybbuk* possession was a minor event that only happened a few times. Hayyim Vital devotes only a few sentences to this issue in his mystical diary the *Book of Visions*, and his concern is with how he was treated by the *dybbuk*. It was only the much-expanded version of the story that was added to the third letter of Shloimel Dresnitz and its publication by J. S. Delmedigo in 1629 that brought the *dybbuk* to the attention of the larger Jewish community. The other document that brought the *dybbuk* story to a larger audience was the letter of Elijah Falco, Luria's erstwhile student. The letter remains problematic in that its provenance and history remain murky, and there is no external contemporaneous evidence to verify the truth of this letter, as there is with the Dresnitz story.

Aside from the questions of history and provenance, there is an important difference between the Vital and Falco stories, and that is the method of exorcism. The narratives of the *dybbuk's* wanderings and adventures are fairly similar and are based on earlier motifs and traditions that need further explication and study. The key difference is how the *dybbuk* is forced to leave the person being possessed. Vital utilized *Yihudim* that he was taught by Rabbi Isaac Luria before he attempted to exorcize the *dybbuk*. In contrast, Falco exorcized the *dybbuk* with the traditional methods of exorcism that were the standard procedure for exorcizing evil spirits and demons in the ancient and medieval periods. In other words, for Falco, the *dybbuk* was just another evil spirit and treated with conventional methods.

Though Luria taught Hayyim Vital the special kabbalistic *yihudim* to deal with the *dybbuk*, he did not personally want to get involved. It was only in the case of Vital's possession that he involved himself, but he had no choice in that case. In the other cases, he found reasons why he could not attend to the situation himself and deputized Vital to act on his behalf. Perhaps Luria did not want to acquire the reputation of being a *ba'al shem*. We see something similar happen more than a century later in Nikolsburg. Rabbi David Oppenheim did not want to become directly involved in the exorcism of the youth but offered the exorcist a manuscript of remedies and magical formulas to help with the exorcism. A related point is the connection between possession and medical issues, like epilepsy and mental illness. Both caused behaviors that people believed were the result of demonic possession. The association of these illnesses with possession is found throughout the whole history of possession and exorcism. The *ba'alei shem* were seen as healers and proto physicians rather than spiritual and religious leaders. This may explain why Luria, Oppenheim, and other major rabbinic figures distanced themselves from direct involvement these incidents.

The Safed *dybbuk* stories were publicized in a number of sources during the seventeenth century through a variety of sources, but the first verifiable accounts of possession after the Safed events did not occur until the end of the seventeenth century and in Central Europe. Sara Zfatman has noted in her important study that several of the central figures involved with these events had or were suspected of Sabbatean connections. More central to our concern is the method of exorcism as described in great detail. What jumps out of the story is that this exorcism was undertaken without any reference to Safed methods of exorcism. It is a classic pre-Safed exorcism, with one important distinction. The evil spirit, which is still called an "evil Spirit" is identified as what we call a *dybbuk*. In other words, we have a new type of Spirit, the Safed *dybbuk*, who is exorcized by the traditional methods, very similar to what we have seen in the Falco Letter. The likeliest explanation is that the *dybbuk* concept caught the popular imagination, but the Safed method of exorcism was not widely known. It was only at the end of the eighteenth century that Lurianic writings began to be widely published and disseminated. The result was a hybrid, the *ba'alei shem* exorcizing a new type of Spirit using the classical methods of exorcism.

The Besht, the founder of Hasidism, was a practicing *ba'al shem* for his whole career, but he was only involved in two *dybbuk* stories. Both were related to his revelation as a major spiritual figure. The Besht did not reveal his spiritual abilities until he was thirty-six years old, the same age as when Rabbi Isaac Luria came to Safed and became a public figure. The two *dybbuk* stories were one way of connecting the Besht to Luria. The whole section of *Shivhei ha-Besht* describing the Besht's life before his revelation was a copy of the Lurianic hagiography *Shivhei ha-AR"I*. One noteworthy aspect of these *dybbuk* stories is that madness is introduced in connection with the possessed persons. It is explicitly stated that madness is a factor in their behavior. The later history of Hasidism includes a number of hagiographical accounts of hasidic leaders exorcizing *dybbukim*, but these are all in story collections that were published beginning in the second half of the nineteenth century and are not reliable historical accounts. The majority of stories in these collections were typological rather than specific to individuals.

There are accounts of *dybbuk* possessions later in the nineteenth century and into the twentieth, but when they are more carefully examined, it is clear that they are cases of mental illness or would be holy men making claims to establish a reputation. These phenomena are the territory of folklorists and anthropologists, not historians. Were it not for the success of Anski's play, these possession and exorcism stories would be just minor oddities of no great significance. As several scholars have noted, the play is more a product of nineteenth-century Russian literature with an overlay of Jewish folklore.[2] Similarly, the centrality of the female character and the significance attached to it for feminist ideology has nothing to do with the historical question of the gender of those possessed. A count of all those possessed in the historical accounts shows that their gender is approximately equally divided between male and female, and age is also not a determining factor. Anski's play is important as a work of literature and art, but it is not a historically accurate account of *dybbuk* possession as it first manifested itself in Safed.

Appendix to Chapter 2

A. Rabbi Joseph Karo, Safed, 1545[1]

Further, I testify that in this year, five thousand and three hundred and five [1545] of creation, here in the upper Galilee, a Spirit entered a young boy and he spoke great things during his epileptic fit. They sent for and assembled many wise men and important people, and I was among them. The sage R. Joseph Karo, of blessed memory, came and spoke with the Spirit. It did not respond to him until he threatened it with the punishment of torture, and it spoke and responded to him. The sage said to him, "What is your name?"

He said, "I do not know my name."
He said to him, "Who are you?"
And he answered, "I am a dog."
"And what were you before this?"
He said to him, "An Ethiopian gentile."
"And before that what were you?"
He said to him, "A Christian gentile."
He said to him, "Before that what were you?"
He said to him, "From those people who know the Hebrew language."
He said to him, "What were your previous deeds?"
He said to him, "I do not remember.
He said to him, "Did you know Torah or Talmud?"
He said to him, "Read the Torah, but I did not know Talmud."
He said to him "Did you pray?"
He said to him, "I did not pray [daily], only on Sabbaths and Festivals."
He said to him, "Did you don phylacteries?"

He said to him, "I never donned phylacteries in my life."
He said to him, "You have no repair."
He said, "They have already decreed against me." He has no repair, and he said that it was two years that he had been out of the body of the dog because the father of the youth had killed the dog that he was in, and he said to the father of the youth: "Because you tormented me by killing the dog that I was in, similarly I will kill your only son." At that time, the sage R. Joseph Karo read [the prayer] *Alenu le-Shabeah* seven times forwards and backwards[2] and decreed torments against him so that he should leave every place where he had transmigrated, and in this way the youth was healed. This is what I saw with my own eyes at that holy event.

B. Exorcisms by Hayyim Vital in the *Book of Visions*

1. The Widow in Safed

a. *Book of Visions* 1.25 (73)

5331 [1571]. When I was in Safed, my teacher z"l taught me how to exorcise evil Spirits with the power of a unification that he had taught me. When I came to him, a woman was lying on the bed. When I sat down by her side and [the evil Spirit] turned his face away from me. I told him to turn his face toward me and speak to me, that he should leave, but he refused. I slapped his face with my hand. He said to me: Because I would not turn my face you hit me?"

I did not do this maliciously, but because your face burns like a great flame and my Soul would be burnt if I looked at you, because of your great holiness.

b. Text of the *Yihud—Sha'ar Ruah ha-Kodesh*. Tel Aviv, 1963, 88d–90d

My teacher, of blessed memory, taught me a *yihud* to be used to remove an evil Spirit, Heaven forbid. On occasion, the soul of a wicked man, whose sins are so numerous that it cannot yet enter Gehenna, may wander here and there. It may sometimes enter the body of some man or woman and subdue it; this is called "the falling sickness" [epilepsy].[3] By means of this *yihud*, his soul is repaired a bit, and it leaves the person's body. And this is the procedure, as I have performed it with my own hands and have experienced it.[4] I take the person's arm, and I place my hand on his pulse, either on the left hand or the right, for there is the site of the garment in which the soul is garbed. I concentrate on that soul that is garbed in that pulse that it should leave from there, with the force of the *yihud*. While still holding his hand at the pulse, I recite this verse, both forward and backward. I concentrate with all the [divine] names that emerge from me, both in the numerical value of each letter, their first letters and their final letters, as is known. Through this, I concentrate that it will leave. And then it speaks from within the body, [responding to] whatever you ask of it, and you command it to depart. Sometimes it is necessary to sound a shofar near his ear, concentrating the [divine] name *qera satan* [rend satan], all with the punctuation of *shwa*. You should also reverse it with At"Bash,[5] and this is the name, DGBNT. Know that that spirit does not come alone. Rather a satan supports him and leads him in his wanderings in this way so that his recompense for his sins may be completed. And it [the Spirit] cannot do anything without its permission for the Holy One has set [the satan] as [the spirit's] overseer, as it is written in *Zohar, Parshat Bo*, "A wicked person is judged by his evil impulse."[6] And that is as Scripture states, "*Appoint a wicked man over him; may an accuser [satan] stand at his right hand*" [Psalm 109:6], that King David, of blessed memory, cursed the evildoers, that the Holy One should punish his evil soul, that [the Spirit] should enter him and harm him. A satan comes with him to stand at the right of the soul of that evildoer, to help [the soul] to remain there. Sometimes the soul leaves, and the satan remains alone, guarding his place. Therefore, the transmigrated soul does not always stay there. It leaves and goes at specified times to be punished. He needs to leave there to receive his punishment. In the meantime, the satan who is appointed to guard his place remains there. The person is not healed from that illness until both of them leave. You should know that the Holy One "*sweetens bitter with bitter.*"[7] On the contrary, the verse that appears as a commandment that the soul of the evildoer should be punished, it is on the contrary, hinted there that his repair is through the *kavvanot* that I will write. I cannot expound at length about this matter here.

[Following is a long section that contains a series of *kavvanot* and mystical names that are used in the exorcism process. I have not translated it because it would make no sense in translation.]

And you should intend that it depart by the force of all those [divine] names. If it does not depart, repeat the aforesaid verse[8] and again intend all the mentioned names, each time concluding by stating forcefully, "*Depart, depart quickly.*" And know that the entire enterprise depends on your being as courageous and strong hearted as a mighty hero. Your heart should not weaken. This will strengthen him, and he will not harken to your words. You must also order [the spirit] not to leave via any site other than between the nail of the big toe and its flesh, so as not to injure the body in which it is situated. And you must order it, with the force of the foregoing names you intended and of excommunication and banning, not to cause any harm and not to reenter the body of any Jew whatsoever. Know that it will refuse very much to speak, in order not to be embarrassed before those hearing it. And know that when it speaks, the person's body remains as still as stone, and the spirit's voice emerges from its mouth without the lips moving, in a tone as soft as that of a small child. Also, when it ascends in the body to the lips to speak, the image of a round gland ascends under the skin of the throat, and similarly when it descends to the large toe of the foot, in order to leave, as has been mentioned. And know that when you ask him who he is and what is his name, he will deceive you and tell you someone else's name—either to mock you or to preclude the effectiveness of your order that he departs. It is therefore necessary that you order him, by [threat of] excommunication and banning, and by force of all the aforesaid names that you intended, that he should not deceive you at all. He will tell you who he is and his name in full truthfulness. You also need to do this in purity, with ritual immersion, in holiness, and with complete intentions.

2. The Daughter of Daniel Romano (*Book of Visions* 2.35 [97])

I saw in a dream a wealthy man who had died here in Damascus, a year before I came. His name was Judah Gano, and I had never seen him. He begged me, for God's sake, that I should repair his Soul, because there is nobody else in this generation who is worthy to repair [Souls]. Tomorrow, I will come to your house, so you can repair me. And I awoke.

The next day, a girl came to my house who was the daughter of Daniel Romano. She was possessed of an evil *Spirit*, and I healed her.

C. The Nephew of Joshua bin Nun

1. *Sefer Meirat Eyna'im*, Shlomo ben Gabbai, Constantinople, 1666, 17a

A STORY IN SAFED, MAY IT BE REBUILT SPEEDILY IN OUR DAYS, DURING THE TIME OF MY TEACHER, MAY HIS MEMORY BE FOR A BLESSING

Know that a certain youth, the son of the sister of the sage, R. Joshua bin Nun. He was eighteen years old and was a student in the yeshiva. My teacher, may his memory be for a blessing, saw him and said to his father, "The youth, your son, has a *Spirit* within him, and don't waste your money on physicians."

"His father said: "Heaven forbid; he only has occasional heartache, and he has had this pain for twelve years. The physicians healed him, and the pain returned to the heart."

My teacher, may his memory be for a blessing, said to him, "You will see that this is a *Spirit*. He commanded him, and the *Spirit* spoke. He said that he had been impregnated in that youth for twelve years. My teacher said to him, "Why have you been impregnated so many years."

The *Spirit* responded: "I was a pauper in Rome and was supported by charity, in that transmigration. This youth was also there, and he was the official in charge of charity. I called out to him that he should support me financially. He refused, and I died of hunger. The Heavenly Tribunal decreed that just as he killed me in that transmigration, so too I will kill him now."

My teacher, may his memory be for a blessing, decreed upon him that he should do him no harm. The *Spirit* said: "If you want that I should leave from here, fulfill one condition. It is, after I leave from here the youth should not see the face of a woman for three days. If the condition is transgressed, I will kill him."

The *Spirit* left, and the father of the youth asked the youth, "How do you feel?"

He responded, "I feel very well."

His father said to him, "My son, he will return."

The youth said, "No, my father, since I feel that I am better than when I was under the care of the physicians." My teacher, may his memory be for a blessing, commanded that the youth be guarded, that they should not let him leave the study house, and that no woman should come near him. The *Spirit* said that he was a deceiver and therefore asked him to fulfill this difficult condition. One day was Rosh Hodesh, and I Hayyim went to prepare a festive meal, and I left my place for Rabbi Joshua bin Nun to guard him. He also left, and the youth was left alone. His mother and aunt came in to see the youth. They saw him and kissed him. In that moment, the *Spirit* returned, entered him, and strangled him. Because of the fear of the nations of the world, that they would say that we killed him, the rabbi, may his memory be for a blessing, miraculously traveled [*kefizat ha-derekh*] on two reeds, in a moment, to Tiberias, and it was at twilight. In Tiberias, my teacher, may his memory be for a blessing, uttered a prayer that this should not be heard among the nations, so that it should not cause harm. We returned to Safed after eight days.

2. Joseph Sambari, *Divrei Yosef*, ed. S. Shtober (Jerusalem: Machon Ben Zvi, 1994), 350–51[9]

There was also a story in the days of the rabbi, may the memory of the righteous be for a blessing, that there was a youth who was sick for a number of years. The physicians came and went, but they could not heal him. The neighbors said to his father, "Perhaps he is possessed by a *Spirit*?"

The father said, "Heaven forbid; he is sick with a great fever, and whoever is possessed by a *Spirit* does not burn with fire as he does." The neighbors implored the father, until the father of the youth went to the rabbi, implored him, and brought him [the youth]. When they came, the Rabbi took hold of his pulse and said that he has a *Spirit*.[10] "If you do not believe me, I will cause him to speak." He immediately adjured the *Spirit* that it should speak before them, and it said that it was so and so. The rabbi asked him, "Why did you enter him?"

The *Spirit* responded that before he was transmigrated, the youth was the official in charge of charity. "I was a poor man and asked him two or three times for charity. He did not want to give me anything, until I died of hunger. Now I have been given permission, since he was the cause of my death, that I will kill him." The Rabbi then said to him that he should leave, since after his soul came into another body, he is considered to be another person, and he is not guilty of anything. The rabbi then told him: "If you will leave voluntarily, it is well. If not, I will expel you by force." When the *Spirit* saw the torments of his soul, he said that he would leave of his own will, but on condition that no woman should appear before this youth until seven consecutive days have passed. "If any woman appears before him, I will kill him." The rabbi said to his father and mother: "Listen to what the *Spirit* is saying. If you can fulfill the condition, I will endeavor to exorcise him. If not, I will cease my efforts."

His father and mother responded, "Let him leave, and we will guard the youth all seven days." The rabbi again warned them a second time, and they agreed with him. The *Spirit* immediately left him, and after three days, the youth was able to get up and walk around the house. His aunt, who was in Sidon, heard about this and came to rejoice with him that he had been healed from his malady. She arrived in Safed, may it speedily be rebuilt, and entered the youth's house, and nobody of the household was in the house. They were busy preparing the meal for the guest who had come, and they left the youth without a guardian. His aunt found the youth, and he was sleeping, and she bent down and kissed him. As she was kissing him, the youth cried out because the *Spirit* had entered his throat and strangled him. When the rabbi heard this, he miraculously traveled [*kefizat ha-derekh*] with him, so that the matter would not become known among the gentiles.

Appendix to Chapter 3

A. The Widow in Safed

The story of the widow in Safed is found in an abbreviated version in Vital, *Sefer Hezyonot*, 1.25 (73). A fuller, more detailed version was published Delmedigo, *Ta'alumot Hokhmah*. Several other sources quoted Delmedigo's text in full or in part. They include:

> Naphtali Bacharach, *Emek ha-Melekh*, Amsterdam, 1648, 16c–17b.
> Menasseh ben Israel, *Nishmat Hayyim*, Amsterdam, 1652, 169a–170b.
> Joseph Sambari, *Divrei Yosef* (Shtober ed.), 351–54. This edition contains significant variations from the Delmedigo text and has been published here in full.

1. J. S. Delmedigo, *Ta'alumot Hokhmah*, Basel, 1629, 49b–50b

A story occurred in the days of the holy and pure Rabbi and divine kabbalist, our teacher, Rabbi Isaac Luria Ashkenazi, of blessed memory, in Safed, may it speedily be rebuilt, concerning a widow into whom a *Spirit* entered. She had great pains and torments. Many people came to her and spoke with her. The *Spirit* responded to each one and told them the afflictions of their heart and what deficiencies they had. Among those who came was a sage by the name of Rabbi Joseph Ashkenazi, of blessed memory.[11] The *Spirit* immediately said to him: "Welcome my teacher and master. Does not my master remember that I was his student for a long time in Egypt? My name is so and so, and my father's name is so and so." When the woman's relatives saw that her pain and anguish were very great, they went to the holy rabbi, our teacher, Rabbi Isaac Luria, of blessed memory, to beg him that he should go with them to the woman and expel the *Spirit* from the woman. However, the rabbi, of blessed memory, was not free to go with them, so he sent his student, Rabbi Hayyim [Vital] Calabrese, of blessed memory, with them. He put his hands on him and transmitted the *kavvanot* and [divine] names. He also commanded him that he should decree bans and excommunications and should expel him against his will. When Rabbi Hayyim, of blessed memory, came in to her, the woman immediately turned her face to the wall. The rabbi [Vital], of blessed memory, said to her, "Evildoer, why have you turned your face away from me?"

The Spirit responded and said to him, "I could not look at your face, since the evildoers cannot look at your face, the face of the Shekhinah."

Rabbi Hayyim Vital, of blessed memory, immediately commanded him to turn his face, and then he turned his face. The Rabbi immediately said to him, "Tell me what sins and transgressions you committed that you were punished with such a severe punishment."

The *Spirit* responded to him, "I committed adultery and I caused bastards [*mamzerim*] to be born. It is now twenty-five years that I am wandering the earth, without even an hour or a moment of rest. Three angels of destruction are always with me everywhere I go. They punish me and flog me mercilessly and announce before me, saying, 'Thus, will be done to a man who increases bastards [*mamzerim*] in Israel." These three angels of destruction are alluded to in the verse "*Appoint a wicked man over him; may an accuser stand at his right side*" [Psalm 109:6]. The *Spirit* said further to the rabbi, of blessed memory, "Does not my master see one standing to my right and one to my left, and they announce before me,[12] and the third one beats me with deadly blows."

The rabbi asked him, and said, "Did not the Talmudic sages say, '*The judgment of evildoers in Gehenna is twelve months?*'"[13]

The *Spirit* responded:

> My master was not precise with regard to the passage mentioned. The Talmudic sages said that the punishment in Gehenna is only after they have suffered all punishments aside from Gehenna, transmigrations, and other harsh decrees. Afterwards, they bring him into Gehenna, and he remains there for twelve months while they purify and perfect them,

in order to remove from them all the stains from their souls, so that they would be prepared and ready to enter the Garden of Eden. For example, it is like an expert physician who puts difficult and bitter potions on the wound so that they should eat the infected flesh in the wound. Afterwards, he puts bandages and bindings on the wound in order to heal and cool the flesh as it was originally. So too is the matter of Gehenna. The pain of Gehenna is not even one part of the fifty parts that the Soul and Animus of the sinner suffer before their entrance into Gehenna.

Then the rabbi, of blessed memory, asked him, "How did you die?"
The *Spirit* responded and said: "My death was by strangulation. Even though the four forms of death by the court have been abrogated, the law of the four deaths has not been abrogated.[14] I went from Alexandria on a ship to Cairo, and the ship sank in the place where the Nile enters the sea. I and other Jews that were with me on the ship drowned."

Then Rabbi Hayyim Vital, of blessed memory, asked him: "Why did you not recite the confession as your Soul left your body? Perhaps it might have helped you?"

The *Spirit* responded to him: "I did not have time to recite the confession because the water immediately choked me in my throat, and I immediately drowned in the water. I was distraught and did not have the presence of mind to confess."

Then the rabbi asked him, "Tell me what happened after you drowned in the sea, and after your Soul left your body?"

The *Spirit* responded and said,

You should know that when the matter became known about the sinking of the ship, the Jews of Cairo immediately went out, entered the water, and took us from the water and buried us. Immediately after the Jews left the cemetery, a cruel angel came with a fiery staff in his hand and strongly smote my grave with the staff. The grave immediately split into two from the blows that were great and mighty. The angel said to me, "Evildoer, evildoer, arise for judgment." He immediately took me and put me in the hollow of the sling and slung me with one shot, from Cairo to before the gate of Gehenna that was in the desert. As I fell there, before the gate of Gehenna, many thousands of evildoers who had been sentenced to Gehenna came out, and all of them shouted at me and said to me, "Go, go, man of blood, leave here troubler of Israel, and continually cursed me with many curses." They said to me, "It is not yet appropriate for you to enter Gehenna, and you do not yet have permission to enter here." They immediately slung me from mountain to mountain and hill to hill, and these three angels of destruction always accompanied me and announced before me and beat me. Also, every time that other angels of destruction, evil spirits, demons, and Lilith's encountered me and heard the announcement that was announced before me, they also beat me with great and terrible blows. These [angels] also dragged me here, and this led me here, until all the vertebrae of my Soul were dislocated. Thus, I wandered the earth until I reached the city of Hormuz,[15] which was a large city close to the land of India. My intention was to enter the body of some Jew. Perhaps I would be spared the blows, torments, and troubles. When I came to that city, I saw some Jews who were evildoers and great sinners against God. They had sexual relations with gentile women and committed other sins. I was not able to enter the body of any of them, because of the many powers of impurity that dwelled in them, and in their environs. If I had entered the body of one of them, I would have added impurity to my own impurity, and damage to my own damage. I again returned to going from mountain to mountain and hill to hill until I came to the desert of Gaza. I found a pregnant doe there, and out of my great anguish and pain, I entered her body. This was after seven years of enduring great and evil troubles. When I entered the body of the doe, I had immense pain, since the Animus of the person and the Animus of an animal are not similar to each other. One of them walks upright, and the other walks horizontally. Also, the Animus of the animal drinks water that is impure and full of despicable things, and it smells bad for the Animus of the person. It also eats food that is not food for a human, and in addition, I had great anguish from the fetus that was in her womb. The doe also had great anguish because of me, and her abdomen was pinched. She ran over hills and valleys until her abdomen split, and she died. I left there and came to the city of Shechem, where I entered the body of a Jew who was a kohen. The kohen immediately sent for the holy men [Kedoshim] and clergy [galohim][16] of the Ishmaelites [Muslims], to increase the incantations and adjurations with impure names, also for amulets with impure names, which they hung around his neck. I was not able to tolerate them and remain in his body. I left him and immediately escaped from there and came here to Safed, may it be speedily rebuilt, and entered the body of this woman. Today is twenty-five years that I have not had tranquility and quiet, but every day they add anguish to my anguish, and pain to my pain.

The rabbi, of blessed memory, said to him, "How long will you have this pain, and is there never any recovery for you?"

The Spirit responded to him and said: "Until all the bastards that I gave birth to would die. As long as they are alive and exist, there is no repair for me. At that moment, all of the people who were present, a very large crowd, cried very much because the fear of Divine Judgment fell upon them. It caused a great awakening in the land because of that event."

The rabbi asked him: "Who gave you permission to enter the body of this woman?"

The Spirit responded and said: "I slept one night in her house, and before dawn this woman got up from her bed to strike a spark from the flint and steel. The tinder did not catch from the sparks and the woman pleaded very much, but she did not succeed. Then the woman became very angry, and she threw the flint and steel and the tinder, everything in her hands, to the ground, and said in great anger, 'Go to Satan.' I was immediately given permission to enter her body.

The rabbi, of blessed memory, asked him and said, "You were given permission to enter her body because of such a small sin?"

The *Spirit* responded and said: "Know my master and sage that this woman was not as she appeared. She does not believe in the miracles that the Holy One did for Israel, and particularly the Exodus from Egypt. Every Passover eve when all Jews are joyous and happy, recite the Great Hallel, and recount the story of the Exodus from Egypt, in her heart she thinks that there never was such a miracle, and it is all a projection and a joke."

The rabbi immediately said to the woman, "So and so, do you believe with complete faith that the one and only Holy One created heaven and earth, and with His hands has the strength and ability to do whatever He wants, and there is nobody who can tell Him what to do?"

The woman responded and said, "Yes, I believe it all with complete faith."

The rabbi, of blessed memory, further said to her, "Do you believe with complete faith that the Holy One took us out of Egypt, from the house of slavery, split the sea for us, and did many miracles for us?"

The woman responded, "Yes, my lord sage, I believe it all with complete faith, and if at times I had other beliefs, I regret it." And the woman began to cry. The rabbi immediately decreed upon the *Spirit* that he should leave, and he should not leave through any organ that would harm her, but through the smallest finger of her left foot. The reason being that the limb through which it leaves might be permanently damaged. The Rabbi concentrated on the [Divine] names that had been taught to him by his teacher, of blessed memory. The finger immediately swelled up and reddened, and it exited through there. Afterwards, for several nights, the *Spirit* came to the windows and door of the house and frightened the woman so that she would let him return and enter her body. The woman's family members went back to the kabbalist, Rabbi Isaac Luria, of blessed memory. The rabbi, of blessed memory, again sent his disciple, our teacher, Rabbi Hayyim [Vital], of blessed memory, and commanded him to examine the *mezuzah*, to see if it was proper or defective. Rabbi Hayyim, of blessed memory, went to check the *mezuzah* and found that the door had no *mezuzah*. The rabbi immediately ordered that a proper *mezuzah* be put on the door. They did so, and from that time forward, [the *Spirit*] never returned.

2. Joseph Sambari, *Divrei Yosef* (Shtober ed.), 351–54

Another story about a *Spirit* that entered a widow and tormented her greatly. At the sound of her shouting, many men and women came to ask the *Spirit* that it should leave the widow at rest since she was a poor woman who needed to work in order to earn a living for herself and her children. The *Spirit* rose before the speakers and told each one of them their evil deeds, with signs and wonders. They were ashamed and left. One day, Rabbi Joseph Ashkenazi came in.[17] The *Spirit* immediately said to him: "Welcome. I was your student for a long time in Egypt?

My name is so and so, and my father's name is so and so. You rebuked me much about my evil deeds, but I did not listen to you. Now I am in great anguish, as my master sees. I have more anguish from angels of destruction than what this woman is suffering. What should I do? 'My punishment is too great to bear' [Genesis, 4:13]." When the relatives of the woman saw the suffering of her soul, they came and prostrated themselves before the rabbi and pleaded with him that he should go with them and exorcise him. Since the rabbi was not free, and also because he was sick, he sent for Rabbi Hayyim Vital. He placed his hands on him and gave him the mystical intentions [kavvanot] to exorcise him. He also commanded him that he should decree bans and excommunications upon him and exorcise him against his will. When Rabbi Hayyim Vital entered the woman's house, she turned her face to the wall. Rabbi Hayyim Vital said, "Evildoer, why have you turned your face to the wall?"

The *Spirit* responded, "Because I could not look at the face of the Shekhinah." He immediately commanded him to turn his face to him, and he did so. Rabbi Hayyim Vital said to him, "What sins and transgressions did you commit that you were punished with such a punishment?"

The *Spirit* responded and said, "I committed adultery, and I caused bastards [mamzerim] to be born from her. It is about twenty-five years that I am wandering the earth, without even an hour or a moment of rest. Three angels of destruction are always with me everywhere I go. They punish me and flog me mercilessly and announce before me, saying, 'This will be done to a man who increases bastards [mamzerim] in Israel.'" The *Spirit* said further to Rabbi Hayyim Vital, "Does not my master see the three of them? One to the right and one to the left," and the third beat him with deadly blows.

Rabbi Hayyim Vital asked him, "Did not the Talmudic sages say, 'The judgment of evildoers in Gehenna is twelve months?'"[18]

The *Spirit* said to him: "The punishment in Gehenna is only after they have suffered all punishments aside from Gehenna, transmigrations, and other harsh decrees. Afterwards, they bring him into Gehenna, and he remains there for twelve months while they purify and perfect them, in order to remove from them all the stains from their souls so that they would be prepared and ready to enter the Garden of Eden, and the pain of Gehenna is not one part of the three parts that they suffer outside of Gehenna."

Rabbi Hayyim Vital asked him further: How did he die? The *Spirit* responded that it was by strangulation. He went from Mana Ammon with many Jews on a ship to Cairo. "When the ship reached the place where the Nile enters the sea, the ship broke up, and I drowned and died." Rabbi Hayyim Vital asked and said to him: "Why did you not recite the confession as your Soul left your body? It would have helped you greatly."

The *Spirit* responded and said to him, "I did not have time to recite the confession because the water immediately choked him in his throat, and he became confused and was not able to confess."

Rabbi Hayyim Vital further asked and said to him, "What happened to you after your Soul left your body?"

The *Spirit* responded and said,

> It is known to my master that when the matter became known to the people of Cairo, burial societies went out and took them from the water and buried them. After they left, a cruel angel immediately came with a fiery staff in his hand and strongly smote the grave. The grave immediately split into two. The angel said to him, "Evildoer, arise for judgment." He immediately took him and put him in the hollow of the sling and slung him with one shot, from Cairo to the gate of Gehenna in the desert. Many thousands came out of Gehenna, and all of them shouted at me and said: "Go, go, you are not yet appropriate to enter here." They immediately slung me from mountain to mountain and hill to hill, and these three angels of destruction always beat me and announced before me.

At every announcement, other angels of destruction, other evil spirits, demons, and Liliths beat him with great and terrible blows in addition to the blows of the three angels of destruction that always accompanied him. These [angels] also dragged him here, and this led him here, until all the vertebrae of his Soul were dislocated. He wandered the earth until he reached the city of Hormuz,[19] which was a large city close to the land of India, and there were many Jews there. My intention was to enter the body of some Jew in order to be [away] from my troubles. I saw that those Jews were complete evildoers, and most of them had sexual relations with menstruating women and committed other sins. I was not able to enter the body of any of them because of the many powers of impurity that dwelled in them, and in their environs. If I had entered the body of one of them, I would have added impurity to my own impurity and damage to my own damage. I again returned to going from mountain to mountain and hill to hill until I came to the desert of Gaza. I found a pregnant doe there, and out of my great anguish and pain, I entered her body. This was after seven years of enduring great and evil troubles. When I entered the body of the doe, I had immense pain since the Animus of the person and the Animus of an animal are not similar to each other. One of them walks upright, and the other walks on all fours, and they cannot relate to each other. I was not able to restrain myself until I drove the doe crazy, and she ran over hills and valleys until she came to Safed, may it speedily be rebuilt. Many people went out to see her, and among those who went out was this widow. When I saw her deeds, that they were pleasant, I entered her body.

It is now two years that he was in her body. He then decreed a great excommunication on the *Spirit* and adjured him with adjurations that had been transmitted to him by the rabbi,[20] of blessed memory, and exorcised him against his will. He came and told the story to friends, and the people were amazed.

Then the rabbi commanded Rabbi Hayyim Vital, of blessed memory, and said to him: "Guard yourself very much and do not go to the market at night or when it is foggy. The *Spirits* are very angry with you, and in particular the *Spirit* that was in the widow goes out every night to kill you, because you exorcised him against his will. You also need to know that you are from the soul spark of Cain,[21] and when you shake your garments, all the evil husks flee from you."

Rabbi Hayyim Vital, of blessed memory, did not pay attention to these words until one time he was at his teacher's house until about two hours after dark, and his teacher said to him, "Sage, R. Hayyim, it has gotten dark, and how will you go home?"

He said to him, "When I leave you, it is like one who separates from life." He then left, and the rabbi accompanied him to the gate of the courtyard. As he was going down the street, he saw a large donkey coming toward him. He was very frightened, but nonetheless he was not deterred from walking on his way. He was going along, and the donkey approached him, and when it reached him, he fell to the ground, and his arm became paralyzed, and he was not able to bring it back. It also appeared to him as if he had fallen into the miry clay.[22] When he shook his garments, it left him. Then he remembered what the rabbi had told him, and he went home. That night, he could not sleep at all because of the pain in his arm. He got up early in the morning and went to the rabbi. As soon as he came in, the rabbi said to him: "How were you saved from that donkey, who was the *Spirit* that was in the widow, and he was greatly angry with you? I knew this, and that is why I accompanied you to the gate of the courtyard, and I did not go back into my house until you came into your house. If I had not done this, I would not have been able to save you from this. Why did you not listen to what I told you? When you shake your garment, all kinds of harmful spirits flee from you." He immediately put his hand on his arm, and the arm returned to normal. From that night onward, he did not go out at night alone, but when he saw that it was getting dark, he remained in the study house of the rabbi, of blessed memory.[23]

B. The Falco Letter

This letter consists of two stories. The primary story is the story of a woman possessed by a *dybbuk* in Safed in 1571. The second story is of a boy who is also possessed by a *dybbuk*. Multiple versions of each story are presented since there are interesting variations between the different versions.

1. Falco Letter—A Spirit Entered a Woman in Safed—1571

This story is found in two versions:

    A. Menasseh ben Israel, *Nishmat Hayyim* (Amsterdam, 1651), 109a–11a.

    B. Joseph Sambari, *Divrei Yosef* (Shtober ed.), 319–24.

A. *Nishmat Hayyim* [Amsterdam, 1651]

[109a][24] A GREAT EVENT OCCURRED IN THE HOLY COMMUNITY OF SAFED, MAY IT BE REBUILT, AND RESTABLISHED SPEEDILY IN OUR DAYS

    Since the person is more drawn to the pleasures of his body and his emotions, rather than following the advice of his soul and the guidance and directions of the Torah, even the believers and those who are punctilious in all things, because the matters of the world to come are not perceived by the intellect. Who will establish all the aspects in his heart, so that it will make an impression on him, to separate himself from every aspect of evil and transgression, in speech, in thought, and deed? Not every person can attain this.

Therefore, I agreed to write this down in order to benefit others, what occurred today, the eleventh of Adar I [in the year] 5331 [1571] of Creation, concerning a woman, into whom entered the Spirit of a Jewish man, as I will explain here. The truth is that whoever was there at that time and heard from the *Spirit*, what he said and revealed, and whoever heard from those who heard them, it would be appropriate for them to align their hearts to Heaven, and should be in awe and fear of the Day of Judgment and the accounting of their soul since all will come to account, and Sheol is not a place of refuge.[25] It became known from one who came from that world and told what happened there. Perhaps the Holy One sent him so that they would be in awe of Him, as the Talmudic sages said, "*God did this so that they should be in awe of Him* [Ecclesiastes, 3:14]—this is a bad dream."[26] This was not a dream, but a waking experience, visible to everyone. I found myself in a large group. There were close to one hundred people there, and scholars and communal leaders among them. Two men who knew adjurations and many other things approached the woman so that the Spirit within the woman should speak. They caused smoke and sulfur to enter her nostrils, but she was unconscious and did not even move her head from the fire or the smoke. Through the adjurations, a voice began to be heard, thick and sustained, like the roar of a lion and the sound of a lion, without moving the tongue or opening the lips. When the voice began to be heard, the two men strengthened and exerted themselves quickly and diligently to do what they [109b] did. They spoke to him [the *Spirit*] in a very loud and quarrelsome tone and said, "Evildoer, speak and say who you are, in clear language." The voice then revealed itself to everyone, and he was a human voice. They again said in a loud voice and in the manner mentioned, "What is your name, evildoer?"

He responded, "So and so [*ploni*]."

"And the family name?"

"So and so."

They asked him, "How do we know that you are so and so?"

He responded that he had died in Tripoli[27] and left behind one son whose name was so and so. He had three wives. The name of the first was so and so, the name of the second one was so and so, and the third one was so and so, and he died while married to the third. She was now married to so and so. He spoke truthfully regarding all the signs that he gave. All of us who were present there recognized that it was the *Spirit* who was speaking. They asked him, "For what sin were you transmigrated into the world of transmigrations?" He answered, for many sins that he committed in his lifetime. They again asked him to give details. He said to them that he did not want to do so since what would be the purpose? Then they pressed him greatly that he should at least give details of his greatest sin. He answered that he had been a heretic and scoffer and had spoken against the Torah of Moses Our Teacher. Concerning this, people publicly testified that he had spoken such things in his lifetime. They asked him, "Do you still hold these opinions now?" He responded, like one groaning, with a bitter voice, shouting and storming, and said, "I recognize that I have sinned, transgressed, and did evil." He asked forgiveness from the Holy One and his perfect Torah, for his many sins. Then the two men began to implore him and force him, by means of everything mentioned above, that he should leave her and should go to a desolate desert. They would also ask for mercy and blow the *shofar* so that he would no longer continue in this transmigration. They said to him, "Do you want that we should ask for mercy, pray, and blow the *shofar* for you?"

He responded: If only [it be so]."

They asked him, "Who should blow the *shofar*?"

He said, "The sage, his honor, Rabbi Solomon ibn Alkabetz."

The above-mentioned sage responded that he was unable to do so. They again asked him, "Do you want someone else?"

He said that it should be the sage, Rabbi Abraham Lahmi.

They also asked him, "Who should pray for you?" He responded that it should be Rabbi Elijah Falco.

They then recited: "God is King [*El Melekh*]" . . . "*And He passed over*" [Exodus 34:6],[28] with blowing of the *shofar*, and it was all done according to his expressed will. They then said to him a second time that he should leave since they had done what he had wanted.

He responded, "I will leave in a while."

They asked him, "Do you want that we should do a *tikkun* for your soul?" He responded that no *tikkun* would help. They said to him, "Do you want that your son should recite the Kaddish or study Torah?" He responded that it would be of no help to him, and his son did not know enough to study Torah.[29] I asked him about the punishment in the grave [hibut ha-kever]. One of those sitting there said, "This one certainly has never been in a grave." The *Spirit* spoke and contradicted his words:

> I entered the grave on the day of burial. I was taken out that night, and never entered it again. It is thirty-three years since that time, and I have been going from mountain to mountain and hill to hill, and I have not found rest anywhere, except for the time I found myself in Shechem, and I entered a certain woman. When she came here, they exorcised me, according to everything that has been written above. However, they immediately placed amulets on her, and I was not able to return to her again."

All of this was true from what we know from others, that it happened in this way.

He then said: "I was wandering in the city, to enter synagogues. Perhaps I would find rest and respite for my soul, but I was not allowed to enter any synagogue."

They asked him who prevented him.

He answered, "The sages."

They further asked him, "Were they alive or dead?"

He said, "Dead. They trampled me and said to me, 'Get out of here, you evildoer."

The questioner further asked him, "Which synagogue did he go to first?"

He said, "To my community."

They said to him, "Which one is it?"

He responded, "Beth Jacob."

They further asked him, "Who is now sitting in your place?"

He responded, "Since they did not allow me to enter, how should I know who is sitting in my place?"

They further asked him, "Who sat beside you when you were alive?"

He responded, "So and so," and everything he said was true. Then they said to him: "How did you enter this woman? Is it not forbidden for you to harm her?"

He said, "What could I do; I did not find rest anywhere, except in her, who is an upright [kosher] woman."

The first two people asked him further, "How did you enter this house?"

"It has a *mezuzah*. I entered through the cellar opening since it had no *mezuzah*."

They asked him, "How did you enter her since she was an upright woman?"

He said: "It was when she was sweeping, and she threw a bit of mud on my head, and through this I was able to enter her. All of this happened on Thursday evening of the previous week." The *Spirit* said all this by himself, and it was so since it was from that time that she felt it herself.

As they stood there and pressured him that he should leave, they said to him: "Why did you not fear the excommunication that you received yesterday to leave and not to return again to her. How could you transgress this? Yes, I left but could not find a place of rest. When I saw that they did not place any amulets on her, I was able to enter her a second time."

They then strengthened themselves and said to him: "Leave, and if not, we will decree against you the excommunication of the *Kol Bo*[30] that you should leave, in any event." They imposed the excommunication of the *Kol Bo* on him, and he swore by the Ten Statements [Aseret ha-Dibrot] that he would leave within one hour. Many people testified that this had been his custom when he was alive, to swear this oath. They waited, and in the meantime, they reproved him and spoke harshly to him: "Are you not afraid of the excommunication, or even of your oath, or even the excommunication of the *Kol Bo*?"

He responded, "What should I do, '*if I am to perish, I shall perish*'" [Esther, 4:16].

After this, one of them wanted to test if it was the Spirit who was speaking and spoke to him in Hebrew, in Arabic, and in Turkish. He responded to each language clearly, as when he had been alive, as those who knew him testified. The woman did not know any of these languages. When he spoke to him in Yiddish, he was not able to respond. He said that he did not know or understand that language. Others asked him, "Who am I?" And he responded to all of them with their names. They also asked him, "What was your trade when you were alive?"

He responded, "The work of *saraflik* [money changing]." And it was so.

They also asked him about ibn Musa, if he had seen him in his journey of transmigration. He responded that he had not seen him at all. They pressured him with the adjurations mentioned above, with the smoke, and with the names mentioned above that he should leave through the large toe of one of her feet. He showed us that he was leaving that day as they had told him, by the movement of quickly raising and lowering her legs, one after the other. As a result of the great movements, which he made with great force, the blanket that was covering her fell off, and she was uncovered and exposed herself before everyone. They approached her to cover her thighs, but she did not feel it at all. Whoever knew her, knew of her great modesty, and now all of her modesty was lost. This was all because she was as dead, and unconscious, as we said above.

They said to him, "The true sign by which we will know that you have gone out completely is that you should extinguish a certain candle that is hanging on the wall, approximately three cubits from her." Through these movements that we mentioned, he wanted to extinguish the candle. He strengthened himself, hastened, and exerted himself to show that he was leaving through the big toe, and extinguish the candle on the wall. Nonetheless, he did not leave. He did not want to leave but wanted to mislead us. Many times, he said [to] bring the candle closer to where it was yesterday so that he could extinguish it there. They said to him: "If you will extinguish the candle where it is, then we will know for certain that you went out. If not, you are mocking us." He again strengthened himself to make movements and movements of the legs, as mentioned, and created air movement through these actions since he did not want to leave and abandon his dwelling place from that place. He was not able to extinguish the candle from there. If he had been closer, he would have been able to extinguish it since the *Spirit* was standing on top of her feet, as he said. Both those who had adjured him and we were able to see that the *Spirit* had come out and was close to her legs. They again adjured him and gave him smoke, fire, and sulfur into the nostrils in order to make him leave completely through the big toe and should completely and absolutely uproot himself and should extinguish the candle, which was three cubits away. He could extinguish it on his way from there on his way to the desolate desert. He said to them many times: "Let this poor Jewish woman be, and do not hurt her."

They said to him: "You are the one who is hurting her. If you have pity on her, leave."

He responded: "Do not continue to force me to leave, for if you force me to leave, I will take out her soul with me." Nonetheless, the above-mentioned adjurers decreed on him that he should leave in any event, but he did not leave. They said: "Sit on the bed and then go out. If you do not want to, we will force you, by the above-mentioned means." He sat on the bed without help. When he was sitting, they said to him in a very loud voice, "Leave evildoer and without her soul." Then he touched the foot himself with his finger as if he was pushing out the spirit through the big toe through this touching. She instantly began to talk, sat up, and said that he had already left. They did not believe her. Perhaps he was speaking through her because they saw that the candle had not been extinguished. She said, "It seems that he forgot to extinguish the candle because of the confusion and his great haste to leave." Nonetheless, they did not believe her and wanted to torment her as before, and she was shouting to her father-in-law and grandmother, "Why do you let them burn me since he has left, and they do not believe me?" She said, "I know that it is true that he has already left."

They said to her, "What is the matter [that you know]?"

She responded, "Must I tell you?" Then they understood that it was not something that should be said in public. Then they said to a woman, "Go to her and she will reveal the matter to you." She did so and learned that the Spirit had exited through her vagina and caused her to bleed as he left. They all agreed to the truth of this sign, and they placed the amulets on her that had been prepared in the house and was assumed to be healed.

An hour later, the sages came to her when the rumor spread in the city that the *Spirit* of a Jewish man was speaking through a woman. When they saw her, they said that it was certain that he had not left. If he had left, he had returned. They said this because of the signs they saw. Her eyes were glazed over, and her breathing was labored. Through these signs they knew that he was still in her. Then the voice returned, the voice of ruin; the spirit was still in her. The two adjurers told me that he had certainly left but reentered her because the amulets that they had placed on her were not written specifically for her, because of the confusion. The whole city, Jews, and Turks, came to see this awesome sight, and it was astonishing to everyone. They hushed up the matter because of the danger of the nations (who were saying that she should be burned), until it would be forgotten in a number of days, and the matter could be resolved. After eight days, the poor woman died because of the *Spirit* who had not left her. They said that he choked her and left with her soul.

Everything I have written above; every detail is written as it was. There is no reason to doubt or question anything since it is all truthfully written and there are no additions or deletions. I have written what I saw and heard. I pleaded with the scholars who were there that they should also put their signatures on this since we live from their mouths so that my words will be believed through their signatures. The eye that sees this writing, and the ear that hears will believe faithfully, as if he had heard directly from the spirit. He will be in fear and awe to believe and fulfill everything that is written in the Torah and the words of our rabbis, of blessed memory. Then he will rest in peace and three groups of angels will go to meet him. One saying, peace, etc., and no plague will approach his tent, and his soul will cleave to God and will return to the place from which it was hewn. Signed by the writer, the young and poor one among the myriads [of Israel], the devoted servant of the fearers of the Lord, and to those who think of his name, Elia Falco.

I was there, and my eyes saw, and my ears heard all this and more, what he saw testifies about them, Shlomo ha-Levi ben Alkabetz.

These words are words of truth which have no measure, so that every man should know about this event and leave his evil ways, and every man [should give up] the wrong of his thoughts before he goes [to the next world] and is not, and he who knows will return, and repent, and come back, and will be healed. The humble one, Abraham ha-Lahmi.

Samuel Bueno.

I too was called to see this matter, and my eyes have seen and my ears have heard, and it is a miraculous thing, to teach us that we should turn back in repentance, says Abraham Arueti.

B. Joseph Sambari, *Divrei Yosef* (Shtober ed.) 319–24.[31]

A story that happened, as I found it in written in the manuscript of the great tamarisk [scholar] Rabbi Elia Falco, may his memory be for a blessing, and this is what it says.

A STORY REGARDING A *SPIRIT*. Since the person is more drawn to the pleasures of his body and his emotions, rather than following the advice of his soul and the guidance and directions of the Torah, even the believers and those who are punctilious in all things, because the matters of the world to come are not perceived by the intellect. Who will establish all the aspects in his heart, so that it will make an impression on him, to separate himself from every aspect of evil and transgression, in speech, in thought, and in deed? Not every person can attain this. Therefore, I agreed to write this down in order to benefit others, what occurred today, the eleventh of Adar I [in the year] 5331 [1571] of Creation, concerning a woman, the daughter of the aged R' Joseph Zarfati, into whom entered the *Spirit* of a Jewish man, as I will explain here. The truth is that whoever was there at that time and heard from the *Spirit*, what he said and revealed, and whoever heard from those who heard them, it would be appropriate for them to align their hearts to Heaven, and should be in awe and fear the Day of Judgment and the accounting of their soul, since all will come to account, and Sheol is not a place of refuge.[32] It became known from one who came who came from that world, and told what happened there, the *Spirit* of a certain man. Perhaps, the Holy One sent him so that they would be in awe of Him, as the Talmudic sages said: "*God did this so that they should be in awe of Him* [Ecclesiastes, 3:14]—this is a bad dream."[33] This was not a dream, but a waking experience, visible to everyone. I found myself in a large group. There were close to one hundred people there, and scholars and communal leaders among them. Two men who knew adjurations and many other things approached the woman so that the *Spirit* within the woman should speak. They caused smoke and sulfur to enter her nostrils, but she was unconscious and did not even move her head from the fire or the smoke. Through the adjurations a voice began to be heard, thick and sustained, like the roar of a lion and the sound of a lion, without moving the tongue or opening the lips. When the voice began to be heard, the two men strengthened and exerted themselves quickly and diligently to do what they did. They spoke to him [the *Spirit*] in a very loud and quarrelsome tone and said: Evildoer, speak and say who you are, in clear language. The voice of the *Spirit* then revealed itself to everyone and he was a human voice. They again said in a loud voice and in the manner mentioned, what is your name, evildoer? He responded: Samuel Zarfati. They asked him: How do we know that you are Samuel Zarfati? He responded that he had died in Tripoli,[34] and left behind one son whose name was so and so. He had three daughters [wives].[35] The name of the first was so and so, the name of the second one was so and so, and the third one was so and so, and he died while married to the third. She was now married to Tuviah de Liriah. He spoke truthfully regarding all the signs that he gave. All of us who were present there recognized that it was the *Spirit* who was speaking. They asked him: For what sin were you transmigrated into the world of transmigrations? He answered: For many sins that I committed in my lifetime. They again asked him to give details. He said that he did not want to do so, since what would be the purpose? Then they pressed him greatly that he should at least give details of his greatest sin. He answered that he had been a heretic and had said that all religions were equal. Concerning this, people publicly testified that he had spoken such things in his lifetime. They asked him: Do you still hold these opinions now? He responded: Like one groaning, with a bitter voice, shouting and storming, and said: I recognize that I have sinned, transgressed, and did evil. He asked forgiveness from the Holy One and his perfect Torah, for his many sins. Then the two men began to implore him and excommunicate him, that he should leave her and should go to a desolate desert, by means of everything mentioned above. They would also ask for mercy for him, pray for him and blow the shofar. They said to him: Do you want that we should ask for mercy, pray, and blow the shofar for you? He responded: if only [it should be so]. They asked him: Who should blow the *shofar*? The Spirit said: the sage, his honor, Rabbi Solomon ibn Alkabetz. The above-mentioned sage responded that he was unable to do so. They again asked him: Do you want someone else? He said that it should be the sage, Rabbi Abraham Lahmi. They also asked him: Who should pray for you? The Spirit responded that it should be Rabbi Elijah Falco. They then recited: "God is King [El Melekh]" . . . "And He passed over" [Exodus 34:6],[36] with blowing of the *shofar*, and it was all done according to his expressed will. They then said to him a second time that he should leave, since they had done what he had wanted. The Spirit responded: I will leave in a while. They said to him: Do you want that your son should recite the *Kaddish* or study Torah?[37] He responded that it would be of no help to him, and his son did not know enough to study Torah. I asked him about the punishment in the grave [hibut ha-kever]. One of those sitting there said: This one certainly has never been in a grave. The *Spirit* spoke and contradicted his words. I entered the grave on the day of burial. I was taken out that night, and never entered it again. It has been close to three years since that time and I have been going from mountain to mountain and hill to hill, and I have not found a place of rest, except for the time I found myself in Shechem and I entered a certain woman. They exorcised me, according to everything that has been written above, and they immediately placed amulets on her. I was not able to return to her again, and I came here. All of this was true from what we know from others, that it happened in this way. Afterwards, I wandered in the city, to enter synagogues. Perhaps I would find rest and respite for my soul, but I was not allowed to enter any synagogue. They asked him: Who prevented him? The *Spirit* answered: the sages. They further asked him: Were they alive or dead? He said: Dead. They trampled me and said to me: Get out of here, you evildoer. The questioner further asked him: Which synagogue did he go to first? He said: To my community. They said to him: Which one is it? He responded: Beth Jacob.[38] They further asked him: Who is now sitting in your place? He responded: Since they did not allow me to enter, how should I know who is sitting in my place[?] They further asked him: Who sat beside you when you were alive? He responded: So and so, and everything he said was true. Then they said to him: How did you enter this woman? Is it not forbidden for you? He said: What could I do; I did not find rest anywhere, except in her. She is an upright [*kasher*] woman. They again asked him: If she is a married woman, were you not concerned about her husband? The *Spirit* responded: What about it, her husband is not here, but is in Salonika. The first two people asked him further: How did you enter this house; it has a *mezuzah*? I entered through the cellar opening, since it had no *mezuzah*. They asked him: How did you enter her, since she was an upright woman? He said: It was when she was sweeping, and she threw a bit of mud on her head, and through this I was able to enter her. All of this happened on Thursday evening of the previous week. The *Spirit* said all this by himself, and it was so, since it was from that time that she felt it herself. As they stood there and pressured him that he should leave, they said to him: Why did you not fear the excommunication that you received yesterday to leave and not to return again to her. How could you transgress this? Yes, I left, but could not find a place of rest. When I saw that they did not place any amulets on her, I was able to enter her a second time. They then strengthened themselves and said to him: Leave, and if not, we will decree against you the excommunication of the *Kol Bo*[39] that you should leave, in any event. They imposed the excommunication of the *Kol Bo* on him, and he swore by the Ten Statements [Aseret ha-Dibrot] that he would leave within one hour. Many people testified that this had been his custom when he was alive, to swear this oath. They waited, and in the meantime, they reproved him and spoke harshly to him. Are you not afraid of the excommunication, or even of your oath, or even the excommunication of the *Kol Bo*? He responded: What should I do, "*if I am to perish, I shall perish*" [Esther, 4:16]. After this, one of them wanted to test if it was the *Spirit* who was speaking, and spoke to him in Hebrew, in Arabic, and in the Islamic language called *morisco*.[40] He responded to each language clearly, as when he had been alive, as those who knew him testified. The woman did not know any of these languages. When he spoke to him in Yiddish, he was not able to respond. He said that he did not know or understand that language. Others asked him: "Who am I[?]" and he responded to all of them with their names. They also asked him, what was your trade when you were alive? He responded: The work of *sarafish* [money changing]. And it was so. They also asked him about ibn Musa, if he had seen him in his journey of transmigration. He responded that he had not seen him at all. They pressured him with the adjurations mentioned above, with the smoke, and with the [divine] names that he should leave through the large toe of one of her feet. He tricked us that he was leaving that day as they had told him, by the movement of quickly raising and lowering her legs, one after the other. As a result of the great movements, which he made with great force, the blanket that was covering her fell off, and she was uncovered and exposed herself to the thighs before everyone. They approached her to cover her thighs, but she did not feel it at all. Whoever knew her, knew of her great modesty, and now all of her modesty was lost. This was all because she was as dead, and unconscious, as we said above. They said to him: the true sign by which we will know that you have gone out completely is that you should extinguish a certain candle that is hanging on the wall, approximately three cubits from her. Through these movements that we mentioned, he wanted to extinguish the candle. He strengthened himself, hastened, and exerted himself to show that he was leaving through the big toe, and extinguish the candle on the wall. Nonetheless, he did not leave. He did not want to leave but wanted to mislead us. Many times, he said: Bring the candle closer to where it was yesterday, so that he could extinguish it there. They said to him: If you will extinguish the candle where it is, then we will know for certain that you went out. If not, you are mocking us. He again strengthened himself to make movements and movements of the legs, as mentioned, and created air movement through these actions, since he did not want to leave and abandon his dwelling place from that place. He was not able to extinguish the candle from there. If he had been closer, he would have been able to extinguish it, since the Spirit was standing on top of her feet, as both those who had adjured him had said. We were able to see that the Spirit had come out and was close to her legs. They again adjured him and gave him smoke, fire, and sulfur into the nostrils in order to make him leave completely through the big toe and should completely and absolutely uproot himself and should extinguish the candle, which was three cubits away. He could extinguish it on his way from there on his way to the desolate desert. He said to them many times: Let this poor Jewish woman be, and do not hurt her. They said to him: you are the one who is hurting her. If you have pity on her, leave. He responded: Do not continue to force me to leave, for if you force me to leave, I will take out her soul with me. Nonetheless, the above-mentioned adjurers decreed on him that he should leave in any event, but he did not leave. They said: Sit on the bed and then go out. If you do not want to, we will force you, by the above-mentioned means. He sat on the bed without help. When he was sitting, they said to him in a very loud voice: Leave evildoer and without her soul. Then he touched the foot himself with his finger as if he was pushing out the spirit through the big toe through this touching. She instantly began to talk, sat up and said that he had already left. They did not believe her. Perhaps he was speaking through her, because they saw that the candle had not been extinguished. She said: It seems that he forgot to extinguish the candle because of the confusion and his great haste to leave. Nonetheless, they did not believe her and wanted to torment her as before, and she was shouting to her father-in-law and grandmother. Why do you let them burn me, since he has left, and they do not believe me? She said: I know that it is true that he has already left. They said to her: What is the matter [that you know]? She responded: Must I tell you? Then they understood that it was not something that should be said in public. Then they said to a woman: Go to her and she will reveal the matter to you. She did so and learned that the *Spirit* had exited through her vagina and caused her to bleed as he left. They all agreed to the truth of this sign, and they placed the amulets on her that had been prepared in the house and was assumed to be healed. An hour later the sages came to her when the rumor spread in the city that the spirit of a Jewish man was speaking through a woman. When they saw her, they said that it was certain that he had not left. If he had left, he had returned. They said this because of the signs they saw. Her eyes were glazed over, and her breathing was labored. Through these signs they knew that he was still in her. Then the voice returned, the voice of ruin; the *Spirit* was still in her. The two adjurers told me that he had certainly left but reentered her because the amulets that they had placed on her were not written specifically for her, because of the confusion. The whole city, Jews, and Turks, came to see this awesome sight, and it was astonishing to everyone. They hushed up the matter because of the danger of the nations, who were saying that she should be burned, until it would be forgotten in a number of days, and the matter could be resolved. After eight days the poor woman died because of the *Spirit* who had not left her. They said that he choked her and left with her soul. Everything I have written above; every detail is written as it was. There is no reason to doubt or question anything, since it is all truthfully written and there are no additions or deletions. I have written what I saw and heard. I pleaded with the scholars who were there that they should also put their signatures on this, since we live from their mouths, so that my words will be believed, through their signatures. The eye that sees this writing, and the ear that hears will believe faithfully, as if he had heard directly from the spirit. He will be in fear and awe to believe and fulfill everything that is written in the Torah and the words of our rabbis, of blessed memory. Then he will rest in peace and three groups of angels will go to meet them. One saying, peace, etc., and no plague will approach his tent, and his soul will cleave to God, and will return to the place from which it was hewn. Signed by the writer, the young and poor one among the myriads [of Israel], the devoted servant of the fearers of the Lord, and to those who think of his name. I the humble one, Elia Falco.

I was there, and my eyes saw, and my ears heard all this and more, what he saw testifies about them. Shlomo ha-Levi Samuel ibn Alkabetz.

These words are words of truth which have no measure, so that every man should know about this event and leave his evil ways, and every man [should give up] the wrong of his thoughts before he goes [to the next world] and is not, and he who knows will return, and repent, and come back, and will be healed. The humble one, Abraham ha-Lahmi.

Signed, Samuel Bueno.

I too was called to see this matter and my eyes have seen and my ears have heard, and it is a miraculous thing, to teach us that we should turn back in repentance. Says, Abraham Arueti.

2. THE *MAYSE BUKH*. BASEL 1602, STORY NUMBER 152

This story is found in three versions:

112 | The *Dybbuk*

A. *Mayse Bukh*, Basel 1602, story number 152. English translation in Moses Gaster, *Ma'aseh Book*. 2 vols. (Philadelphia: Jewish Publication Society, 1934), 1: 301–3.

B. Menasseh ben Israel, *Nishmat Hayyim* (Amsterdam, 1651), 111a–11b.

C. Joseph Sambari, *Divrei Yosef* (Shtober ed.), 324–25.

A. *Mayse Bukh*, Basel 1602, story number 152

A story happened that an evil spirit entered the body of a young man. Thereupon he [the evil *Spirit*] was adjured to reveal his name or that of his wife. When they mentioned his wife, he began to scream and said that his wife was an *agunah*, which means that she had no right to marry, for he had lost his life at sea and the sages could not give her permission to remarry; that he had requested the sages to give her permission to marry again and gave them many indications that he had been lost at sea, but they did not know where his home had been. The sages said: We cannot give her the permission. He was crying because she had become a harlot because she could not obtain permission to marry.

The sages asked him why he could not rest in peace and what sins he had committed? He replied that he had committed adultery. The sages said: What happened to the woman with whom he had committed adultery? He did not want to say, as she has been dead a long time and it would not help if I told. He said, I am in the position of the man about whom the sages say that he who is guilty of adultery should have the four kinds of capital punishment inflicted upon him, but I have not been punished in that way.

While they were talking, the young man stood up on his feet. The sages asked him: why have you stood up now? The youth replied: because a great sage is coming in. As they looked around, the sage entered, as the young man had said. A company of young men followed him into the house and wanted to hear what was happening. Then the evil *Spirit* said why have you come in here to see me? There are those among you who have done the same thing as I and will become like me. The youths became terribly frightened. Then the evil *Spirit* said: Why are you so astounded? That youth who is standing among you dressed in white clothes, has slept with a man, which is as bad as adultery. The youths became terrified and looked at one another. Thereupon the young man dressed in white clothes began screaming and said: It is because of our many sins, true, I did it. And the other youths also confessed their evil deeds. Then one of the sages asked: How did you know what they did? The evil spirit began to laugh and said: It is written: *"It is as a sign on every man's hand"* [Job, 37:7]. In Yiddish this is, every man has written on his hand what deeds he has done. Then they asked him: How can you see their hands? They are under their cloaks? The evil spirit again laughed and said: I can see everywhere. Then they asked him how he came into the young man. He replied that he had no rest in the water. The fish ate his body, and then his soul departed from him and entered a cow. The cow became insane, and the gentile owner sold it to a Jew who slaughtered it, and as the youth was standing nearby, he flew straight into him. Thereupon the sages adjured him, and he left the youth and flew away.

B. Menashe ben Israel, *Nishmat Hayyim*, Amsterdam, 1652, 111a–11b

Another story of this sort happened at the same time. A *Spirit* also entered a certain youth. They adjured him in the same way as mentioned above. He also mentioned his name, the name of his city, and his wife's name. Every time he mentioned his wife, he cried. He said that his wife had been left an *agunah*, because he had drowned in the sea. The sages were not able to allow her to remarry, and she had illicit sexual relations. He asked the sages who were standing there that they should free her, and he gave many signs for his words.[41] They said to him that even with all this, it was still forbidden. He had a learned discussion with them about this, from rabbinic sources, etc. They asked him what his transgression had been. He said that he had committed adultery in Constantinople, and what happened to him was what the Talmudic rabbis said, *"The four forms of capital punishment have not ceased, etc."*[42]

They said to him, "What was the name of that woman?" He did not want to reveal it. She had already died, and what purpose would be served by revealing it? In the middle of this, he stood up. They said to him, "Why did you stand up?"

He said to them, "Because of a certain scholar who was coming in." So it was, immediately afterwards, he came in, as he had said. After this, a group of young men came in. He said: "Why have these come here to see me? They have done deeds like I have done and have behaved like me!" The young men were astonished. He said to those standing there:

"Why are you surprised? The one who is dressed in a white garment, did he not commit adultery with a woman in Constantinople? And the one next to him did he not do such and such?"

They were even more astonished and looked at each other. The one dressed in a white garment began to cry greatly and said, "He is telling the truth." All of them admitted and confessed their misdeeds. Then one of the sages who was present asked him and said to him, "How do you know about all of these sins?"

He began to laugh and said to him, "Does not Scripture say, 'It is as a sign on every man's hand' " [Job, 37:7].

They said to him: "But their hands are inside their sleeves. How do you see what is on their hands?"

He laughed again and said, "What don't I see, even in the most secret places?" One of the sages who was standing there said to him, "Tell me, what are my deeds?"

He said to him, "Concerning you sir, we do not have permission to say anything." They asked the youth who had the *Spirit* within him: "Why does the *Spirit* speak with your mouth and your lips, as if you are the one who is speaking? He should speak for himself."

He laughed again and said: "Did not the Talmudic sages say in tractate *Baba Kamma*, on a certain page: *'The representative of a person is like the person, etc.'* "[43] Then they asked him, in what manner did he enter this youth? He responded that he had drowned in a certain place. The fish ate his flesh, and his spirit wandered the earth. He hid and concealed himself in all sorts of creatures. All of them caused him all sorts of discomfort, until he entered a cow. Then the cow became mad. When the owner saw what the cow was doing, he sold it to a Jew, and the Jew slaughtered it. The youth was standing nearby when the cow was being slaughtered, and he left the cow and entered the youth. Many testified that this was what happened. Immediately after the cow was slaughtered, the youth felt that the *Spirit* was troubling him. The youth died within eight days. Therefore, the one who fears the word of God will repent of his sins that he has committed and will implore his Creator. Perhaps, God will hear him and will heal him. Until here.

C. Sambari, *Divrei Yosef* (Shtober ed.), 324–25

Another story of this sort happened a second time in Safed. A *Spirit* also entered a certain youth. They adjured him in the same way as mentioned above. He also mentioned his name, his wife's name. They asked him what his transgression had been. He said that he had committed adultery in Constantinople. In the middle of this he stood up. They said to him, "Why did you stand up?"

He said to them, "Because of a certain scholar who was coming in, and so it was." After this, a group of young men came in. He said: "Why have these come here to see me? Why have you come here to see me? The cup [of punishment] will soon pass to you since we all participated in this sin, and I am surprised at these since that which is self-evident needs no proof. However, I am amazed at the one who makes himself out as a pietist, who dresses in white garments, and he glows with evil. He does the deeds of Zimri and wants the reward of Phinehas. He did not commit adultery with a woman in Constantinople." They were even more astonished. The one dressed in a white garment began to cry greatly, and they admitted and confessed their misdeeds. Then one of the sages said to him, "How do you know?"

He said to him, "Is it not written, '*It is as a sign on every man's hand*'" [Job, 37:7]? He said, "I know, even what is in the most secret places."

Then they asked him, "In what manner did he enter the youth?" He responded that he had drowned in a certain place. The fish ate his flesh, and his spirit wandered the earth until he entered a cow, and the cow became mad. When the owner saw what the cow was doing, he sold it to a Jew, and the Jew slaughtered it. The youth was passing nearby when the cow was being slaughtered, and he left the cow and entered the youth. Many testified that this was what happened. Immediately after the cow was slaughtered, the youth felt that the Spirit was troubling him. The youth died within eight days. Therefore, the one who fears the word of God will repent of his sins that he has committed and will implore his Creator. Perhaps God will hear him and will heal him. Until here what happened in the city of Safed in the year five thousand and three hundred and seventy-one of Creation.

3. SHMUEL VITAL, *SHA'AR HA-GILGULIM* (JERUSALEM, 1963), 186A–87B

STORY OF THE SPIRIT

The humble Samuel Vital said:

I will expound the riddle that happened to me in Cairo, may the Lord found it well, with regard to a story that happened to Esther, blessed among women, the daughter of Rabbi Judah Veisil, may God protect and preserve him, who was injured and remained injured and heartbroken more than two months after she married. Then they came to me one day and pleaded with me that I should go and visit her. I went to visit her, and I found her to be injured, and I was uncertain if it was a mischievous spirit [*mazik*], or a demon or a Jewish evil *Spirit*. I advised them to bring a judge from the gentiles to visit her, and they did so. In the middle of this, the mischievous spirit that was within her said in a loud voice that he was a gentile and he had entered her, because of his desire for her. In the course of his words, he said that he had lightly hit me in the thigh, and because of this I was injured in the thigh, so that I should not be able to go and heal her. Afterwards, the gentile judge occupied himself with her, and he said that he had already imprisoned the mischievous spirit in a small bottle and buried it in the ground, as was customarily done with them.

Afterwards, a voice suddenly shouted from the girl and said: "I have been left alone in the body of the girl, and I am a Jewish *Spirit*. Therefore, hurry and call the sage, R. Samuel Vital, may God protect and preserve him, so that he would heal me and take me out of her." They immediately called me, and I was compelled to go to her because of the honor of those who came. When I came to her, it had not been confirmed if he was a Jewish *Spirit*, a demon, or a mischievous spirit. I sat by her side, and she was lying like a stone, covered by a white blanket. Concerning the doubt, I said, "Peace to Israel."

The girl's lips immediately moved and responded to me: "Blessed is the one who comes, peace unto you, blessings, and goodness."

I said to him, "If you are a Jew, recite, 'Hear O Israel.'"

He replied, "Hear O Israel" etc. Then I began to speak to him, and he responded appropriately to me concerning everything I asked of him. I asked him: "Who his father was, from what land was he, when did he die, where was he buried, how many years did he live, what was his punishment, what was his sin, who was it that had transmigrated here, the Soul or the Spirit? Who was in charge of him? Was he dwelling here alone, or did he have someone guarding him?" He responded to everything appropriately and in order. There was no deceit or twisting in his words, and [there was no] need to decree a decree against him, like the other Spirits, whose ways are known to those who know this discipline.

Afterwards, I asked him, "What do you want?"

He responded to me that I should repair him and exorcise him with my great wisdom from this body. He recognized me from what had been announced about me in heaven. I said to him, "If so, how is it that you were so proud and said, 'I hit the sage in his thigh so that he would no longer come to me?'"

He responded, "It was not I; heaven forbid. Rather it was that gentile who harmed me and said that he would beat me." It is false; he said this to boast about himself, but he had no ability, heaven forbid, to harm me.

I said to him, "If so, why did you come to me in a dream on Tuesday night, the seventeenth of Tammuz, and you troubled me?"

He responded, "It is true that I came, but the one who troubled you was that gentile mischievous spirit, and I did not sin against you at all."

I said to him, "Why did you come with him?"

He responded, "To ask you for a repair."

Finally, I said to him, "What do you want now?"

He responded, "My desire is that you should repair my Soul and my Spirit and exorcise me from this body."

I said to him, "Yes, I will do this tomorrow."

He again said to me, "Why will you leave two Spirits in anguish like this, my Spirit, and the Spirit of this young woman? You have the ability to do this." He pleaded with me greatly, and finally adjured him with a severe adjuration that he should not lie and leave and enter her again. Also, that he should not harm the young woman, members of her family, or those present when he departs from her, and no other Jewish person. Further, he should not dwell here in Cairo but should immediately go on his way to Gehenna, to be healed there.

Aside from this, I decreed all of the above with bans and excommunication, etc. Afterwards, I said to him that he should give us a true sign of his departure and that he should say "Peace unto you" when he left. He did so and said it three times. Afterwards, I called ten scholars to be present. I began to press on the pulse point of the right hand, and I concentrated on the verse *"Appoint a wicked man over him; may an accuser stand at his right hand"* [Psalm 109:6], at length, as I have written, and also other mystical intentions that are known to me in order to repair his Soul and his Spirit. Afterwards, he moved his lips and recited with us in a loud voice, first the whole psalm *"May the Lord answer you in time of trouble"*[44]; the psalm *"May the favor of the Lord, etc."*[45] "O you *who dwell in the shelter of the Most High, etc."*[46]; *"By the power of [Ana be-Koah], etc.,"*[47] and I concentrated on the name "Destroy Satan"[48] and afterwards, *"Answer me when I call, O Lord my vindicator, etc."*[49]

Afterwards, this prayer,

> In the name of the only God, You are great, and Your name is great in might. Please honored and awesome One who is adorned, magnificent, and sanctified. Who is elevated and blessed, who examines and investigates. Who is upright and exalted. The hidden and concealed One, who pulses with seventy-two names. The only God, the bright and the pure One, who hears calls to Him, who receives prayers, who answers those in trouble, harken Your ear to my prayer, to my petition and my request that I pray before You and ask of You. You will hear from heaven, the place of Your dwelling, and receive with mercy and grace, this Spirit who stands before us, who has transmigrated into this girl, who is called so and so, daughter of so and so, who is called so and so. Accept our prayer that we are praying on his behalf to repair his Soul and Spirit and to take him out of this transmigration. Afterwards, bring him into the judgment of Gehenna and deliver his Soul and his Spirit from the sling of the mischievous spirits and its torments. This transmigration and this shame that he has experienced should be considered as an expiation for his sins, transgressions, and crimes. May my words be words of defense before You, for this Soul and Spirit, and may Your mercy overcome Your attributes concerning him, as we mention the thirteen attributes of mercy, *God King who sits on the Throne of Mercy*, etc. *And He passed over*, etc.[50]

When the thirteen attributes, *God gracious and compassionate*, are recited, it is customary and appropriate to blow the *shofar*, as is the custom with all the *selichot*. Afterwards, one should recite the thirteen attributes of the prophet Micah, *"Who is a God like you, etc."*[51] And the verse, *"When all manner of sins overwhelm me, etc."*[52] And the verse, *"Happy is the man You choose and bring near to dwell in Your courts, etc."*[53] And the verse, *"Then all these courtiers of yours shall come down to me, etc."*[54] And I recited this verse three times. Afterwards, I said, "Leave, leave, leave," and I concentrated on the mystical intentions that are in this verse that is written here. Immediately after I concluded the word leave, three times the left leg of the girl was raised before all the assembled, and it left through the small toe of her leg and shouted in a loud voice and said three times, "Peace unto you."

I responded to him three times, "And peace unto you."

The young woman immediately sat down, opened her eyes, looked at me, and was ashamed. She asked what the people were doing since she did not know anything about what we had done. She kissed my hands, ate, and drank.

All of this was done by me on Thursday, the 25th of Tammuz, in the year 5426 of Creation (1666), here in Cairo, may the Lord find it well. I have written this as a memento for those who will come after us so that they will know that there is a God in Israel.

The humble, Samuel Vital, Sephardi Tahor.

Appendix to Chapter 4

1. The *Dybbuk* in Prague (c. 1690)[55]

Since we will be talking about a spirit, we will tell what the pious, famous, distinguished in Torah, Rabbi Hirsch Segal, rabbinic judge in the holy community of Nikolsburg told me:

When he was rabbi in the holy community of Rostitz[56]—he went to Prague. There was a maiden there, a maiden in whom there was a *Spirit*. Many novel things were told about the maiden, that the Spirit in her had spoken. They went to him, and as soon as the *Spirit* saw them coming, he said, "Welcome gentlemen"; and he immediately said to the two parents—since they were sitting on a bench, and the maiden sat on the bed; she said to her father, "You blind one, get up and let the rabbis sit." The pious R. Hirsch, the judge, began, "Listen you evildoer, we do not come to sit, rather we want to know what sins you committed, that you came to this situation; do not cause us to decree many excommunications against you, or that we should mention many *holy names*,[57] but tell us what you have done."

He said, "My dear gentlemen, I will tell everything in sequence as it occurred." He had *transgressed* the religion of the Torah of Moses and had many children with non-Jews—then he died; and as soon as he came to his grave, an angel of destruction came and created him; he stood up from his grave, and the angel of destruction said to him: "What did you think, when you angered your Creator in this way? Woe and wind, how will it go for you?" Immediately, many thousands of angels came, and they all looked like frogs. They bit him on all parts of his body—until he died again. They immediately created him again. Afterwards, angels of destruction came who looked like mice, and bit him on all parts of his body—until he died, and they immediately created him again. Then came *angels of destruction* who looked like cats, and they tore at his flesh—until he died. Afterwards, angels of destruction came who looked like dogs and tore his flesh apart. Then he was created again. Then came angels of destruction who looked like wolves, and they tore him apart. Then he was created again. Other angels of destruction came and tore him apart. They all looked like different animals, until there was no creature in the world that did not have dominion over him. In the end, the angel of destruction led him to the gate of Gehenna. As soon as he came to the gate of Gehenna, *several thousand* people came out of Gehenna, and they shouted and cried: "Go, you evildoer, what do you want among us? You want to add sorrow and troubles on us and all who are here?"

The angels of destruction began to say to him, "No, you evildoer, you are not worthy that you should come into Gehenna, you must come into the *hollow of the sling*."

The Spirit asked the pious Rabbi Hirsch and Rabbi Feibush if they knew what the *hollow of the sling* was, *God protect us*. Rabbi Hirsch responded to him, "We do not know other than that a *person*—God protect us from it—is placed in a sling and is thrown from one end of the world to the other end."

The *Spirit* responded to him, "Dear Rabbi, you don't know how it is." He could, because of our many sins, tell him about this because he experienced it. There are two angels who are so large that each one goes from one end of the world to the other end of the world and reaches from heaven to the earth. One angel went and swallowed him, and before he reached the feet of the angel, he was smashed. Each time the angel spat him into the mouth of the other one, like someone spits phlegm from his mouth. Each time he was created, an angel spit him out. They did this to him for eighteen years, and he did not see any light, until one time, several years ago, they did something for him from heaven. He saw his father and mother and heard how his mother said: "Woe is shouted over that hour when I had relations with my husband. Woe is shouted over the moment that I became pregnant with him and that I gave birth to such a descendant." The spirit said that this was a spiritual satisfaction, even though I had great anguish from the words. Yet, it was a spiritual satisfaction because he had seen a little light. Afterwards, he did not see any until several months later. The one appointed over him led him to a place and he rested in a sewer [Koit Leck].[58] The maiden crossed it, and the one appointed over him gave him permission to enter her, because she was untidy and slovenly, and that is how he came into her. However, the maiden was pious, but her parents were sinful people, and that is why he came into her.

The rabbis said to him, "Go out; we will do penance for you, will fast and study on your behalf, and will recite Kaddish for your sake."

The *Spirit*, responding with troubled words, said, "Dear gentlemen, you cannot help me *as long as* his daughter lives—he cannot be an expiation for his *transgressions*." The *Spirit* did not leave the maiden until she died.

Therefore, dear people and dear friends, take notice and understand my words; think about the great Day of Judgment that God, blessed be He, judges, and absolves no person; *from great to small*, each one must give an accounting.

2. Nikolsburg[59]

[TITLE PAGE]

The Story of the *Spirit* in the Holy Community of Nikolsburg in the year 456 (1696), in the small counting.

Listen dear people, whether near or far. Hear and see what happened in the holy community in the land of Moravia, which is called Nikolsburg.[60] A story occurred, and how did it happen? A youth came to the community, and he shouted and murmured day and night since there was an impure *Spirit* within him, as you will read herein. The hair on your head will stand on end. A story like this never occurred again. Each person should run to it and should buy it for much money. When one will read in it, the tears will flow from your eyes. Every person who will hear this will turn their heart to repentance speedily and quickly, about the wondrous sign that God, blessed be He, sent into the world. This was seen and heard by Jews and Christians, what the impure *Spirit* did and avoided. It is impossible to write his words, that he did expel. How the kabbalist Rabbi Moses Prager was able to exorcize, and he was no longer able to remain in the youth. He vanquished him with adjurations and holy names. The Holy One, blessed be He, also accepted the prayers of the holy community, as they had prayed. The pious youth was rescued through this. With this we will all turn our eyes to God, blessed be He, and the Holy One will publicly redeem us. Amen.

124 | The *Dybbuk*

[Printer's Introduction. Verso of title page.]

The printer said, Since I was present at *the great miracle and sanctification of God's name*, that happened among Jews and gentiles in the holy community of Nikolsburg. It has not happened in many hundreds of years that *many famous scholars* were present at *the great miracle and sanctification of God's name*. They said that this *miracle and sanctification of God's name* was literally the equivalent of the splitting of the Red Sea. Many hundreds of people who saw the rod of chastisement for the transgressions they committed in their youth, they repented. I am bringing this into print, for the sake of heaven, so that the audience should accept a moral lesson. Even though someone arose and printed a letter about this great story, and this letter was copied from one end of the land to the other.[61] However, one can put this aside since he has not printed a tenth of it and wrote many falsehoods. Therefore, since I am benefiting the public for *the sake of heaven* and want to properly bring this great story into print. I was present from the beginning to the end, present at all the warnings and adjurations. I stood next to Rabbi Moshe Prager, the kabbalist, may his Creator protect him, and wrote, thank God. All the members of the holy community of Nikolsburg can testify that all this is the truth. It is not comparable when one was present and watched over everything, as opposed to someone writing a letter hundreds of miles away. Therefore, I want to print the truth and, at length, everything that occurred. I want to benefit the public so that people should awaken and repent. The Holy One gives the evildoers strength to accept their punishment. Similarly, He gives the righteous strength that they should be able to receive their reward in the world to come. May He send us the righteous Redeemer, speedily in our days, amen.

[Preface]

[1][62] "*The works of the Lord are great, within reach of all who desire them*" [Psalm 111:2]. "*God has brought to pass that men revere Him*" [Ecclesiastes 3:14]. "*How awesome is Your name*" [Psalm 66:3]. In Yiddish this is: "How great are the works of God. They are available to all who desire it. God who created all this so that the people should fear Him. [2a] How awesome are His works. '*That you may recount it to a future age*' [Psalm 48:14]. There is divine justice on earth" [Psalm 58:12]. In Yiddish this is, "God does everything so that the children who come afterwards should tell that God's Divine Providence is over all people, and He pays

each one their reward and punishment—each one according to what they have earned."

[CIRCUMSTANCES FOR THE ENTRY OF THE SPIRIT: URINATING ON UNUSABLE RITUAL FRINGES (ZIZIT PASUL) AND SPITTING ON A GARBAGE PILE; SHEPISH, C. 1690.]

[2] How did this great story occur here, that has not happened in hundreds of years, to a youth whose name was Abram son of Rabbi Hayyim, may his Creator protect him, from the holy community of Shepish, in the land of Poland. The youth went to urinate on a mound of garbage and was wearing *zizit* that were not usable [*pasul*]. He urinated on the *zizit*, and after he finished urinating, he expectorated on the garbage, exactly where the *Spirit* was resting on the garbage. Thus, those appointed over him gave him permission to enter into that youth. It was like a fiery serpent had run into his mouth.

[THE SYMPTOMS.]

[3] The *Spirit* was very quiet in the youth at first, but one time the youth suddenly fainted. Later, when he gained better control over the youth, he did not allow him to eat. He also did not allow him to lie in his bed, but every night he threw him out of the bed. His father became angry with the youth since he was falling out of the bed, "Are you a child, that you are falling out of the bed?" Nobody knew what the matter was with the youth.

[4] Finally, the *Spirit* did not allow him to pray or study nor to don phylacteries or wear *zizit* or tolerate any other sacred thing. He began to speak out from him, hit people, and began to harm people—when someone said a word to him, the youth began to produce strong responses. He threw him down three or four times in one day, in the middle of the street. He blew him up so that his neck became like a thick puffed-up pigeon, and his stomach became like a barrel. Everything within him ran back and forth, up and down—they saw how he ran up and down within him, from the stomach to the throat, into his head, and his head became very thick—like a great water flow. His tongue hung down to his heart, and the foam flowed from his mouth—like a foaming barrel of beer.

[5] When he threw him down in the streets, he took a stone of at least a hundred pounds and began to confess what kinds of sins he had committed in his days. He stood there and sang at length, "my

neighbor is a donkey," "I will commemorate the day of his dying—not his death."[63] Also, "*He holds the measure of judgment in His hand,*" and "*Who will live,*"[64] in a pleasant voice like a cantor. Afterwards, the confession of sins [*vidui*]. He hit himself with the stone after each sin. When he mentioned something he had done, he lifted the stone with both hands, as high as he could, and hit himself four or five times with the stone. The blows could be heard at a distance of a hundred meters. If the heart was a strong as iron, it would have had to shatter according to nature. He hit himself in this way between each sin that he mentioned—as I will write further—and shouted, oy, oy, oy, and sang in a pleasant voice. This had not been seen or heard in his day from any spirit.

[TRAVELS TO *BA'ALEI SHEM* THROUGHOUT POLAND. A MEETING WITH THE *BA'AL SHEM* OF BRISK (OF KAWAI).]

[6] The father of the youth saw this, and Rabbi Hayyim, may his Creator protect him, traveled with his son Abram around all of Poland, to all of the *ba'alei shem*, and to all of the houses of study to help his son, the above-mentioned Abram. The *Spirit* engaged in mischief and great evil that cannot be written about. A number of times, in the greatest winters, the youth would go into the forest, naked and barefoot. He sat in the greatest snows and sat for three days up to his neck in the snow. He did this a number of times so that they did not know what had happened to him. In brief, all of these *ba'alei shem* in all of Poland covered him with adjurations and other remedies and could not accomplish anything with him. On the contrary, they made it worse, and the youth's condition worsened: He threw a child against the wall, and he bashed in his brains. He chased people with a knife.

[7] He chased a hundred people to the holy community of Brisk. They adjured him. The *ba'al shem* wanted to give him something to eat—the *Spirit* took the pot and hit the *ba'al shem* in the head with it, almost splitting his head open. The scholars in the holy community prepared a letter that no *ba'al shem* should attempt to adjure him because he harms people. They had the letter sewn into the youth's hat.

[WANDERINGS THROUGH POLAND WITH THE FATHER FOR THREE YEARS, RETURN HOME, SENT FROM POLAND.]

[8] Thus, his father, Rabbi Hayyim, may his Creator protect him, traveled with him for three years through all of the land of Poland. There was no

help for him, because of our many sins. On the contrary, he tormented the youth even more because of our sins and attacked him three or four times a day, and he did not let him sleep at night. His father came home with him and locked him alone in a room. There was a stone lying in the room that he used to hit himself with, and if someone moved the stone, he came close to destroying the house, broke out windows and bashed pots and other vessels.

[9] After this, the father saw the great piteousness of his son, and he said to his son: "Listen my child, we cannot help you. I traveled with you for three years all over. I became impoverished because of you. I have [other] children—God help them. I see great anguish in you, your death is better than your life. My child, go into the world alone, where you want, perhaps God, blessed be He, will send you a salvation."

[PRAGUE AND NEARBY BOHEMIAN LEIBEN]

[10] In brief, he traveled to Bohemia, and he was sent to the holy community of Prague. He came to the holy community of Prague. He got away from the community and ran in one run until Bohemian Leiben, a distance of five miles. He ran from Bohemian Leiben, and he was sent to Moravia.

[NIKOLSBURG, FRIDAY OF SHABBAT SHUVAH (FRIDAY, 9 TISHREI 456 (1696), WOLF FISHOFF INSTEAD OF OPPENHEIM.]

[11] When he came to the holy community of Nikolsburg, just before Shabbat Shuva of 456 [Sept. 1695], the great rabbi of the city and the province was not in Nikolsburg.[65] He was visiting his father-in-law in the holy community of Hannover. Thus, the noble Rabbi Wolf Fishoff preached. The youth fell down in front of the synagogue on a mound of sand. He rolled around in the sand and put white sand into his mouth. There was a commotion around the youth, and nobody understood the youth, and nobody knew what this was. Some said that he was having an epileptic fit. In the meantime, they took him to the almshouse.

[SENT TO HUNGARY WITH AN ESCORT.]

[12] After the Sabbath, the youth was sent away, and he traveled to the country of Hungary. In this way, he suffered all sorts of torments. The youth had been sent with an escort, and the spirit took the escort away

128 | The *Dybbuk*

and put him in the highest tree. [From here to the end of the sentence the text is damaged.] The escort looked around and saw the youth. Suddenly, he threw him down from the tree, and the escort thought that he had broken his neck. He [the youth] immediately grabbed a stone and hit himself with it. The escort ran away from him several times. He came to the community and swore that he would never be an escort for a Jew again.

[MATTERSDORF. SELF-HARM: HITTING HIMSELF WITH A STONE, BANGING HIS HEAD AGAINST A WALL, PUTTING SAND IN HIS MOUTH.]

[13] In the holy community of Mattersdorf, he [the Spirit] carried him up the stairs into the women's section and threw him down on his head. Everybody thought that he had broken his neck. He [the *Spirit*] immediately grabbed a mighty stone and hit him for more than two hours. This piteous thing was seen by Jews and gentiles. After this beating, he hit his head against the wall ten or twelve times so that they thought that his brains might fall out. He bit him on the hands, arms, and feet so that the blood flowed afterwards. He dug up handfuls of earth and put it into his mouth.

[PRESSBURG (STAYED WITH A GENTILE FOR TEN DAYS).]

[14] Afterwards, he came to Pressburg; they hired a gentile that he should stay with the gentile, only to sleep there. They had to give the gentile a gulden every day. He stayed there for ten days. He ran away from Pressburg and was missing for three days, and nobody knew where he had gone. They searched everywhere for him, to find what happened to the youth. They sent messengers in all directions, and they could not find him. The youth came back after three days, and all of his clothes were soaking wet. The *Spirit* had led him away near the shore of the Danube, and he placed him on the highest tree. He let him sit there for three days, without eating or drinking. On the third day, he threw him down from the tree into the Danube, with his head down and his feet up. The water covered him, and his head got stuck in the mud—for more than an hour. Then, [the Spirit] got out of the water with him and led him into Pressburg. In this way his hat with the letter disappeared, that he had from the holy community of Brisk, that no *ba'al shem* should

adjure him because he harms people. When he came back to Pressburg, they gave him other clothes.

[STAMPA: CONFRONTATION WITH THE GENTILE SCHOLARS AND THE LOCAL NOBLEWOMAN. THE ATTEMPT TO EXORCISE HIM BY R. MEIR EISENSTADT.]

[15] They sent him to Stampa. There he [the Spirit] pushed him around. The mouth cannot describe and the heart understand that Jews and gentiles ran to this. The noblewoman became aware of this, and she sent to Falve, three or four miles away, to bring the most important and senior scholars to come and adjure him. Thus, they led him to the synagogue in Stampa. The scholars brought their things into the synagogue, and the noblewoman entered the synagogue with them. They wanted to speak with him. He said such things to them that were extraordinary to hear, all before the noblewoman. The scholars were fined several hundreds, because of the embarrassment that he shamed them before the noblewoman. *It is forbidden to put it in writing.* To the senior one he said: "Listen you whore chaser, you will not succeed with me with your things. Rather, go home; your whores are waiting for you, you defrauders of land and people. If I wasn't concerned about the noblewoman, I would throw your things at your heads and might cause your brains to fall out. I will end because of the noblewoman. You are worse pigeons than I am—so get off my neck, or I will show you the road." Thus, they slunk away from him with great shame.

[16] After this, Rabbi Meir Eisenstadt, may his Creator protect him, who was rabbi in Stampa,[66] took out a Torah scroll and wanted to go toward him with the Torah scroll. He became so enraged that he tore all the seats from the walls and destroyed all the lecterns. He broke and destroyed everything. He chased out all the people from the synagogue—people were almost killed. He destroyed the whole synagogue. He took revenge against the youth and hit him with a stone that weighed ninety pounds and gave himself more than a hundred strokes and blows on his heart. If it had been made of iron, it would have had to break. He hit his head on the ground again so that his brains should have come out. He had earth and excrement in his hands and shoved it into his mouth. He said to himself, "Thief, you must eat earth because I do everything to spite you, and they want that I should leave you." He bit him in his

hands and feet, and blood flowed. He stabbed himself with a knife that was long enough to enter his heart. However, no blood flowed. Jews and gentiles witnessed this greatly piteous event.

[17] The noblewoman said, "If it will help the youth, I am willing to spend a hundred Hungarian ducats."

The *Spirit* responded in the following way: "Your graciousness would not be adequate even with a thousand Hungarian ducats. Nobody in the world will bring me out of my fortress. I am protected by the angels of destruction. I laugh at and mock the whole world. Nobody will bring me out; I sit with strength. If someone says even one word to me—I will take my revenge on this youth. I will also harm the lives of these people—as I did to a number of people in Poland. Therefore, I warn the people, if they will not let me go peacefully, I will take the youth to Steiermark, where there is no Jew.[67] I will torment him there so that the whole world will know to talk about it. Therefore, I say to you, nobody should say a word to me about what I am doing to the youth. I hit him with a stone of a hundred pounds, and I give him a hundred strokes with all my strength—and he has no sign of it. I stick the knife into his heart—and no blood flows from it. You can be troubled by this; I do nothing to the youth. I do everything to myself, because of my great sins that I committed."

[RETURN TO NIKOLSBURG. IN THE ALMSHOUSE OF LEIBELE BASHKES, MAY HIS CREATOR PROTECT HIM. THE MONOLOGUE OF THE *SPIRIT*. THE ALPHABETICAL CONFESSION.]

[18] In brief, they sent the youth again to Nikolsburg. They rented a place for him in the almshouse of Leibele Bashkes, may his Creator protect him. He caused the youth such suffering—*that were not heard and not seen* in his days, such an impure spirit difficult impurity. One day he even threw him two or three times to the ground on his back and dragged him along on his back—like a frog drags along on its stomach, until he came to a stone. He held on to the stone with both hands and began to sing in a loud voice—like a cantor, in a pleasant voice, in Hebrew, but I am writing it in Yiddish so that the women should be able to understand it.

[68]**I am guilty**. I ate pork that is forbidden from the Torah. Afterwards, I drank wine offered to idols that is forbidden by the rabbis.

I have been treasonous. I ate meat together with milk. I boiled—specifically, seethed a goat in its mother's milk.

I spoke with a married woman. I spoke with her intentionally so that I would think about her.

I robbed. Freely and publicly. *I was a treasurer.* I was a treasurer and quietly took money from the charity box.

I cut the curtain of the Torah Ark. I stabbed at the curtain of the Torah Ark, just like Titus the evildoer.

I spoke scornfully. I spoke obscenely, even between *Baruch sheamar* and the *Amidah*[69] spitefully.

I was corrupt. I was the head of a land, and afterwards I lost my faith. I used to be a very important person. Now I am an impure Spirit.

I destroyed. I caused two communities to be exiled. *I made a cattle stall from a synagogue*—this is a cattle stall. Afterwards, a building of impurity was built there.

I killed two rabbis. Rabbi Isaac R. Hendel and Rabbi Aaron R. Leib. I buried them in the courtyard of the gentiles and placed something that is not proper on their graves.

I caused evil among Jews. *I was an evildoer*, and I did not want to obey those who punished me and was insolent before them.

I was malicious. I *threw a Torah scroll and phylacteries* into the outhouse, woe is me, woe is me.

I was oppressive. "*I dug pits, ditches and caves*"[70] on the Sabbath—I dug pits, caves, and cellars, specifically in spite on the Sabbath.

I changed my clothes on "the day of their disaster" [Deuteronomy, 32:35]. I changed my clothes on a Christian holiday.[71] Also,

I desired the money of others. I desired the money and goods of other people.

I libeled. *I slaughtered two children.* I slaughtered two children, and I buried them in the courtyard of the gentiles. Also,

I put excrement on the holy Ark out of spite.

I gave bad advice. I gave bad advice concerning Jews. I poured. I poured into impure vessels from holy vessels.

I lied. I denied the fundamental principles of Judaism.

I bowed. I bowed to the worship of idolators.

I rebelled. In particular, I handed over the money of Jews to violent robbers for secular uses. I rebelled against the words of the Torah and the rabbis.

I acted perversely. *I acted perversely in two communities.* I destroyed two communities and caused them to be exiled.

I planted vineyards on the Sabbath out of spite. I planted vineyards on the sabbath out of spite.

I was defiant. I was "*wayward and defiant*" [Deuteronomy, 21:18].

I have given fine flour into impure bread.[72]

I acted perversely. *I was involved with cattle.* I had to do with cattle, and I placed an idolator in the holy Ark.[73]

I was faithless. Uncovered, I went to the idol worshipers. I walked bareheaded in front of the idol worship.

I insulted the Jews. I insulted all of the Jews.

I was stiff necked. I behaved in a frivolous manner in the synagogues and houses of study.

I have behaved wickedly. I was the leader of a land; now I am an evil spirit.

I was corrupted. *I slept with a menstruant woman and a married woman.*

I burned a Torah scroll.

I lusted. *I transgressed all six hundred and thirteen commandments. Therefore, I was handed to wrath and scorn. For all the sins that I am guilty of, I was placed into the hollow of the sling.*[74]

[20] I was handed over to the angels of destruction. They pushed me, tore me, hit me, splintered me, broke me, struck me, plucked me, and tore me to shreds with iron tongs, with rods and spears. I did not derive any benefit. Oy, oy, oy, children come and see the great revenge taken on me. Punish your children with me. I was a Jew for forty years, the head of a land. Afterwards, I fell away from my faith and became a hegemon.

And for the sins that I am punishable by the four deaths of the court.

[THE CONTINUATION OF THE SPIRIT'S MONOLOGUE. TORMENTS AT THE HANDS OF THE ANGELS OF DESTRUCTION AND THE HOLLOW OF THE SLING.]

[21] I became ninety years old. Afterwards, the destroyers came over me in the middle of the street, and they tore my impure spirit out of my body. Afterwards, thousands and tens of thousands of angels of destruction, of all sorts of creatures in the world, like mice and rats, and all sorts of insects in the world, tore me, bit me, ate me, and spit me out again. Afterwards, angels of destruction came over me, from all sorts of poisonous and burning snakes. They tore me and bit me. My impure spirit was torn to shreds. Afterwards, all kinds of wild animals and impure domestic animals, particularly pigs as big as mountains. They dragged me to Gehenna, through all wildernesses, mountains, and valleys. I thought I would have rest—if I came to Gehenna.

[22] First, they put me into the hollow of the sling. Large fiery dogs came out of Gehenna and barked at me. They bit me and tore at me and scratched at me. I was given into the hands of the destroyers in this state, who hurried and pushed me. One destroyer placed himself where the world ends and took me into his mouth and spat me out. I flew to the other end of the world. Another destroyer was standing there, and he caught me in his mouth and swallowed me. He again spit me out to the mouth of the other destroyer. Another destroyer stood in the middle of the world with a fiery sword. Each time they spit me back and forth, the destroyer that stood in the middle of the world hit me several times with the fiery sword and cut me apart as I was flying. This hurt me more than anything else. This lasted six years.

[CONTINUATION OF THE SPIRIT'S MONOLOGUE. HIS TRANSMIGRATION INTO VARIOUS OBJECTS. (A RAW APPLE, A PIG, A MILLSTONE, AN ADULTEROUS MARRIED WOMAN.)]

[23] Afterwards, I came into a ripe apple. If it was ripe and came to a Jew, and if he recited a blessing over the apple—I would have some merit. First, the apple was ripe and fell off [the tree] and was eaten by a pig.

[24] Thus, I was in the pig for four to five months. I did not want to suffer that the pig should snack on garbage and such things. Every day I ran with the pig for three to four miles into the forest, until I caused the pig's stomach to explode, and the pig dropped dead. I came into the hands of the destroyers again. They punished me with all the torments and harsh judgments, that had never been seen or heard before.

[25] Afterwards, I came into a mill wheel. I caused great troubles for the miller. I drove the wheel into the water. When he wanted to make the wheel stand still—when he wanted it to run quickly—I made it stand still. I broke his wheel out of spite. The miller almost killed himself out of his suffering. I caused all the millers to run away from the mill. In this way, I spent six years in the mill, because I denigrated the washing of hands.

[26] Afterwards, I came into an adulterous woman, I had no rest in her because she was with impure and unclean men.[75] I took revenge on her. I broke her foot, knocked out an eye, and I went out of her.

[27] However, now I am in a holy and pure body, in a worthy inn, because I see the master who will bring me out after twenty-six years. I still need to be in the youth for twenty-six years.

[Continuation of the Spirit's monologue. Confession with the tunes of various piyyutim. Giving "explanations."]

[28] When the Spirit came to "*stoning, burning, beheading, and strangulation*," he lifted a stone with both hands and all his might and hit himself ten or twelve times with all his might. All of the bystanders had to shed tears, out of great pity. When he came to *strangulation*, he threw him into the lake that was near the almshouse, with his head down and his feet above. He stood in this way more than half an hour, or about three quarters of an hour, with his head in the water. Afterwards, he went out of the water, and he again threw him down on the ground. He again grabbed the stone and hit himself with the stone.

[29] After the confession, he began to sing, "Dwellers in houses of clay, why do you tolerate sin?"[76]

> Woe is me, I, the impure Spirit.
> Why can my eyes not see the heaven?
> Why do those appointed over me not allow me to see the heaven.
> Ha, ha, if I were worthy to see heaven—I would be far along the way.
> Woe, woe shouted.
> How I was a manager and head of a land, afterwards I became a hegemon.
> How they gave me every honor in the world.
> How they laid me only on golden cushions.
> Woe, woe, how they carried me to my grave, impure.
> O, woe is me, how they went before me with drums, trumpets, and flags.
> O, how the destroyers and angels of destruction ran at my side, and many thousands and tens of thousands, ran, laughed, jumped, and danced over me.

Afterwards, they laid me in the grave impure.[77] The people went away from me, and the destroyers came and captured me. They took me out of the grave with great cruelty. Whoever of them that could reach me hit me with wrath, anger, and fury, with fiery rods and iron bars. Afterwards, they ground me between two millstones. This is how they punished me for many years, punished me four times a day, until I came into the body of Abram, a holy and pure body.

O woe, thousands, and tens of thousands of angels of destruction and all sorts of destroyers stood around me. O woe, how they screamed, how can I not raise up my face to heaven. Ha, ha, take your revenge on me.

[30] Afterwards, he began to sing, "I remember the day I dropped dead," not the day I died—"the day I dropped dead."[78]

Oy, Oy, the angels of destruction tore me out of the impure body and tore me apart and shredded me.

O, woe, I was so high and important. I was the head of a land. Afterwards, I was a hegemon and did not think about the end of days. Oy, oy, oy.

"My wife became a stranger to me" Woe, woe, my wife became an evil Spirit, may her name be blotted out.

How did she talk me into all the evil?

"I was detested by the children of my loins." Woe, when I think about my two impure offspring, when they do all the repairs on the Sabbath, and light a fire, my heart breaks and cracks.

"About my limbs and body." Woe, woe, my limbs have become snakes and adders. They must only eat earth.[79]

Thus, the spirit took handfuls of earth and poured it into the mouth of the youth.

[31] Afterwards, he began to sing, "He grasps the attribute of judgment in His hand":[80]

Oh, you dear people, how is each person paid for his punishment and judgment?

Gentlemen, chastise your children so that they will not come into the hands of the destroyers.

Gentlemen, be like those appointed over me, who check and coerce, and tear, splinter, and bite.

[32] Afterwards, he began, "Who will live, who will die?"[81] When he came to, "Who by stoning?" he hit himself again ten or twelve times so severely with the stone that it was heard at a distance.

When he came to "Who by strangulation," he jumped into the lake, with his head down and his feet up. When he went out, he again lay down on his back, he held the stone in his hand and sang further.

When he came to "Who will be raised up and who will be humbled?" he said, "Dear gentlemen, this you might certainly know: whoever is important in this world—he is humbled in the next world, and the one who is humbled in this world—is very important in the next world."

Then the *Spirit* said: *"They have ended my life in a pit, and cast stones at me"* [Lamentations, 3:53], and he placed the stone on himself, and the stone rolled back and forth by itself.

[33] Afterwards, he began to give interpretations: "Dear gentlemen, why is it written in the Torah, *'the half shekel'* [Exodus, 30:13]? Why is it written in the Torah, 'half shekel'? I will tell you: This is what the Torah means by "a half" [mahazit]? It begins with a *mem* at the beginning and *tav* at the end—this makes *met* [dead]. Afterwards, after the *mem* is written *het*, and before the *tav* a *yud*—this makes *hai* [live]. In the middle there is a *zaddik* [righteous person]. This shows us that the *zaddik* has everything in his hand.

[34] Afterwards, the *Spirit* began, "Concerning me, Scripture says, *'Though he goes along weeping, carrying the seed bag, he shall come back with songs of joy'*" [Psalm 126:6]. He said the following: "'He goes along'—I go and fly around the world and cry. 'Carrying the seed bag'—because my impure seeds have been sown. However, when they will drop dead and will disappear from the world, 'shall come back with song': I will come back with song."

He gave several interpretations about himself in this way. Is this not a wonder not to be written?

[BEHAVIOR ON THE SABBATH IN CONTRAST TO SUNDAY AND CHRISTIAN HOLIDAYS. MEETING WITH WOLF FISCHOFF AND HIS WIFE.]

[35] When Rabbi Wolf Fischoff came to this, how he had hit himself on the Sabbath. On the Sabbath, he used to hit himself for the most part. Sometimes, he hit him four times on the Sabbath: As soon as they began to recite the Kiddush—he took him out into the garden and hit him. Sometimes, he took him out and led him around the streets and hit him, in the middle of the night. Also, two times on the Sabbath during the day. On the Sabbath, he did not allow him to eat anything the whole day. "Bread with ashes must you eat." He said to the youth

on the Sabbath, "No meat, no fish, nothing at all cooked." He let him rest on Sunday, and always on Christian holidays, he also let him rest.

[36] In brief, the noble Rabbi Wolf Fischoff came to this, how he hit himself severely on the Sabbath with a large stone and dug up earth and put handfuls of it into the youth's mouth. The noble Rabbi Wolf asked him the following: "Listen you impure *Spirit*, you confess your sins, and hit yourself mostly on the Sabbath. You are desecrating the Sabbath. The evildoers have rest on the Sabbath!"[82]

The spirit responded in this way: "Don't you know what is written in the *Zohar*? The evildoers who desecrated the Sabbath—they are punished mostly on the Sabbath!"[83] The wife of Rabbi Wolf said: "Is there no repair for you? We will give charity for your sake!"

The *Spirit* responded with great mockery and laughter: "Ha, ha—your charity! Yes, rather, buy me a large stone to hit with!" He quoted the verse, *"They ended my life in a pit, and cast stones at me"* [Lamentations 3:53].

[CONTINUATION OF HIS PRACTICES ON THE SABBATH: CONFESSION DURING THE TIME OF THE TORAH READING. MEETING WITH SIMEON WADISHLIF, OF BLESSED MEMORY.]

[37] Most of the time, he went to the synagogue on the Sabbath and remained there until the Kedushah was recited. Then he went out from the synagogue and laid down in front of the synagogue, held a large stone, and confessed, while hitting himself with all his might. This occurred during the whole Torah reading, and several hundred people ran out of the synagogue and did not listen to the Torah reading and watched him because of our great sins.

[38] The noble Rabbi Simeon Wadishlif, of blessed memory, used to join them. The Spirit spoke to him in the following way: "Concerning you, broad beard, I am very saddened. How do you run out of the synagogue and run to me, to the impurity?" This Rabbi Simeon had argued with him a number of times [about] why he had tormented the youth so much—he should rather leave him alone. They would do penance for him, and he would have rest—he said: "You, broad beard, when I will leave—I will enter you. Your repentance will not help very much!"

One time, this Rabbi Simeon came one Sabbath morning, and he was hitting himself so hard that the above-mentioned R. Simeon had strong words with him. The Spirit said to R. Simeon: "Yesterday, an appointed one over me left and only one appointed one remained over me. The appointed one who remained gave me permission, whoever talks to me or comes to me—I may harm them. If you had come to me yesterday directly, you have a great army, but today I no longer have any power to harm. The one appointed over me came back to me early this morning."

[PRACTICES ON SABBATH EVE.]

[39] Several times the spirit left when they began to recite the *kiddush* on Friday night. The *Spirit* left immediately and grabbed a stone with both hands and said, "So, my appointed ones, are you not giving me the strength to hit?" He said this three times consecutively, "So, my appointed ones, will you give me the strength to hit?" He threw the stone away and went into the house and sat for an hour in the house. Afterwards, he went out again and began to scream: "Ha, ha, ha. Come here, take revenge on me, and throw the youth into the lake with the head down and the feet up. A half hour is one time." Afterwards, he took him out of the lake, and laid him on the ground, and hit him until two hours after dark.

[40] He hit him this way every Friday night, and during the day of the Sabbath, he ordinarily hit him three or four times. He did not let him eat on the whole Sabbath. On Christian holidays, he did not do anything to him, and allowed him to eat anything he wanted. During the week, he only hit him twice a day. He did not allow him to eat meat, and he did not allow him to eat any meat from the hindquarter. On Monday and Thursday, he usually led him before the synagogue when people were coming out [after services] in the morning. He laid him in front of the synagogues and beat him.

[MEETING WITH HIRSCH SEGAL.]

[41] Rabbi Hirsch Segal, the judge, came and with great compassion watched what he had done to the youth. The above-mentioned Rabbi Hirsch, the judge, spoke to the Spirit: "Listen you evildoer, you impure *Spirit*. Why do you add sin to transgression and torment the youth so much? You desecrate the name of God on the Sabbath, you hit the youth, and you confess. You desecrate the Sabbath, you break the stone, and dig up the earth and pour it into the mouth of the youth."

The *Spirit* responded, "You broad beard, just for spite, I want to do it even more."

The above-mentioned Rabbi Hirsch said, "Tell us rather how we can repair you so that you can have rest."

The *Spirit* said, "You cannot repair me as there is no hope for me."

The noble Rabbi Hirsch, the judge, said, "Will you not let the youth rest—I want to put a garment on you that is full of divine names!"

The *Spirit* said, "I will jump into the fire and burn myself along with the youth."

The above-mentioned Rabbi Hirsch, the judge, said, "You evildoer, you lie, you cannot come into Gehenna—how will you be able to burn yourself?" The *Spirit* gave the above-mentioned Rabbi Hirsch, the judge, evil things and pulled out a knife and chased several hundred people who stampeded in great fright, and he did not harm anyone. The above-mentioned Rabbi Hirsch, the judge, remained standing.

[MOSHE PRAGER: IN BROD, RETURN TO NIKOLSBURG.]

[42] Everything evolved when the noble Rabbi Moshe Prager, may his Creator protect him, a kabbalist, was not at home. He had left on a journey and had wanted to have his book published, his book *Vaykhel Moshe*.[84] God, blessed be He, caused that when he came to the holy community of Brod, and preached there on the Torah portion, *Lekh Lekha*. After the sermon, important people together with the great scholar, the rabbi of the community, Israel, the son of the late Rabbi Kopel Segal, one of the exiles from Vienna, asked the above-mentioned Rabbi Moshe that he should remain in the community, and they would learn Kabbalah from him. Therefore, the above-mentioned Rabbi Moshe remained in the community for approximately eight weeks. The noble Rabbi Moshe had decided to travel from the holy community of Brod to Breslau, to bring his holy book into print. A letter arrived from the noble Rabbi Hirsch Segal, the judge, that the noble Rabbi Moshe Prager, may his Creator protect him, should come home quickly [because] the wife of the above-mentioned Rabbi Moshe was sick. When the above-mentioned Rabbi Moshe came back to Nikolsburg, his wife, thank God, had recovered.

[THE ARRIVAL OF PRAGER TO NIKOLSBURG: THE APPOINTMENT BY DAVID OPPENHEIM AND THE RECEIPT OF A BOOK OF MAGIC.]

[43] The wife of Rabbi Moshe asked him, for the sake of mercy, that he should not allow himself to be talked into going to the Spirit by any person. There are many *ba'alei shem* in all of Poland, and not one

of them could do anything against him, and he harmed many of them. There has not been such a difficult *Spirit* and *kelipah* in all of his days. Rabbi Moshe was in Nikolsburg for eight days and did not want to go to the *Spirit*.

[44] The noble Rabbi Moshe went to the sage, the chief rabbi of the land, Rabbi David Oppenheim, may God bless and protect him. The sage said to Rabbi Moshe: "I ask R. Moshe, confront the *Spirit*. It will cause such a sanctification of God's name that has not happened among Jews and Christians for a hundred years. I have the books for this, and I will give them to you." Many important people implored Rabbi Moshe greatly that he should sanctify the name of God and vanquish him.

[THE EVE OF ROSH HODESH SHEVAT, 29 TEVET, JANUARY 4, IN THE MORNING AT THE ALMSHOUSE: THE FIRST MEETING WITH PRAGER.][85]

[45] It was the eve of Rosh Hodesh Shevat, 456 [1696], in the small counting. The noble Rabbi Moshe left the synagogue in the morning. Several scholars waited at the synagogue. They implored the above-mentioned Rabbi Moshe that he should forgive them and go with them to the almshouse to the *Spirit*. They will see what he [the *Spirit*] will say to him. Rabbi Moses and the scholars entered the room where he was. The youth was sitting behind the oven, eating bread and butter. The noble Rabbi Simeon Widishlif, of blessed memory, said to him, "Abram come out from behind the oven, I'm bringing you a Jew—that you have never seen in your life."

The *Spirit* said, "Certainly, a Jew from the other world, a lord." The youth came out from behind the oven and was eating.

Rabbi Moshe said to the youth, "Did you wash [your hands] before eating?"

The *Spirit* said: "How did you think about washing? He has not washed [his hands] in six years. This one will certainly make me pious!"

[46] Rabbi Moshe said, "Listen, I want to show you something that you have not seen in your lifetime." Rabbi Moshe took out his *bretl*[86] of holy names and showed it to the *Spirit*. As soon as the *Spirit* saw the names, he ran out of the room, running past Rabbi Moshe and back in, bringing a large stick, and past Rabbi Moshe again. He thought he would frighten Rabbi Moshe, like he had frightened and chased all the people. However, Rabbi Moshe did not allow himself to be frightened,

though he was a small person. He remained standing and hit him with both hands and his stick. He said to him, "*You impure Spirit, you came to me with a stick—I came against you with the name of the Lord of Hosts.*"[87] He immediately let the stick fall and ran out of the room. However, the other scholars, who were afraid, did not want to approach. Rabbi Moshe stood opposite him, and the *Spirit* did not want to go into the room before Rabbi Moshe. However, the *Spirit* stabbed at the door of the room with a knife, and he said, "Come out and I will slaughter you." However, Rabbi Moshe did not fear him and went to the door of the room and wanted to go out to him. The *Spirit* ran away from R. Moshe, from the door and ran into the other room.

[47] Afterwards, he again came into the room and said to Shalom: "Is Leibele dearer than your son? You are a greater evildoer than I am. Why do you allow such people to come in to me? I told you a hundred times that you should not allow such people to come in. I watched out for R. Moshe Prager in all of Hungary, and where I sensed him, I ran away two miles distant, and he follows me! However, he will not succeed with me. He thinks, because he was somewhere else with a *Spirit* that he was able to exorcise—he will also exorcise me! Ha, ha, ha, ha—he will not succeed with me. The same one was shot with silent gunpowder.[88] Don't worry, I also want to shoot R. Moshe." The *Spirit* ran away and did not want to go into the room where R. Moshe was, under [any] circumstances.

[48] In brief, Rabbi Moshe went away again with the scholars. The *Spirit* was angry the whole day about the people in the almshouse and also sinned with the youth. He said to the people: "They let such people in to me—those who can storm worlds. Those appointed over me are also frightened of this R. Moshe."

[THE FIRST WARNING: THURSDAY, 8 SHEVAT, JANUARY 12, IN THE ALMSHOUSE. PROMISES OF ACTIONS TO DO *TIKKUN*. FEAR OF THE ADJURATIONS.]

[49] After this, Rabbi Moshe went and gathered scholars and all the yeshiva students, with the knowledge of the sage, the chief rabbi of the land, went to the spirit and formally warned him, *with the people who were present and the people who were not present, that he should leave the body of the youth, Abram, without harm or pain, with the following words:*

> You evildoer and impure Spirit, I warn you with the knowledge of the sage, the chief rabbi, and with the knowledge of the whole community, and with association of the Holy One, His Shekhinah and the whole heavenly family and the heavenly court.

He had notified all the worlds and holy names, all the angels who rule over all the worlds. He also notified all the ministers and those appointed over the spirits and demons who are under them—or in their realm.

> I join them all to this warning. They should all agree with me, with the warning that I have issued. You should leave the body of the youth Abram, who was born from Yetta, with no harm or pain. You should leave by way of the small finger of the left foot. You should not harm any Jew, whether they are here, whether they are not here, whether man or woman, whether child or adult, whoever it might be. You should have no dominion over the holy names [missing?] that someone's hair stood on end, out of great fear, that Rabbi Moshe described.

If you will leave—it will be good. I will take on a fast for your sake for a whole year, from day to day, except for the days when Tahanun is not recited. I will recite Kaddish for you and will teach classes for your sake, so that you will have expiation. They will take you out of the hands of the destroyers and the demons. You will have a temporary rest until the time that it will be decreed by the heavenly court that you must leave this world as a wanderer. You will have rest from the demons until the time that you will come into Gehenna. I came to you with the holy community for your good. We will benefit you that you will have a repair, "*so that no one may be kept banished*" [II Samuel 14:14]. You will thank me for this, and you will be a memorial to R. Moshe Prager.

If not—you evildoer, impure spirit, if you will not leave, and will not leave with good—you must leave. I have no doubt about this. I will teach you good manners, nothing more—the difference is, if you will leave with good or not. If I will need the adjurations and great names for you, and will storm the worlds, above and below, because of you, afterwards, you will have no repair. Therefore, I advise you a good thing. I would rather only be good. Therefore, please leave.

And if not—I will excommunicate you and those appointed over you and ban you with *all sorts of excommunications, ostracisms, bans, and curses, and all sorts of adjurations,* with seven Torah scrolls, seven *shofars,* and seven children who have not yet had a nocturnal emission. I will send against you and those appointed over you such armies—who will tear out you and those appointed over you from the body of *the youth Abram, born of Yetta,* and you will be thrown into the depths of the abyss away from the world. You and those appointed over you will derive no benefit from the light of the sun and the moon. There will be no hope or recovery from your catastrophe.

[50] The *Spirit* began to shout very loudly and bitterly. Ha, ha, ha, ha. I laugh at you, I laugh at you; I mock you; I don't ask for you. When I will leave him—I will enter you. You will not bring me out. I will leave in twenty-six years. Ha, ha, ha, ha. You will not bring me out—I have taken in this mockery. No, no, you will not bring me out, in twenty-six years—when it comes time to leave him, I will first tear out his heart, and then I will go out. How do you warn me in the name of the sage? The rabbi is not here; he has moved to Vienna!

Rabbi Moshe responded, "You evildoer, impure *Spirit,* it is true that the rabbi has moved to Vienna, but before he moved from here, he gave me permission and asked me that I should go against you *with great adjurations and with excommunications, ostracisms, curses, and bans.*"

[51] The *Spirit* responded: "You thief, Moshe Prager, why are you not dealing with your book? You are bringing a book to print! Why do you not let me rest? If you will not let me rest—I will not allow this youth to have any rest. I will hit him with a large millstone. I will not let him eat or drink or sleep. I will cause you such mischief—I will stick and bite him and hit him continually on the Sabbath. He must only eat earth for me. I laugh at you; I mock you. I am not afraid of you." He mischievously said bad things about each person to spite them. "Ha, ha, ha, ha, I am afraid of nothing. I have brought it far enough. I have been in the hollow of the sling and withstood other punishments, and I still have much to endure!"

[52] Rabbi Moshe began: "You evildoer, repent, and we will repair you. We will give charity on your behalf and will fast for your sake." He began to laugh and to mock: "*Will not repent, will not repent.* No repair can help me. The blood of the prophet Zechariah boils.[89] I have killed two rabbis, R. Itzik R. Hendels and R. Aaron R. Leibush."

[53] They said to him: "We will ask them to allow us to ask forgiveness for your sake. We will send in meat for you." The *Spirit* responded: "You must be a denier [of God] if you want to ask for forgiveness. I had them buried in a courtyard and had an image[90] placed on their

grave. My impure offspring do not suffer so that I should have a repair. Therefore, I am not going out. I will leave in twenty-six years, and I first want to tear out the heart of the youth. Ha, ha, ha, ha. I will not go out. I am in a good inn, in good quarters. Not out, not out, not out, inside, inside. If I would have to leave otherwise, I will harm a number of souls. Then I will enter you." This was on Thursday, 8 Shevat, 456 [1696], in the small counting.

[MONDAY, 12 SHEVAT, JANUARY 16. DRASENHOFEN IN AUSTRIA. MEETING WITH APOTHECARY, PHYSICIAN, GOVERNOR.]

[54] On Monday, Rabbi Moshe again went to the spirit with a holy group.[91] He wanted to give him another warning. As soon as the *Spirit* became aware that Rabbi Moshe was coming with a holy group and thousands ran before them, God protect them. When the *Spirit* saw the people come running—the youth went into the room. There was a small hole in the wall, barely enough for a cat to crawl through. The *Spirit* lowered the youth through the hole—it was a miracle—and ran away with the youth. It was not possible that a bird could fly after him—all without shoes, barefoot, in socks. Six people on horses rode after him the whole time.

He ran to Drasenhofen in Austria. There he sat among the mountains, not thinking that they would ride after him. They surrounded him, and when he saw them, he took out a knife and chased them around the field. In brief, they captured him and threw the knife away in the field. They tied him to a horse and brought him back to the holy community of Nikolsburg.

[55] Rabbi Moshe did not go to him until eight days later, because Rabbi Moshe had heard how people spoke disgraceful things. They said they should let him go since they would not be able to overcome him. As a result, a desecration of God's name might come of it, heaven forbid. Several people also spoke about disgraceful things, and this might cause a libel against the community. The day that he was involved in hitting himself in the communal garden, several hundred gentiles were present. There were also several officials, including a cavalry officer and many soldiers. They reached a conclusion. When he would hit himself with the stone—they would take the stone away from him. As soon as he lay down on his back and grabbed a stone of ten pounds and began to confess with his pleasant voice—as was his norm—a fear fell upon the gentiles, and nobody wanted to touch him.

[56] However, the apothecary began talking with him in Latin. He wanted to send the scholars to him, and they would adjure him. He responded to him in Latin. You put a rope around your neck. They will adjure me? You have not come enough to me—will they also come to me? Who stands behind you? Why do you not leave a poor sinner in peace? Go only with good on your streets! The apothecary was ashamed to respond even a word to him.

[57] The doctor said to him he wanted to take him to his house. He would adjure him at home and drive him out. He said to the doctor: "Do you whore with your whore? You made your wife a whore first, and then you married her. Did you not make her a whore—whoever wanted her could have relations with her! How will you be able to exorcise me! You will first bring ten devils into yourself—before you exorcise me." He had to remain silent.

The governor also said something. He [the *Spirit*] picked up the stone and threw it at him. He hit him—he hit the spot that he threw at. Many people said: "He will cause a great libel against the community. He should be sent away to another community." Thus, Rabbi Moshe almost did not want to go to him. Rabbi Moshe did not go to him for eight days.

[SHABBAT, 10 SHEVAT, JANUARY 14 (AFTER THE FIRST WARNING). INTENSIFICATION OF THE VIOLENCE—BANGING HIS HEAD AGAINST THE WALL, THROWING HIMSELF INTO THE RIVER.]

[59] The Sabbath after the first warning, the spirit tormented the youth the whole day. From the time they called for Kabbalat Shabbat, he did not let him rest until the Sabbath ended, hitting, biting, and sticking him. He hit his head against the wall and threw him into the lake. He said: "This is all out of spite because you had brought Rabbi Moshe to adjure me. On the contrary, I will torment him more, out of spite." In all the six years he did not torment him as he had on the Sabbath as he did on that Sabbath—the Sabbath of the first warning. Rabbi Moshe heard about the spite that the spirit had engaged in, and the mockery. The above-mentioned Rabbi Moshe said: "I am zealous against you, for God's sake I will sacrifice myself. '*The zeal of the Lord of Hosts shall bring this to pass*' [II Kings 19:31; Isaiah 9:6, 37:32]; '*My help comes from the Lord, maker of heaven and earth*' [Psalm 121:2]. I will not let you go, and some people can say what they want!"

[THURSDAY, 15 SHEVAT, JANUARY 19: THE SECOND WARNING AND AFTERWARDS. FROM THE ALMSHOUSE TO THE OLD SYNAGOGUE.]

[60] Rabbi Moshe again went to him with a holy community on Thursday and gave him the second warning. He pulled out a knife and chased several hundred [people] out of the house. He locked the room and made a mess of the rooms. He broke all the tables and broke all the beds. He tore open all the cushions and poured out all the feathers. Rabbi Moshe ordered the rooms to be broken open, and they took a rope to bind him, and a great wonder happened. They took a knife away from him and searched in his sacks. In a short while, he again had a knife. The wonder is indescribable. When they bound him, he sank to the ground, and he defecated for more than half an hour. Rabbi Moshe recited holy names and names of angels for more than an hour and united and combined all the worlds—that they should assist in sanctifying the Great Name so that the impure spirit, the difficult spiritual impurity, should be torn of out of the body of *Abram, born of Yetta, with a strong hand, and anger and wrath poured out, without harming and without pain, the people that are present and the people that are not present*. He recited permutations of names, psalms, and added a *"May it be Your will"*—this had not been seen or heard from any *baal shem* in a hundred years. He ordered that they should ignite sulfur and put the smoke under his nose.

[61] The *Spirit* began to shout: "Ha, ha, ha, ha. Here I am, here I am, not out, not out. I will leave in twenty-six years. Then I will kill the youth. Ha, ha, ha, ha. See the revenge taken on me. I was the head of a land; then I became a hegemon. How important I was—how lowly have I become. I have no rest in the whole world. Similarly, when I was in a pig—they gave me no rest. Here I am in a good inn—where should I leave to?"

[62] Rabbi Moshe said: "We come for your welfare and benefit. We will repair you so that you will be able to enter Gehenna."

The spirit began to laugh and mock:

Yes, he wants to repair me! Concerning me it was said, *"a twisted thing cannot be made straight"* [Ecclesiastes 1:15]—until my impure offspring will become an expiation. There are still two in this world. I still have to fly around in the world for another fifty years; afterwards, perhaps there will be hope.

Punish your children with me. I had only one glance at the next world. I saw in this world such small, squashed Jews, how important they are in the next world. I would rather have been God's servant in this world. How important I was in the world with my friends who fly together in the world and have no rest in the whole world! I have been a spirit for forty years. Ha, ha, ha, ha, what I have endured!

[63] Rabbi Moshe asked him about his name. He said, "Soon I will tell him my name; he is ready." However, Rabbi Moshe answered [that] he had a report that he was called Antfer, Samuel, or Abram. He was a cantor, and afterwards became head of the land. Afterwards, he became embittered, and afterwards he became a hegemon.

Rabbi Moshe said: "You evildoer, do I not know your name? Were you not a famous cantor? Your name is Antfer, Abram, or Samuel."

He laughed more and said, "You are lying, I was head of a land—not a cantor." He became frightened before Rabbi Moshe and said with great arrogance: "How do you know me? You were hanging on the gallows, and I flew by! Since that time, you know me." He said evil things to each one, and blew up the youth like a barrel, and spit on everyone. R. Moshe slapped him in the face. The *Spirit* said: "Who are you hitting? The body is not mine. I am only a *Spirit*; the body belongs to the youth!"

[64] He said bad things about each one of them. One Jew was standing in the back. He said to him: "This evildoer came here to see me, and he is wearing *zizit* with an unfit string. If Abram did not have unfit *zizit*—I would not have come into him." The Jew searched all over and did not find anything wrong. The *Spirit* said: "Did you check the upper corners?" It was true that the *zizit* were damaged in one of the corners.

[65] However, after the second warning, he became very submissive and was very fearful of Rabbi Moshe. He no longer hit him during the day—but only at night. He picked up a stone and led him before the new synagogue in the middle of the night, hit him for two hours, and confessed. He did not hit him again during the day.

[66] One time, people came to him and said, "Rabbi Moshe Prager has left in order to have his book printed." He danced around in the dust of the room out of great joy. Afterwards, he learned that someone had fooled him. That person did not dare appear before him. He wanted to kill him.

[TUESDAY, 20 SHEVAT, JANUARY 24. THE THIRD WARNING IN THE ALMSHOUSE. A REQUEST TO DEFER IT UNTIL THURSDAY.]

[67] In brief, Rabbi Moshe again went to him with his holy group on the next Tuesday to give him the third warning, *after which there is nothing more*. When Rabbi Moshe came into the room, he asked him: "I ask you, my dear rabbi, leave me alone today, there is no Torah reading today. I plead with you, leave it until Thursday." Rabbi Moshe responded:

> No, you evildoer, I do not give you any time. I give you the warning today [that] you should voluntarily leave the body of the youth, Abram, born of Yetta, *without harm or pain, the people who are present and the people who are not present. Only by way of the small finger of the left foot*. In this way, we will repair you, and you will have rest from the *destroyers and the demons of destruction*. I take upon myself for your sake to fast every for a year, except for the days that Tahanun is not recited. I will recite kaddish for you and will organize classes for your sake, and give charity for your sake, so that in time you will be able to be repaired. However, you will have rest from the *destroyers and the demons of destruction*. They will no longer punish you severely and will no longer persecute you as previously. I promise you all this in exchange for this. If you will not leave voluntarily—I will take you on Thursday, *may it come upon us for good*, into the synagogue, and I will deal with you and those appointed over you with great adjurations, with excommunications and bans and great curses, and will cause a great noise against you and those appointed over you, in heaven and on earth, and there will be no *redemption for your downfall*.

[68] The *Spirit* began to shout, weeping, mumbling, and lamenting:

> O woe, you have great mercy on the youth. You are merciful people—why do you have no mercy on me? Where should I go to, where should I enter—*where should I take my disgrace?* I will not go out, not out, I sit with strength. Just today they have given me a third one appointed over me. I ask you please, very, very much, let me go. I am no longer torment-

ing the youth. If you do not let me go—I will take revenge on the youth. I let him don phylacteries today and let him pray—something he has not done for years. Will you not let me go—so that I will have to leave, I will kill the youth, tear out his heart. You are killing the youth.

[69] Rabbi Moshe responded:

You evildoer, you *Spirit* of impurity, how can you be so stubborn and add sin to offense, to the transgressions that you did during your lifetime? You say that you want to kill the youth. You will not have the power together with those appointed over you. With God's help, you can have three appointed ones or ten—I don't care. Afterwards, I will—praise God, blessed be He—I will vanquish you and those appointed over you. You must leave, and you are not allowed to harm the youth in any limb of his two hundred and forty-eight organs, and not any other Jew in the whole world. You have no more time than from today until the Thursday *that will come upon us for good*. I will go against you and those appointed over you with great and severe adjurations that have not been seen or heard in several hundred years. I give you my word, before the holy group, that if you leave according to my words—I guarantee you before the holy group, *may their Creator and Redeemer protect them*, you will have a repair through me. Your punishment will be lightened. The destroyers and demons of destruction will no longer pursue you as they did previously. The prayer of the community is great. We will fast together and pray for your sake, but only leave according to my words. I only want what is good for you. You know well that in all my days, I *have only been good to those who are near and those who are far. Everyone who hears me will agree.*

[70] The *Spirit* began to shout and lament. He says, never, no spiteful word, just never. He leaves the youth in peace during the day. However, at night, when everybody is asleep, he leads him out of the almshouse and takes a mighty, large stone, leads him to the new synagogue, and beats him. However, during the day he leaves him at peace.

[Wednesday, 21 Shevat, January 25. Monologue by the youth about events since Rosh Hodesh Shevat.]

[71] In brief, on Wednesday, Rabbi Moshe went with only ten to fifteen people to the Spirit and wanted to hear what the Spirit had to say, and what he had considered. R. Moshe wanted to use the adjuration tomorrow, Thursday. Rabbi Moshe spoke to the *Spirit*, but the *Spirit* did not respond with a single word. Rabi Moshe told him great names into his ear. Rabbi Moshe put phylacteries on the youth. He let him lie, but he did not want to say a single name. The youth said: "My dear Rabbi, I cannot mention any names. I am afraid of him!" Rabbi Moshe became angry with the youth. Why did he not want to mention any names? He said,

> My dear rabbi, do with me what you want; I will not mention any names. I must engage with him. I obey him, and he obeys me in return. You do not feel this. When I do not obey him and want to mention names or do a religious act—he takes revenge on me. He hurts me in my main organs, like a cat with copper nails is rolling around inside me and stabs me like with a sharp nail. I faint—my death is better than my life. I wish I was dead—I would have rest from him. My life is no life.

[72] Fourteen days ago, a volume of tractate *Berakhot* lay on the table. I looked into it and just read in the text: "*Rabbi Eliezer said: There are three watches in the night and at every watch the Holy One roars like a lion.*"[92] As soon as I said this, he said to me, "Come out with me!" I came out, and he said to me, "Lie down quietly, or I will go up three stories with you, and I will throw you down!" He said to me: "I want to teach you good manners. Do you want to begin something with me? You want to study Talmud? Come here, I want to teach you! He hit me, stabbed me, bit me, and scratched my feet—for many years he did not do anything. For the last eight days everything repeated itself, "You want to study Talmud with me—don't ever come to me with your Talmud!"

[73] Three weeks ago, on Rosh Hodesh, he allowed me to go to the old synagogue. The congregation was reciting the Hallel, and I also began to recite it. He said to me: "Come out! You donned phylacteries, and you are also reciting Hallel; I will teach you proper manners! He

tore off the phylacteries from my head and tore them to pieces and led me to the lake and threw me over the wall into the lake and left me in the lake for more than half an hour with my head down." He said to me: "If you do this to me one more time, I will kill you. Watch yourself with me—I say this for your good!"

[74] Three weeks ago, I washed myself a little for the Sabbath. He said to me, "You are starting something new with me—come outside, I will wash you properly!" He took me out, took a knife and stabbed me in my hands and washed me with the blood, "Wash yourself this way; this is called proper washing!" So, dear rabbi, how should I recite names? I dare not, dear rabbi.

The *Spirit* did not say anything this time and allowed the youth to speak.

[75] Rabbi Moshe asked the youth: "My child, tell me what does he talk with you? Or, what does he say—when does he want to leave?"

The youth said: "Chirping like a chick, and repeating, he always said to me, 'Obey me; everything I want to have—I will leave you in four weeks.' When the time comes, as he said, he laughs at me, and he says to me, 'I gave you exercises, and you did not properly obey me.' He laughed at me in this way."

Rabbi Moshe said, "Does he show you inside you, what kind of face he has?"

The youth said:

At night he does not let me sleep, except on a bench. He used to throw me off the bench—and I lay on the bare earth. When he did let me sleep—he used to appear to me like a large black cat, full of eyes.

[76] But dear rabbi, I want to tell you what happened one previous night after another. Today, after the middle of the night, somebody called me from outside the window, Abram—and I was lying in front of the oven. I was called this way three times.

They spoke to me, "When we call you—why do you not go out?"

So, I went out. The people in the rooms asked, "Abram, where are you going now?" They can all testify that everything I am saying is true.

I said to the people inside, "I must go out; I am being called." I went out and sat down on the chair in front of the house. As I was sitting there, soldiers came down from the castle, thousands, and tens of thousands, they were innumerable, with weapons, swords, and spears. There were large men and small men among them. All of them were so big that they pole vaulted over the houses with their spears. This lasted for two hours. The soldiers marched past me in one column. I sat on the chair the whole time until a great fear came over me.

The *Spirit* said to me, "Do not be afraid, they won't do anything to you." After they all passed, it was about two [a.m.]. He said to me, "Take the stone and hold on to it and come with me." He led me to the new synagogue and hit me there until about four [a.m.]. Afterwards, he let me go home again. He did this to me two nights in a row.

[77] Rabbi Moshe said:

My dear child, this all means that he will, God willing, have to leave you soon. I hope to God, blessed be He, that I will soon be able to complete this incident. I am awake the whole night over this, and do, thank God, blessed be He, my actions. *The God of my father will help me*, I will soon bring him out, without harming you or the community. The angels of destruction and the destroyers are coming for him, but I will save him from the angels of destruction. They will no longer have him in their hands if he will come out peacefully.

[78] The *Spirit* did not say anything and allowed the youth to speak with Rabbi Moshe. However, when Rabbi Moshe and the people left, the *Spirit* became angry with the youth. "Why did you reveal all the secrets? I did not allow it." He hit him, bit him, and hit his head against the wall many times. "You should not disclose what I tell you!"

[THURSDAY, 22 SHEVAT, JANUARY 26. THE FIRST ADJURATION, THE NEW SYNAGOGUE. SABBATH, 24 SHEVAT, JANUARY 28, AGGRAVATION.]

[79] In brief, the next day, Thursday of the Torah portion Yitro, they took the youth to the new synagogue for the first adjuration. They cut off all of the youth's hair and led him into the synagogue. All of the scholars who were there, particularly the noble judges, went with Rabbi Moshe to the adjuration in the new synagogue. God help us—almost a

thousand people filled the synagogue, and the women's section was also full. Several hundred people stood outside in the community's garden and listened to wondrous things.

[80] The youth said to Rabbi Moshe:

Dear rabbi, I am ready to die, if only he can be vanquished, even if he would tear my heart out—I would not worry about it. My life is not a life like this. I will sacrifice myself, like Isaac at the Akedah. However, if you will not vanquish him—he will take even more revenge on me and cause me great anguish that is indescribable. He scratches me in my bowels—like I was being scratched with copper nails. He burns me inside, like someone was being burned with glowing irons. My death is ten times dearer than my life, as happened to me a number of times in Poland. All the ba'alei shem were over me and could not help me. They made it worse for me. They only angered him, and he took revenge on me and caused me great trouble.

[81] Rabbi Moshe consoled the youth and said, "My child, do not fear. 'My help comes from the Lord, maker of heaven and earth' [Psalm 121:2]. I hope to God, blessed be He, I will vanquish him, and will not have to do any harm to you and no other Jew, both those that are here and those that are not here. Thank God, blessed be He, I always go from the potential to the actual, that he should no longer cause you any trouble as he did in the past."

They took the youth and sat him high on the Torah reading table, above the seats, near the holy Ark. They tied his hands and feet and tied him to an iron window frame.

[82] Rabbi Moshe began:

Listen, you impure evildoer, great and difficult spark of impurity. I warn you one more time out of compassion, with the warning that has nothing after it. I have already given you three warnings. I have already spoken enough with kindness. God knows that I am only interested in your good. I want to benefit you, that you will have rest from the destroyers and accusers. I will say Kaddish for you, and I will fast for you every day for a year—except for the days that Tahanun is not recited. We will have study sessions for your sake. All of us who are here—God protect them—in the synagogue, nobody should neglect; all must give charity, one more, one less. If not this way—we and the holy group, with the association of the Holy One, His Shekhinah, and the whole heavenly family, will adjure you and those appointed over you, will excommunicate and ban, will anathemize and curse, and will decree and adjure the lords who are those appointed over you.

Since R. Moshe already had a report what lords were over the appointed ones, and what type they were, he had already seen in his movements in his deeds. "Thus, I decree against them, that they will tear you out *with wrath, anger, and destruction, and without harm, from the body of the youth, Abram born of Yetta*." The spirit did not respond at all and made himself dead for more than half an hour.

[83] This what Rabbi Moshe ordered. They should take sulfur and devil's dung,[93] have them turned to smoke, and place it under his nose.

[84] The *Spirit* began to blow up the youth and his head and throat became the same thickness—like a water bucket. It ran up and down him, and [he] tore a rope that was two fingers thick, and he began to shout:

Ha, ha, ha, ha. Here I am, I like this very much. Burn more of it—I like the smell. Not out, not out, in the inside. I do not give up at all. I must remain in him for another twenty-six years, and then I will tear out his heart. Ha, ha, ha, ha. You should let me go in peace or I will harm people—as I harmed people in Poland. I want to torment him specifically on the Sabbath and throw him in water and in fire. I want to go with him to the top of the house and throw him down and to run with him into the wild forest. I want to tear out trees and grass, and we must only eat earth and dung.

[85] This is what the noble Rabbi Hirsch Segal, the judge, said to him: "You evildoer, better that you should sanctify the name [of God] publicly and leave—you will have expiation. If you confess and desecrate the Sabbath—what does your confession help?"

He responded: "Ha, ha, ha, ha. This is also a sanctification of [God's] name, that I know how I am punished on the Sabbath. Take a moral lesson from me; punish your children with me!"

They negotiated with him for more than an hour. The *Spirit* kept shouting, "Not out, not out, *will not recant!*"

[86] In brief, Rabbi Moshe ordered that they should take out seven Torah scrolls, seven shofars, and seven children. All the scholars surrounded them. Rabbi Moshe ordered that the whole community should begin to recite the "Song of Ascents"[94] together, and mentioned what intentions they should have, and recited other Psalms. He mentioned all the [divine] names that come from these Psalms. In addition, he recited a prayer, a "*May it be Your will*,"[95] and the whole congregation recited amen with all their might. They also recited the prayer, "*May the favor*" [*Vayehi Noam*],[96] seven times. Rabbi Moshe mentioned the name that issued from this—a person's hair stood on end from great fear.

[87] Afterwards, Rabbi Moshe asked for his name and the names of those appointed over him. If you will not tell me peacefully—you will have to tell me over your [*dnk*—word uncertain]. He mentioned more than one hundred names. Think, which one is it? He only spoke spitefully, "I don't care about all of you; I don't care about you!"

[88] Rabbi Moshe began to give the great excommunication against him and those appointed over him that he should *leave the body of the youth Abram, born of Yetta, without harm and without pain, only through the small finger of the left foot, without harming the people who are present and the people who are not present*. He damned and cursed him and those appointed over him in all the months and constellations, all the days and hours, and named all the lords and those appointed. This took more than an hour.

[89] Afterwards, the community said amen with all their strength and shouted in unison seven times, "*Go out impure one; go forth impure one!*" Rabbi Moshe had previously told them what intention they should have and should extinguish the candles. The seven *shofars* blew *shevarim*[97] seven times.

[90] The *Spirit* started to shout so loud that it was heard at the old synagogue. Such lamentable sounds had never been heard in his days. He made all kinds of noises and blew up the youth like a barrel and flew in him here and there, up and down, from head to foot and foot to head. It was a great novelty to see, and smoke came out of his mouth. Such a thing was not seen or heard in his day. The smoke that came out of his mouth was literally like a rainbow—blue, black, and red came out of his mouth, and nothing other than groats. He shouted: "I don't ask for it! I don't ask for it! I am not going out! How can you

repair me? The list of my transgressions is very long. Three were already erased. I want to compromise with you. I will leave the youth rest on the Sabbath. I will let him eat what he wants, and I will do nothing to him on the Sabbath."

[91] There were many great scholars in the synagogue, and they truly wanted that Rabbi Moshe should compromise with him, lest they [could] not bring him out—the sanctification of God's name would, heaven forbid, become a desecration of God's name. Rabbi Moshe said: "I do not make compromises. He must come out. *My trust is in God.* I will teach him good manners so that he won't do anything to him on the Sabbath. Before the Sabbath I will have him bound and hang him high [off the ground], and he must hang in this way the whole Sabbath."

[92] The noble Rabbi Hirsch Segal, the judge, said, "We will immediately adjure the [divine] name that is over the stones so that he will not be able to take any stone in his hand."

[93] In brief, Rabbi Moshe again spoke with him peacefully and negotiated with him how to help him—he again responded to him with great insolence. Rabbi Moshe renewed his adjurations again and again invoked the great excommunication against him and against those appointed over him. The *Spirit* shouted again several times that was not seen or heard in his day. The lamentable sounds that the *Spirit* made, such sounds had not seen or heard in his day. He made noises of all sorts of creatures and blew up the youth and threw and spit on everyone.

[94] In brief, Rabbi Moshe wanted to adjure him for a third time and impose the excommunication on him and those appointed over him. The *Spirit* began to shout in a loud voice, "Remain quiet for a little while; remain quiet for a little while!"

Rabbi Moshe remained quiet for a while and said to him: "So, evildoer, repent and sanctify the great name of God publicly, and leave *the body of the youth Abram, born of Yetta, without harm and without pain, to the people who are here and the people who are not here.* If he would sanctify the name of God, it would certainly be an expiation for all the desecrations of God's name, that you did in all your days."

The *Spirit* responded: "How will you have a greater sanctification of God's name, when you see how I am punished? I do not want to torment the youth anymore. I ask you, let me go. Don't be angry, I am still taking revenge on the youth. You are making everything worse. I will allow him to eat whatever he wants, just let me go!"

Rabbi Moshe did not agree to any of it and again began to recite holy names, and again imposed the great excommunication on him. He again began to shout as before. This went on until midday that they urged everything on him.

[FRIDAY–SABBATH, 23–24 SHEVAT, JANUARY 27–28. IN THE ALMSHOUSE (THE DAY AFTER THE FIRST ADJURATION.)]

[96] Afterwards, he went from the adjuration, and the youth went to the almshouse. However, the spirit was humble and submissive immediately after the adjuration and had no strength. The youth's bowels were not troubled the following Friday. On Friday night he allowed him to pray, wash, and recite the *kiddush*, and allowed him to eat and drink. He allowed him to be joyful and recite the grace after meals with a group. It was a great joy for the youth and for the people since he tormented him mostly on the Sabbath and did not allow him to eat the whole Sabbath. The youth literally became like a newly born person. The youth, thank God, blessed be He, enjoyed keeping the Sabbath and eating and drinking—something he had missed for six years.

[SUNDAY, 25 SHEVAT, JANUARY 29. IN THE NEW SYNAGOGUE, WARNING, AND PRAYER.]

[97] In brief, on Sunday, an hour before the afternoon service, Rabbi Moshe went and again took the youth and led him to the new synagogue. He took along twenty or thirty scholars. They placed the youth on the Torah reading table, and again, peacefully, began to speak with him, in a positive way:

> Listen to me, impure evildoer of impurity, great and difficult spark of impurity. How obstinate you are. You don't want to obey? I am only interested in your good, so that I will save you from demons of destruction and the accusers. You only have to leave the body of the youth Abram, son of Yetta, without harm or pain, and the people who are here and the people who are not here. If you will leave for me—tomorrow I will, tomorrow will be this sign, I will go against you with great adjurations that have not been seen or heard and will

storm worlds against you, and those appointed over you, in the upper and lower worlds, that you will have to leave by force. I will allow you to be thrown into the heart of the great abyss, and you will have no redemption from your catastrophe. Therefore, it is better if you leave peacefully, according to my words. I want to show you the prayer that Rabbi Hirsch Segal, the judge, has composed, that I will recite in the amidah for your sake. I want to read it to you, word for word. Listen to me:

[98] Lord of the Universe, Merciful Father, Lord of penitence, God, King merciful and compassionate, who behaves mercifully to all of His creatures. We have come with prayer and petition before You, that You should let flow the good flow [shefa]. Act beyond the letter of the Law with this spirit, who has cleaved and come to this youth, Abram, born of Yetta, and he is confused within him. Please, Merciful father, lighten his punishment, and even if he has punishments from his severe transgressions or light ones. You are the Lord of Mercy too. Give him unearned mercy that he should not be banished permanently. May our prayers ascend before Your Throne of Glory, to remember with good memories of all the good merits that the spirit himself did or the merit of his ancestors. To join our prayers, that they should be accepted before You like the incense [of the Temple], and like a pleasant odor, to influence mercy and compassion on him. Do not remember his sins and transgressions. Put aside the sins and transgressions that he transgressed and the sins that he committed, both by himself and with others. Raise up our prayers before You, as if he had prayed for himself. May he have rescue and redemption from all the demons and accusers that were appointed over him to punish him, according to the punishments that were imposed on him. May he have a place of true rest. In the manner and on the condition: If he does not return to him, and does not harm any Jewish person, whether male or female—with Your great mercy and forgiveness, please forgive and take pity on him, to give him tranquility and rest, and may he have a repair. You, the one who hears the prayers of Your people, Israel, with mercy—You should hear our prayers.

May the words of my mouth be acceptable before You—God, our Rock and Redeemer, amen.[98]

[99] As soon as he heard the prayer, he began to shout, "The prayer is good for me, and also immediately recite psalms on my behalf!"

Rabbi Moshe recited approximately six psalms, and the spirit began to shout: "Enough, recite Kaddish immediately for my sake. It does not depend on saying much or saying little—just say Kaddish immediately!" The *Spirit* shouted: "Rabbi, recite Kaddish immediately. Immediately also study for my sake!"

Rabbi Moshe studied for his sake and also recited Kaddish.

[100] The *Spirit* spoke: "I want to leave but give me three days. I want to look around the world, to see where I can have a place of rest. Do you not see how many thousands and tens of thousands of angels of destruction and destroyers are standing around me? They are sitting and looking forward to my going out. They will again punish me with great and difficult punishments!"

Rabbi Moshe said: "Do not fear, do not worry; just leave. I will save you from the angels of destruction. You will have in all your days a memorial in me—just go out!"

The *Spirit* said, "I will leave, but if they will not keep with me what is given to me—I will come back into him in three days!"

Rabbi Moshe promised this to him, that everything will be observed as he had been promised. He would do even more for his sake, that he had not promised—so that he should have rest. Rabbi Moshe allowed the youth to go back to the almshouse.

[MONDAY, 26 SHEVAT, JANUARY 30. THE SECOND ADJURATION (THE TRANSFER FROM THE MORNING UNTIL AFTERNOON, AND FROM THE NEW SYNAGOGUE TO THE OLD ONE.)]

[101] They wanted to adjure the *Spirit* the next day, Monday, in the new synagogue. Thousands of people gathered in the synagogue so that it was not possible for Rabbi Moshe and the rabbinical court to enter the synagogue. They left and put off the adjuration until the afternoon. They thought that the crowd would disperse in the meantime, but the crowd—God protect them—remained in the synagogue. In brief, in the afternoon, it was even harder to enter the synagogue. On the contrary, the crowd had increased.

[102] In brief, the communal leaders and the notables along with Rabbi Moshe and the rabbinical court led him to the old synagogue. The old synagogue was full in the blink of an eye. The whole women's section was full of Jews and gentiles—everybody ran there. In brief, they took down the chandelier that hung between the holy Ark and the reading table, and they suspended the youth in a chair before the holy Ark. Rabbi Moshe warned him in the name of the holy group, *with the association of the upper and lower worlds*, as I mentioned above. He should leave *the body of the youth Abram, born of Yetta, without anguish or harm, and the people who are here and the people who are not here, only by way of the small finger of the left foot.* If—if he will go out peacefully and will sanctify the name of God before Jews and gentiles—the sanctification of God's name will atone for the desecration of God's name that you have in all your days, desecrated the name of God! Several hundred gentiles were standing around the synagogue at the windows of the synagogue wanting to see what the outcome would be.

[103] In brief, Rabbi Moshe began to recite adjurations that had not been seen or heard, and each one aroused a fear. The *Spirit* made such noises that had never been heard in his lifetime. He became subservient and did not say an angry word to anyone. He only spoke to Rabbi Moshe—he cried during the adjuration—he said to him, "Cry your eyes out of your head!" However, beyond that he did not utter an angry word. In brief, Rabbi Moshe did not imagine stopping. This time he must leave.

The *Spirit* began to shout: "Be quiet once. I want to leave. I want to leave. Only remove those appointed over me from the excommunication; they give me no rest anymore!"

[104] Rabbi Moshe said: "You and those appointed over you remain in the great excommunication until you will leave the youth *without harm and without pain* from all of his two hundred and forty-eight organs. *From the principle, you hear a prohibition*: If you will leave—then the excommunication ends. Not only that, but we will also keep what we promised you—the whole community will accept a fast upon themselves on the eve of the new month,[99] or the one that will come upon us in the future. All those who began to fast, with the exception of pregnant and nursing women, and nobody should leave the synagogue without giving charity for your sake."

[105] The *Spirit* began to shout: "Woe, charity does not help me at all. You should measure the cemetery and give the candles in all

three synagogues for my sake.[100] I want to leave; I want to leave. Where should I go out of such a holy and pure body, out of such a good hostel? I waited for him for three weeks, until he came and urinated on the pile of dung and on his defective *zizit*. This is how they gave me permission to enter him. What a nice rest I had in him! I ask you: Give me another twelve months' time!"

Rabbi Moshe said, "Not even a half hour; we are not ceasing with you; you must leave immediately!"

He shouted again, "No, twelve days, give me time!"

Rabbi Moshe responded, "You evildoer, we previously told you, we are not giving any more time."

The *Spirit* again responded, "You must give me twelve hours; I cannot leave for another twelve hours."

[106] Rabbi Hirsch Segal, the judge, said, "How will we know that you have left?"

The *Spirit* said, "If I will leave through the small toe, I will break a window pane and will fly out."

Rabbi Hirsch Segal, the judge, said, "Give us an oath by the Supernal God that you will leave."

The Spirit responded, shouting: "Ha, ha, ha, ha, if I was ready to say the words—I would be far along; I dare not say the words yet. However, I can give you a handshake that I will keep my word, that I will leave in twelve hours."

[107] They untied his hands, and he extended his left hand. Rabbi Hirsch Segal, the judge, said to him: "You evildoer, here we see your deception! Do you want to deceive us? Why do you not extend your right hand?"

The *Spirit* shouted, "I am lefthanded, I am lefthanded!"

Rabbi Hirsch Segal, the judge, said to him, "No, you must give the right hand."

[108] He extended his right hand that he would leave in twelve hours, in the manner and with the conditions that they will hold him to what he had promised. That is, Rabbi Moshe Prager would fast for his sake for a whole year, day to day, except for the days when Tahanun is not recited, and for thirty days they will recite Kaddish for him in the new synagogue, and Rabbi Hirsch, the judge, in the old synagogue. Specifically Psalms and Kaddish because they cut of all the accusers and all the destroyers. Rabbi Moshe must sit on the mourner's bench, ashamed, and the youth must recite Kaddish for a whole year. Lectures

should be given for my sake, and also Kaddish recited at the end. The cemetery should be measured for my sake and candles donated to the synagogues. Thirty candles should burn in the synagogue for me. When all of this will be kept—I will leave in twelve hours—as I shook hands on it. If not—when what I have been promised is not kept—I will enter him again in three days.

[109] They asked him, "When we will pray for you, we have to mention your name, so tell us your name."

He began to shout, certainly ten or twelve times consecutively, "My name is Samuel!"

Then they asked him, "What is your father's name?"

The first time he said, "Michel."

Then Rabbi Hirsch Segal, the judge, asked him, "Tell me again, what is your name?"

He shouted ten times, "Samuel!"

They asked him again about his father and he shouted, "Mendel!"

They said to him: "You evildoer, earlier you said, Michel!"

He said: "I was mistaken. My master is called Michel, and my father is called Mendel."

They asked him what was his mother's name? He shouted several times: "Beilah. Her soul left her, and she is an expiation for all of Israel!"

They said to him, "You evildoer, how do you curse your mother?"

He responded: "She became an expiation; she incited me into all the evil things she became, may her memory be blotted out. *I increased silver and gold, and it became an idol.*[101] She gave me money for controversies; she led me into all evil."

[110] In brief, it was about four in the afternoon, and it was time for the afternoon prayers. They prayed the afternoon prayer. They left the youth suspended there, and they prayed the afternoon and evening prayers. The *Spirit* ran back and forth in the youth and blew him up, thick as a barrel. His tongue hung down to his heart, and a foam covered his mouth. When they shouted amen with all their might, he shouted several times—that had never been heard before. Afterwards, they allowed the youth to return to the almshouse.

[MONDAY, 26 SHEVAT, JANUARY 30, AT NIGHT IN THE ALMSHOUSE. THE OCCURRENCES BEFORE THE DEPARTURE OF THE *SPIRIT*.]

[111] In brief, that night there was a great novelty: That night there was such an unfortunate occurrence in the holy community of Nikolsburg that

had not happened in many years. Nobody could sleep the whole night because of the noises that were heard on the castle hill and in the garden. All the dogs in the holy community of Nikolsburg were under the windows of Rabbi Moshe, and they nearly tore themselves apart with barking.

[112] The spirit pushed the youth the whole night and gave him no rest. He ran with him from room to room and banged on all the doors—so that the house trembled and shook. The people in the almshouse became very afraid. He had never done this before. The youth said to the people in the almshouse: "My dear people, I ask your pardon. I know for certain that I will not survive the night. He will certainly tear my heart out today. He has never in his life done such things."

[TUESDAY, 27 SHEVAT, JANUARY 31, BEFORE MORNING IN THE ALMSHOUSE. THE DEPARTURE OF THE *SPIRIT*.]

[113] This lasted until about four in the morning. Just as the twelve hours ended, as the *Spirit* had shaken hands on, that he would leave, the youth sat down in the front row bench. The *Spirit* began to shout with a loud voice: "Go away from the window. I will harm anyone who stands near the window!" He shouted three or four times.

[114] Suddenly, there was banging on the wall near the window. They thought that the wall would fall down. The youth said, "These were the ones appointed over him, in the lead." Afterwards, there was a crack in the windowpane—just like one had shot a rifle. Something fell out of the pane as large as a gold piece, a round hole in the middle. Around the hole were a few cracks, like a star. The *Spirit* had left. The youth had received a small cut under the nail of his small toe of his right foot. When they cut open the skin, the shoe was full of blood. Here, the *Spirit* had left.

[TUESDAY, 27 SHEVAT, JANUARY 31, IN THE ALMSHOUSE. THE BEHAVIOR OF THE YOUTH AND THE COMMUNITY AFTER THE DEPARTURE OF THE *SPIRIT*.]

[115] The youth began to pray and don phylacteries and began to mention all the holy names and later to do religious activities that previously had not been possible for him to do. The youth began to see things in the heavens that were not possible to see. Immediately, the whole crowd—God protect them—began to enter the almshouse and saw the new aspect of the youth, where the spirit had left.

[DURING THE MONTH AFTER THE DEPARTURE OF THE *SPIRIT* (UNTIL WEDNESDAY, 26 ADAR I, FEBRUARY 29). THE COMPLETION OF THE CONDITIONS THAT HAD BEEN PROMISED TO THE *SPIRIT*.]

[116] They immediately formed a quorum [*minyan*], and Rabbi Moshe girded himself and the following days [Tuesday, 27 (Shevat), January 31; Wednesday, 28 (Shevat), February 1]. They burned candles all thirty days in the almshouse and also in the new synagogue for the full thirty days. The women measured the cemetery four times during the thirty days. They began a class to study Mishnah for his sake and recite Kaddish. Rabbi Hirsch Segal, the judge, recited all the holy psalms in the old synagogue the whole thirty days. Rabbi Moshe recited all the holy psalms in the new synagogue. He also sat on the mourner's bench in the synagogue and fasted for his sake for a year, from day to day, except for the days that Tahanun was not recited. The rabbinical court decreed a fast on the eve of the new month of Adar [Thursday, 29 Shevat, February 2]. All began the fast—except for pregnant and nursing women, for the sake of the Spirit. He also utilized holy names.

[AFTER THE DEPARTURE OF THE *SPIRIT* (TUESDAY, 27 SHEVAT, JANUARY 31) FROM THE ALMSHOUSE TO GUARDING IN THE BET MIDRASH FOR EIGHT DAYS.]

[117] The communal leaders and the rabbinical court took the youth out of the almshouse and put him in the bet midrash so that Rabbi Moshe should watch over him, at least for eight days.

[118] The communal leaders together with the rabbinical court sent their assistants to all the synagogues and had them announce, "In the end—since the *Spirit* has left and has gone out of *the body of the youth Abram, without harm or pain*—therefore, he and those appointed over him are no longer excommunicated."

[119] All the youth's strength was taken away from all of the two hundred and forty-eight organs. The youth had no strength in any of his limbs and could not move. The proof is: The youth said that he must die, he has no strength anymore in his body. They took away the youth's clothes and gave him completely different clothes. They also advised the youth that he should go and immerse in the mikvah, but he did not have the strength to go and immerse himself. Rabbi Moshe had them pour nine measures of warm water over him.

[THE NEXT NIGHT (WEDNESDAY, 28 SHEVAT, AT NIGHT) THE APPEARANCE OF THE *SPIRIT* TO THE EMISSARY, NAPHTALI BEN MOSHE DACH OF VIENNA.]

[120] In brief, the next night the *Spirit* came into the house of Rabbi Ber Beck, the head of the community, may his Creator protect him, to a Jerusalemite named Rabbi Naphtali the son of Rabbi Moshe Dach of Vienna. He came and wanted to destroy the house. He said, "He was *between Usha and Shefaram*."[102] This is how they chased him back with his appointed ones. He had no rest in the whole world. He was still excommunicated with those appointed over him.

[121] He spoke to him again: Yesterday we had the communal assistants announce the excommunication! The *Spirit* responded: "No, it is not valid. *The mouth that forbids is the mouth that permits.* Rabbi Moshe Prager who excommunicated me—he must bring me out again; otherwise, it has not helped me."

[WEDNESDAY, 28 SHEVAT, FEBRUARY 2. THE DECISION CONCERNING THE ABROGATION OF HIS EXCOMMUNICATION BY PRAGER ON THURSDAY AND FRIDAY.]

[122] The communal leaders along with the noble judges composed an announcement, and Rabbi Moshe Prager, may his Creator protect him, went to all the synagogues and made the announcement personally: "Tomorrow morning, on Thursday, the eve of the new month of *Adar*, without a fast—in the old synagogue, in the afternoon service—in the new synagogue, and the next day, on the new moon of *Adar*—in the study house [*bet midrash*]."

[123] The announcement was in the following words:

> Holy community, here we announce and make known since every eye sees: "The Lord is near to all who call upon Him, to all who call Him with sincerity. He fulfills the wishes of those who fear Him; He hears their cry and delivers them" [Psalm 145:18–19]. With regard to the exorcism of the Spirit, which has happened, that excommunications and great and awesome bans were given against the Spirit and those appointed over him, at great length, in all matters and with strength, and given with a condition: when he will

leave—the excommunication should be abrogated completely and should be like a broken clay pot, which is not in effect and does not continue in effect. Therefore, we announce the above-mentioned announcement in all the synagogues, in association with the Holy One, His Shekhinah, and the Heavenly Hosts, and all this is the word of God. With the condition that it will be fulfilled that the youth Abram born of Yetta will remain in this state in the future, without any harm or pain, and to every Jew who is here and who is not here, that all of them should remain without harm or pain from the above-mentioned Spirit, who mentioned that his name was Samuel born of Beilah, or any other name that he has, and was in the youth Abram born of Yetta—All the bans, excommunications, and shunning that was given, both on the spirit and on those appointed over him, are completely abrogated like a broken pot, and there is no curse, ban, or excommunication on them. They are innocent of all the bans, excommunications, and shunning that was imposed on them, here in the holy community of Nikolsburg. In the manner that the spirit should not enter any person in the world, both awake and in dreams, whether man or woman, youth, or maiden, boy or girl, old man, or old woman, whether in this land or in another land, in civilized space or wilderness, seas or rivers. All of the people should give into their hearts to walk in the worship of the exalted Name and to worship Him with awe and love. May the Lord give the good flow and mercy. Amen, amen, amen, selah, selah, selah.

This is the announcement that Rabbi Moshe Prager announced in all the synagogues in the holy community of Nikolsburg.

[124] The youth became sicker and became very feverish, like the fire of Gehenna. They despaired of him.

[MONDAY NIGHT (THURSDAY, 29 SHEVAT?) IN THE STUDY HOUSE: THE APPEARANCE OF THE *SPIRIT* TO THE YOUTH.]

[125] In brief, he came again to the youth on the third night, and Rabbi Moshe Preger was watching over the youth in the study house and was

studying. The youth began to shout, *"Hear O Israel"* [Deuteronomy, 6:4] and frightened all the people in the study house. Rabbi Moshe asked, "Abram, why are you shouting?"

> The youth responded: "The Spirit came to me and was carrying a large millstone on his back. He said: 'The conditions that have been promised to me have not been kept—I want to go into you, and I want to beat you with this millstone!" However, the Spirit was standing far from me. He was not allowed to come within four ells of me—because of the power of the Names that Rabbi Moshe had hung on him.

[126] He said to me: The first child that I will have—I should name him after him. He warned me that I should be God-fearing, should guard myself from transgressions, and should recite psalms instead.

[127] He tried to provoke me and said to me: "Your part and your share, I was within you for six years, and no hand, head, or foot hurt you. Now, since I am outside of you—your share is to be deathly ill. Put the Names aside and give me permission again for me to come into you—you will immediately become well again."

[128] He also said to me: He has been a *Spirit* for forty years, and he must be a *Spirit* for another thirty years. Afterwards, he will receive his judgment, with what kinds of punishments he will be punished. He also asked that all of the conditions should be observed. Otherwise, he was punished four times a day. Now he was only punished two times a day. When they keep the conditions that they gave him as gift—he will have rest, and he will have a place in the wilderness where there are also other *Spirits*, and the accusers and demons of destruction do not pursue him so strongly.

[129] The *Spirit* also came to Rabbi Hirsch, the judge, and said to him that he will no longer harm any Jewish person or come into them.

[THE SITUATION OF THE YOUTH WORSENED: FEVER AND CONSTIPATION.]

[130] The youth became very sick. They despaired of his recovery. He had a high fever and was very badly constipated. Because the *Spirit* had been in him for six years, he had not had any bowel movements for

the whole six years. The *Spirit* had consumed everything within him. This is how he had eaten enough for six people and had no bowel movement, because the *Spirit* had been in him. However, he did allow him to urinate, but when he collapsed the bladder, he could not urinate. Afterwards, when he left him, his innards became overgrown, and his bowels became very watery. The holy community of Nikolsburg provided great remedies for him and gave him a number of enemas, until his bowels moved naturally. They gave him several gold coins worth of almond oil to drink, and several other things that he needed, that no other community had provided. *There is no greater sanctification of God's name than this before Jews and gentiles.*

[THE CONCLUSION OF THE AFFAIR. BECOMING HEALTHY AND TORAH STUDY.]

[131] In brief, the youth, thank God, became fresh and healthy in his body and his limbs. He had—with God's help—acquired a different appearance. Previously, he had been very pale in his face. He did not have a drop of blood within him and walked stooped—corpselike, literally with his head between his feet. He could not see the sky. However, now—God's help—straight, with red cheeks, a dignified person, like a king, and sits day and night over his sacred texts. Rabbi Moshe studied with him personally, until he moved away. He was very pious and holy. He was beloved by those above him and pleasant to those below. He was esteemed—thank God—in the eyes of God and man.

[EPILOGUE: THE MORAL LESSON—REWARD AND PUNISHMENT.]

[132] Such a story and public miracle has not occurred in many hundreds of years. Hundreds of people saw this great story, and awakened to repentance, as if the Holy One had sent a number of prophets to the world. "*God has brought to pass that men revere Him*" [Ecclesiastes 3:14].

"*The sum of the matter, when all is said and done: revere God and observe His commandments. For this applies to all mankind*" [Ecclesiastes 12:13]—every person should implement this on their heart. The Holy One gives a *reward to all who do His will* and *punishes those who transgress His will*. We should be worthy of the redemption by the Messiah, speedily in our days, amen.

[CONCLUSION OF THE PRINTER.]

[133] Therefore, I had this book printed for the sake of heaven so that everyone who will read it—they will certainly take a lesson, and should not rely on anyone, as the *Spirit* always shouted, "Take a good lesson from me, punish your children with me!" Therefore, I want to benefit the community with this, [so I] brought it to print. I spent a large amount, and important rabbis agreed that I should bring to print this great miracle and sanctification of God's Name. Therefore, it is decreed with the great excommunication that was imposed on the *Spirit*, that nobody, no stranger, should reprint, for at least ten years, from the year 456 [1696], in the small counting, until the year 466 [1706]. In the meantime, we will be worthy of the redemption that will be fulfilled through, "*I will give My spirit into you*" [Ezekiel 37:14], *speedily in our days, amen.*

3. Koretz

Sara Zfatman, "Tale of an Exorcism in Koretz: A New Stage in the Development of a Folk-Literary Genre," *Jerusalem Studies in Jewish Folklore* 2 (1982): 35–65.

[1a][103] A TALE OF A SPIRIT IN THE HOLY COMMUNITY OF KORETZ DURING THE TUMULT OF WAR

The story happened in our days. The whole world knows to tell about it. Inform yourself about it since in all his days such wonders and miracles have not happened. Therefore, every person should buy this story. He will know to tell many novel things, what happened here, in our days. Through this we will be worthy to come to the Holy Land, and concerning this, let us say amen:

An incident happened in the holy community of Kotelnia to a pious man called Rabbi Elia. His daughter that he raised was beautiful and fine and clear in her deeds like the shining sun. The maiden's name was Mindel. It was not known that there was a *Spirit* within her. She was afflicted with a strange illness for close to three years. When it was within her for a full year, her pain increased from year to year. At times she broke her bones, and mother and father were left in tears at the great trouble.

[1b] They could not find a sage who might recognize the voice of the *Spirit*. Father and mother began to ask, what will come of this

trouble? They traveled with the young woman to sorceresses and doctors. Some said that she suffered from epilepsy, and some said that she was mentally ill. Nobody knew what the truth was, until the impure *Spirit* became stronger from day to day. Many people said that this was the greatest truth, that one should not comb her hair.

At the end of the three years, the impure *Spirit* began to display strange activities. Many times, it tugged at her heart so that the maiden fainted from great pain. There was not even a drop of blood in her face. At times, he made her stand upside down and began to laugh with great pleasure. See gentlemen, who can imitate me with such skill, that I make her stand upside down and her dress still clings to her? Whoever sees this great wonder, everyone should cry greatly. Sometimes the maiden lay with her mouth open when the *Spirit* ran into her head. It was very painful for the maiden [2a] because the *Spirit* shouted from her body with a great shout. Her lips did not move, but the voice of the *Spirit* was heard. Nonetheless, there was no sage or soothsayer who would go there and who could recognize the voice. The great deeds that the *Spirit* engaged in cannot be told.

It was close to the New Year. The people of Kotelnia wanted to send for Rabbi Isaac, the sexton of the holy community of Priluka. Rabbi Isaac, the sexton, was skilled in cursing the *Spirit* with excommunication and curses, in order to cast fear and confusion upon the *Spirit*. Rabbi Isaac assembled a quorum of ten worthy men, who were holy and pure, to excommunicate the *Spirit* and warn him with a great warning. Rabbi Isaac decreed a great decree against the *Spirit*, that he should tell him immediately who he was, in the maiden. He should immediately tell me and my assembled group. Are you a harmful spirit of the demons or a Soul that is impure? I order you that you should immediately tell me your name.

[2b] The *Spirit* began, with a bitter outcry and lament. Woe is me, who brought you to me that you should bring such troubles upon me? Why are you asking for my name? I will definitely never tell you, my name. Rabbi Isaac, the sexton, again decreed the great excommunication, that he should tell him his name before all the people. The *Spirit* began a great outcry: "Woe is me, how have I fallen into such a great trouble? Whom should I accuse, that they are even pursuing my troubles? I have taken possession of all the veins and organs. How should I leave and fall into the hands of harmful spirits again?"

He excommunicated and adjured him so long, until he had to tell him that his name was Jacob Jacobowitz, and he could not recover from this. Rabbi Isaac pushed him even further at that time, until the *Spirit* begged him. In truth, he excommunicated and adjured him in other ways. He could not recover from him. *In the meantime*, when it was revealed that he was the oppressing *Spirit*, her mother and father lamented greatly. *Woe to us*, how has such a calamity happened to us, among all of Israel?

[3a] They consulted with each other and took the maiden to the holy community of Pavlovich. In this way it began that the rabbi of the community began to expel with holy names and with his prayers. The rabbi cried about this that *the Spirit, may his name be obliterated*, out of spite against the adjurations, began to break the body of the maiden. At times he bent her spine back until it bent back to her knees. She called out, "Hear O Israel" [Deuteronomy 6:4], so that she was heard far away. Answer me God in my trouble, listen to my prayer. All the *troubles and torments* cannot be described, all that the maiden accused him. The *Spirit* did not stop his troubles, until he strengthened his hand, with full force, to attack the maiden in her head and mind.

When all the heads of the lands[104] saw the troubles of the maiden, they sent for Rabbi Abraham Baal Shem of the holy community of Przemyśl since he was skilled in such matters. Afterwards, our Lord God did not show His grace, and the maiden had greater torments. When Rabbi Abraham saw that he could not overcome him, he fumigated him [the *Spirit*] with sulfur and put bitter wormwood on the fire. [3b] Rabbi Abraham soon returned to his home since the *Spirit*, may his name be obliterated, had mocked him, as he desired.

When the people saw the troubles of the maiden, they turned to the holy community of Lubartov. There, the *ba'alei shem* did their work with purity, to expel the *Spirit* from the pure soul. This was in the year in the tumult of war in Small Poland.[105] The satanic *Spirit* continued to strengthen for the worse, as I will write about her evil luck. How many times were overturned *our works to nothing*? First, they started to fumigate, but he swallowed the smoke, and it disappeared into her thigh. Thus, he callously broke the bone of her foot. When the *impure Spirit* came down into her thigh, the head of the maiden turned around, and her face changed. Her voice was heard whimpering because of the evildoer. Her voice was heard with crying and lamenting. She raised both hands to God, blessed be He, with great lamenting. [4a] *Woe is me* I have been turned into a drunkard, but not from wine, rather from my troubles and pain.

Therefore, dear gentlemen I will reveal for you her prayer, which came out of the mouth of the maiden. Even though it is not the same, *hearing to seeing*, nonetheless it is just to write the words of the maiden's prayer.

Before the King God, high and uplifted. She began to shout with her outcry. *God Almighty*, Almighty God, how long will my troubles continue in this way. *God, Lord of Israel*, it is revealed and known before You, before I went out into the air of the world, the evildoer, the evildoer had transgressed the whole Torah that was given in the whole world. Since this evildoer has transgressed the whole Torah, why should I suffer for his sake, the great troubles? What are my great sins, that such great troubles have found me? If You want to remember the sins of the parents on the children?[106] Why should I suffer travails for five long years? Your way is to defer Your wrath. Why should I be desolate and hidden before You? Even though You respond to the greatest sins *the most severe heavenly judgment*, [4b] nonetheless, he does not suffer more than twelve months.[107] You have commanded, "*His mercy is on all of His creatures*" [Psalm 145:9]. Why have You averted Your compassion from me? Am I then among the greatest *sinners of Israel* that You have allowed me to drink the bitter goblet of wine?

After the prayer, she opened her mouth with wisdom. She adjured the *Spirit* with excommunication and with curses, with holy names that she had heard from the adjurers. She adjured the *Spirit* by herself with all her strength. She adjured him with the Name of forty-two holy and pure letters[108] and with the angels who serve before God, blessed be He, who are called Adiel and Naor.[109] Also with the name of seven letters that was on the metal plate of Aaron the priest. Also with the text written in the Torah scroll of Rabbi Hanina ben Teradion with twenty-two letters.[110] She also adjured him with the great name that came out of the mouth of the high priest on Yom Kippur.

Now I will reveal before the whole community how the maiden organized her prayer, with the merit of the binding of Isaac. She began to pray:

"God, God, Merciful and Compassionate Lord [Exodus 34:6]. How long will You continue to cover my prayer in clouds?[111] [5a] Remember that You tested Abraham our Patriarch, and because of this test, Sarah, our mother, died.[112] Lord of the Universe, it is revealed and known before You that You said to Abraham our Patriarch: Take your only son to Me.[113] You told him to take him so that he should increase into a multitude of people. On the contrary, if he would slaughter his son, then the blessing would not have been fulfilled. But certainly, You were not after Isaac his son, and Your intention was not Isaac his son, but the lamb that was substituted for him. Your primary intention was the offering so that his merit should be for every community, that Your highly praised name should be sanctified among the nations. That it should be known that You are stronger than all the gods.[114] Now, Lord of the Universe, You have tested me with this evil Spirit so that every sinful person will see my troubles and will have the courage to repent in his thoughts.

Therefore, now, Lord of the Universe, it is just to have compassion on me, and send me my redeemer. It has been five years that I have been bound before You with this evil thorn. You, highly praised God, hear my prayer. [5b] In the past, the people of Sodom committed great sins. Nonetheless, You said, when ten righteous people will be found there, I will forgive their sins.[115] Lord of the Universe, will you not find here ten people in the whole community who will pray and fast for my sake, the afflicted maid, *bereaved and lonely*? You are called the Guardian of Israel. I will take an *inference from minor to major* from the Egyptians. See Lord of the Universe, the Egyptians rebelled against You. Nonetheless, You did not order the recitation of Hallel on *the last days of Passover* because creations of Your hands were drowned in the sea on that day. And I, Lord of the Universe, am a maiden of Israel. And I am a creation of Your hands. And should I be worse than the Egyptians in Your thoughts."

And the evil *Spirit* heard all the words of the maiden and ran into her head immediately. And she began to scream: "Am I obligated to suffer from all the words of the accursed impure one? I will cause her great suffering, and [he] began to pluck out her hair and wanted to completely break her body."

When we the holy group saw the great pain of the maiden, [6a] we cursed the evil *Spirit* that he should be cursed by the special God. They began to fumigate her with bitter wormwood. He descended into her thigh with great fear of the wormwood. In the middle of this, they brought Rabbi Jacob, the rabbi of the community of Mirapol. When the spirit saw him, a great sickness befell him. Before he entered the room, he arranged the Name of Fear in the proper order. When Rabbi Jacob began to adjure the *Spirit*, he immediately descended into the thigh, because of his great pain. When the *Spirit* descended, the maiden began to praise our Lord God again. She sang the whole "Great, Threatening, Awesome,"[116] because of her great anguish, When the song ended, she began to pray and began to say:

Lord of the Universe, why are all the gates locked and the gates of tears are open?[117] All of Israel are crying when they see my anguish, and they hope for Your compassion. Now, Lord of the Universe, do it for the sake of Your honor, so that Your holy name should be sanctified. [6b] Almighty God, if this is a decree before You, let me know my end. Thus, I will accept the punishment from You with love. Why should they mention the holy names for nothing when You will not build this building?

A disaster almost came upon the *Spirit*. A fire broke out in the holy community of Lubartov, and my group ran out [of the town]. They thought that the fire might descend upon us. The foolish *Spirit* jumped into her head and ran to the fire to see everything. Thus, because of our many sins, our work was for naught. The *Spirit* rejoiced at this because the luck of the maiden was bad. It is impossible to describe what a great joy this was for the evil *Spirit*.

On Wednesday, there was a libel in the community. The non-Jews were going to the governor accusing the maiden, saying that the spirit with the maiden set fire to the city. The governor issued a decree. If they will find the maiden, she should be burned quickly. [7a] His decree was also against those who had adjured her. Thus, the community had to think how they would get the maiden and the adjurers out of the city before they came from the nobleman to search for the maiden. The community sent the maiden away to the holy community of Koretz since there was an *upright and just man* who was wise and wealthy and who followed *the just path*.

My dear brothers, I will inform you about the great story about our Lord God, that God, blessed be He, blessed this man that even the spirit did not disobey his commands. This man was called our master and rabbi, Rabbi Baruch Kot. God, blessed be He, gave him honor and greatness, like he had earned from God. Now I will inform the whole world how the *Spirit confessed* before Rabbi Baruch and confessed everything before him.

On the first day of Passover, Rabbi Baruch began to overpower the *Spirit*. The first time Rabbi Baruch came was on Sunday. In God's name, *He does not slumber and does not sleep*.[118] When Rabbi Baruch came into the room, [7b] the people said, "Welcome Rabbi Baruch, as is customary among many people." When the *Spirit* heard that the name of Rabbi Baruch was mentioned, he *immediately* ran into the head of the maiden.

He began to speak: "Is this the Rabbi Baruch whose fame goes from one end of the world to the other end, as I have heard it said? I see this now with my own eyes, that I have been worthy to have an important person before me. Now I ask of you, sit at my right hand and accept a blessing from me, since it is appropriate to honor a man like you. Therefore, I am also honoring you."

Rabbi Baruch responded to the *Spirit*: "The highly beloved God who is honored and sanctified, who is the ruler over us, to Him is the honor and glory. We are all *mortal*. We are here today, and tomorrow we are in the grave. However, because of our sins, woeful things come upon us. Therefore, I ask you, give me this gift. I must now go to the synagogue to pray. Until I come back to you, allow the maiden to rest."

[8a] The *Spirit* responded to Rabbi Baruch: "Sir, I am willing to do for you whatever you ask me. Perhaps you will give charity on my behalf, and this will help me. From now on and further I will not do anything against you."

Rabbi Baruch went to pray, and the *Spirit* did not do anything to the maiden in the meantime. When Rabbi Baruch finished his prayers, he came back to the maiden. No scribe can write down the whole conversation that Rabbi Baruch had with the *Spirit*. Rather, it is just to write that the power of Rabbi Baruch was able to expel the *Spirit* from the maiden.

Rabbi Baruch said to the *Spirit*: I ask you not to weaken the strength of the maiden. Today is a holiday for us, and we are obligated to eat our bread that has been prepared for us with joy.:

The *Spirit* responded, "At present I see that your good words will bring me much suffering."

Rabbi Baruch said to the *Spirit*: "Do it for my sake and let the maiden rest. I will also come to you after my meal, [8b] and everything that your soul will desire from me, I will do for your sake."

The *Spirit* responded to Rabbi Baruch: "Sir, go eat your bread with joy and drink your wine with a good-hearted mood. I will wait here, as you wish."

Rabbi Baruch went home in peace, and the *Spirit* sat quietly until Rabbi Baruch came back to him. When Rabbi Baruch finished eating and drinking, he went back to the maiden since he gladly wanted to chase out the *Spirit*.

When the *Spirit* saw Rabbi Baruch, he began to speak: "Since I have been in the darkness *a long time* for your sake, therefore, in addition, my good sir, Rabbi Baruch, if you want that I should go out of the maiden, *on this condition*, when you will give charity, fast, and you will recite Kaddish yourself. At that time, I will leave her."

Rabbi Baruch said to the *Spirit*: Do good and trust in God, and [know] that I will certainly not act against his commandments. I will give charity on your behalf. I will rescue your *Spirit* from all the *trouble and distress* since charity rescues from death.[119] Therefore, also do good and save yourself from your need." [9a] Rabbi Baruch began again to ask the *Spirit*, slowly and without force: "My [ ][120] tell me the truth. Is Jacob your real name?"

The *Spirit* responded to Rabbi Baruch: "My dear sir, your many words will bring me to much suffering. Why are you asking about my name? Nonetheless, let me inform you that the truth is that Jacob is my real name."

Rabbi Jacob continued to ask the *Spirit*: "I ask you, who extracted your soul from you, and what was done to you after your death? Tell me."

The Spirit responded:

> My dear Rabbi Baruch, I will tell you the wondrous secret of what you are asking me. I will pass over my death. The angels of destruction came for me. They tore my soul out of me with their horns, with great cruelty and lack of compassion. Before they hurried me to my grave, the demons plucked at each of my organs separately. When I was buried, the demons carried me away and brought me before the lord of destruction, malice, and jealousy. [9b] He issued a severe decree against me, according to my evil deeds. At first, I thought that they would take me to Gehenna. My heart began to rejoice within me. After a while, they even threw me out of Gehenna, and my joy turned to sorrow. Then I was given into the hands

of a male demon. His face was very strange; half was like a dog, and half like a cow. The demon was called Golahav.[121] His form and his face were twisted into a strange shape. He swallowed my soul and began to bite my body. After the swallowing, he spit me out a long distance. Directly, an angel who destroys with strength and might came and quickly swallowed me. Then he also spit me out a great distance. Then a devil came and also swallowed me. The face of that devil was very strange and caused me much pain. The devil had a face like a reptile that is called a turtle in Hebrew. In Yiddish it is called a turtle and in Russian it is called a turtle. [10a] This demon bit and plucked me more than all the other demons. He made holes and cracks in my flesh. Afterwards, he swallowed me, and it was very painful. He also spit me out for a great distance. Then another devil came, and his face was half human and half dog. He also bit my body and soul. I cried and grumbled greatly. Then he also swallowed me, and they all caused me great pain, like bears and lions. Then he also spit me out. All kinds of demons came and plucked at my body and soul. They seated me as if I were still alive and they choked me in various ways. Afterwards, they punished me in a variety of ways. They carried me and left me standing in a stream. They took me out of there with fear and panic. They ground my body and soul between mill stones, and they dragged me out with troubles and obstacles, and made my body and soul whole again. They punished me severely again, as I had deserved. [10b] They cast me again from one end of the world to the other end of the world,[122] for the sins that I did in secret. I escaped and came into the body of a pig. There, too, my pain increased since the demons wounded the pig with fire and lightning. The pig died in this way. Thus, I was not removed from my troubles. I continued to suffer the pains for nine years. Then I escaped into a cow that is ritually clean [kosher]. I thought to myself that I will have an expiation there. I thought that the cow would be slaughtered by a Jew, and I will be redeemed by the blessing of the ritual slaughterer [shochet]. First my evil luck caused that the cow was killed by a non-Jew. That is how I got out of the cow. At first fear and fright came upon me, and

I wound up in a cellar. The adulteress, the married woman whom I had relations with during my lifetime, also became a Spirit like me.[123] [11a] From her great pain, she also came to hide in this cellar. In a while, two maidens came who were sisters. I entered one maiden alone, and the adulteress was a woman who had a weak mind and long hair. She immediately killed her. I hid in the body of the maiden until I was able to strengthen each of my limbs. Now my dear Rabbi Baruch, as you have heard from me, to suffer such pain is not better for me that I should be in the dark. Before I should leave the maiden, I should tell you about my sins. I transgressed everything that one can find in the Torah. However, because of the one merit that I once saved a Jew from robbers, the one appointed over me ordered me to enter a pure body.

Rabbi Baruch responded to the *Spirit*: You should trust in Almighty God. I will help you to the extent of my abilities. I will redeem you with prayer and charity. Now, go down to the thigh, slowly and without difficulty."

[11b] He descended slowly and not forcefully. Afterwards, when we, the holy group, saw that he did not return to all the fear of the *Spirit*, we began the following sequence. First, we took a large barrel, and we made a floor in the middle of the barrel. Then we made holes in the floor. We had the maiden sit above this floor. We placed incense on the floor, that is, white resin, sulfur, bitter wormwood, and put a fire on it. The *Spirit* went away from the incense through the holes until we weakened him. Sunday, when we wanted to place the maiden on it, the *Spirit* ascended combatively and began to speak, "What kind of barrel do I see before me?"

We responded to him, "We will place the maiden in it along with you, and we will expel you from her.:

The *Spirit* said: "Of those I see, who will put me in there? Out of spite, I will not go into the thigh, and I will break the barrel into pieces."

Rabbi Baruch said to the *Spirit*, [12a] "Don't you know that you have to enter the barrel without force."

The *Spirit* began with a shout: "Now I know well that from you the troubles come upon me. A parable about what you are doing to me. It is just like one person holds another by the hand, and the other one hits him. You are doing the same to me. You tell me to get into the barrel, and they will excommunicate and curse me. I will definitely not go into it. I will break the body and bones of the maiden."

Rabbi Baruch said to the *Spirit*, "I will decree against you with force that you should go into the barrel by yourself, even though you only see the troubles through your eyes alone." Finally, Rabbi Baruch compelled him with his power so that the *Spirit* had to go in by himself. When we began to fumigate with the smoke of the incense, the *Spirit* ran into the head because of great troubles. We immediately fumigated with sulfur under the nose. He saw that he had no rest, so he descended to his original place. The *Spirit* began to torment the maiden with all his power. [12b] He caused the maiden to faint as if she was dead. She was in the state of fainting for more than five hours without stop. When the *Spirit* saw that we did not attend to the fainting, he ran into her head without compassion and began to shout: "You are called *compassionate people* [*bnei rahmanim*] for no good reason. You are nothing but *perverse evildoers and cruel people*. You see that the maiden is quite dead, and none of you has compassion for the maiden in her need."

We responded to the *Spirit* in unison: "Be silent, we will bring more *awe and fear* upon you. When the *Spirit* heard their words, he immediately descended because he was suffering."

The maiden began to speak out of great anguish: "Dear gentlemen, why do you avert your eyes from me in my suffering? How long will you punish me in Gehenna? You are burning me with fire and sulfur."

Thus, they took the maiden out of the barrel and laid her on a bed. They immediately excommunicated and adjured him, *according to the proper procedure*. [13a] The maiden began to scream greatly, "The *Spirit* has left me, and he is on the bed."

Rabbi Baruch said to the maiden, "Dear daughter, tell me, what kind of face does he have?"

She responded: "Like an insect that is called a cricket. He jumped on my hand and my head." We then began to excommunicate and adjure him and to blow *shofars*. *In the middle of this*, the maiden began to lament, "*Woe is me*; he has returned and is hiding within me."

At that time, our joy turned into mourning. We had a discussion. With what should we expel the spirit? First, between Ashrei and u-Vo le-Zion,[124] we excommunicated him in the synagogue, with seven Torah scrolls, blew seven shofars, and extinguished the candles each time. The spirit heard how the small children shouted amen. After the excommunication and after the *shofar* blowing, a great trembling fell upon him.

From the synagogue, we went to the maiden, to see if the *Spirit* turned to the excommunication or to the curse.

[13b] The maiden began to say, "From the day that you began to excommunicate him with excommunication and curse, such a fear and confusion has not come upon him, and I don't know *what the reason is*." She did not know that the whole community had gone against him *defiantly*. We, the holy group, sent the sexton to the spirit with a warning, to tell him that they had excommunicated him. We will hear what the *Spirit* will respond to the warning.

The sexton came to the *Spirit*:

> Listen Spirit, the ba'alei shem inform you that you have been excommunicated in the synagogue with the blowing of shofars and the extinguishing of candles. Therefore, will you respond to the excommunication and will go out of the maiden. They will abrogate all the excommunications and curses. If you do not want to leave the maiden, they will quickly send to the great court that they should also excommunicate you there. They will also send it to all regions, areas, villages, and communities that you should be excommunicated everywhere. Between Ashrei and u-Vo le-Zion, blowing the shofars, and extinguishing the candles, the small children should shout amen about this. [14a] You will be not come to rest from your troubles all your days. Therefore, I will give you some advice. Follow the holy group and go out of the maiden and sanctify the honored and awesome Name [of God]. At that time, God, blessed be He, will have mercy on you and will act charitably with you. Rabbi Baruch will also keep what he promised you, that you will come to your rest.

The *Spirit* began to shout with a bitter cry: "*Woe is me*, why are you bringing such troubles upon me? I would gladly go out of her, but there is someone appointed over me, who stops me and does not let me leave."

The father of the maiden began to speak: "Tell me the name of the one who is appointed over you. We will also excommunicate him with an excommunication and curse."

The *Spirit* began to say: "His name is Duha. We searched and researched among the names until we learned that he is called Nietuha."[125]
[14b] When the name of the one appointed over him was made known

to us, we praised God, blessed be He, that he has given us *intelligence and understanding* to expel the *Spirit* along with the one appointed over him.

Immediately after the warning, we went into the field together with the whole holy group, to adjure the one appointed over him, and to completely expel the *Spirit*. When we came to the maiden in the field, she began to say, "From the time that you are in the field, the *Spirit* has been sitting in great fear." When we heard the words of the maiden, we began to excommunicate the *Spirit*, groups in the synagogue and groups in the house of the maiden. Our group adjured the one appointed over him, and that time we weakened the power of the *Spirit*, and he could not be saved from it. On Thursday evening, we excommunicated and adjured the *Spirit* until the middle of the night. The *Spirit* thought of many deceitful things, as to how he could be rid of us that night. He ran into the head of the maiden, in order to abrogate our actions.

He began to speak to us with humility: "Dear gentlemen, I ask you, let me rest this night, and do not adjure me anymore. [15a] I will immediately leave the maiden as soon as the roosters will crow."

We, the holy group, responded and said to the *Spirit*, "You must leave the maiden without power *immediately*."

He shouted: "I ask you, I will go out at daybreak when the roosters crow, as I said. If I change what I said, then you should bring my suffering upon me."

We, the holy group, had a discussion. Perhaps, in truth, he is in fear and dread, and he must leave the maiden. We cannot continue because of our fasting. We will go home, and the spirit will rejoice in our leaving.

The next morning, on Friday, our holy group prayed to God, blessed be He, and after the prayers, we went to the maiden, to see if the *Spirit* had fulfilled his oath and had left the maiden. We went into the room, and the spirit began to speak in the following way, "*Welcome gentlemen.*"

Rabbi Jacob responded, "You *Spirit*, how long will you continue to hold on to your double impurity, and not fulfill your words?"

The *Spirit* said: [15b] "My sir, Rabbi Baruch, listen to my words. If I am unexpected then my suffering should come upon me. Yesterday after your departure, they tormented me for most of the night. Thus, I saw that they do not leave me alone. Then I thought something else, and I said to them: When the roosters crow, I will leave the maiden. So, my dear Rabbi Baruch, what is my fault? If the rooster had crowed, I would have certainly left her, as I said I would do. However, neither the rooster nor the hens crowed. Therefore, I won't go out of her anymore."

Rabbi Baruch said, "I decree a decree upon you that you should quickly descend."

Friday night after synagogue services, the *Spirit* began to talk to the father of the maiden: "Call Rabbi Baruch soon, I have many things to speak with him, that he should be my benefactor following his words since I am forced to leave the maiden. I have no rest before the one who is appointed over me. Therefore, I am going and will not tarry."

The father ran to Rabbi Baruch immediately.

The spirit spoke immediately:

> My sir, Rabbi Baruch, I will leave her this night, and I will no longer meet with you. [16a] Therefore, I had you called to me, that you should be my benefactor. Remember what you said: "I will help you to the extent of my reach. I will redeem you with prayer, charity, and fasting." Now my sir, Rabbi Baruch, I ask your learned excellency that you should fulfill your words, that you should be a friend to me. You should save my spirit from all troubles and torments. I will leave the maiden, a beloved soul, slowly and not forcefully.

Rabbi Baruch responded to the *Spirit*, "If only it will be as your words, and I will certainly do as you desire."

The Spirit said to R. Baruch: "Confirm the agreement that I can rely on it. Then I will leave, and the charity that you promised should be for the maiden."

Rabbi Baruch confirmed the agreement. The Spirit bowed to R. Baruch and went into the foot. Rabbi Baruch went to his house in peace. The spirit remained quiet. When everyone in the house was asleep, the *Spirit* left the maiden. The maiden did not know and did not hear how he left through her foot and where he exited from her.

[16b] The next morning, there was an uproar that the *Spirit* had left the maiden. There was great rejoicing in the community. All the adjurers, along with R. Baruch, came and brought a Torah scroll to the maiden. They also hung holy names around the neck of the maiden. I, the writer, remained sitting with her alone so that the *Spirit* should not return and enter her again. Rabbi Baruch fulfilled what he had promised him, with fasting and the recitation of Kaddish. The maiden had great joy, and the maiden remained alive through him. She found a husband.

Therefore, dear gentlemen, you have heard how God did for the maiden and through Rabbi Baruch remained alive. Therefore, we should also benefit from his merit, and we should be worthy to fulfill such commandments and charity and come to the Holy Land in the days of the Messiah. On this, we will say amen.

Appendix to Chapter 5

Shivhei ha-Besht

INTRODUCTION

Shivhei ha-Besht, the hagiographic collection of stories about the Besht, was first published in 1814 in Hebrew. This text has been the standard starting point for discussions about the biography and activities of the Besht. Less well known is that a year later a different version of *Shivhei ha-Besht* was published in Yiddish. In their recent research, Prof. Jonatan Meir and his colleagues have been charting a new path in the study of *Shivhei ha-Besht*, and one of their innovations has been to incorporate the Yiddish materials. In this spirit, I have decided to present the Yiddish versions of the two *dybbuk* stories in *Shivhei ha-Besht*. The text of the Hebrew version is readily available in several Hebrew editions and an English translation. The Yiddish text is found in two early recensions, Ostrog, 1815 and Koretz, 1815. The Ostrog edition was considered lost but was recently discovered. The Yiddish text of the Koretz edition of *Shivhei ha-Besht* has been published by Karl E. Grözinger, *Die Geschichten vom Ba'al Schem Tov Schivche ha-Bescht*. 2 vols. The relevant passages will be translated from this edition of the Yiddish *Shivhei ha-Besht*.

1. THE *DYBBUK* AND THE WOMAN[126]

[sect. 30] This chapter tells how the Besht began to be famous.
Chapter 13.
There was once a crazy woman in the city who was possessed by a spirit. She used to tell everyone who came to her their good and bad

traits. When the *ba'al shem* came to the city, Rabbi Gershon asked the rabbi of Kutov that he should take his brother-in-law to the woman. Perhaps he might get some *musar* [ethical teachings or rebuke] from her. Even though the rabbi of Kutov already knew the *ba'al shem*, as mentioned above, he had to satisfy R. Gershon and went with the *ba'al shem*, and everyone accompanied them.

The rabbi of Kutov entered first, and the woman said, "Welcome holy and pure one." Also, to everyone who entered, she told each one their attributes. R. Israel Ba'al Shem Tov entered last. He was a young man. She said to him: "Welcome R. Israel. Perhaps you think that I fear you? No, I am not afraid of you. I know that you have been sworn from above in heaven, that you should not engage with holy names until you will be thirty-six years old."

The people asked her, "What are you saying?" She said it again, but the crowd did not understand what she was saying. She repeated it several times, until the Besht shouted at her, "If you will not be silent, I will seat a court, and they will permit me,[127] and I will expel you from the woman." When his friends heard this, they began to ask him that he should allow them to permit him, but he did not want to do it. He said that it was dangerous for him if he would ask them to permit him. He pleaded with them that they should not permit him.

The Besht said to her: "Do you see what you caused with your words? Therefore, I ask you that you should go out of the woman yourself, and we will study on your behalf." The *Spirit* promised to leave with good will. The Besht asked the spirit, "Tell me, who are you?"

He responded: "At the present I cannot tell you because it would be a disgrace for my children who are in this city. There is plenty of time; I will tell you when they leave." It was so, when they left, he told him who he was. He obeyed the Besht and quietly left, with good will, from the woman. After this, the Besht became somewhat important, but they did not know what this was and what it meant, but everyone considered him a simple person and an ignoramus.

2. THE *DYBBUK* AND THE MADMAN[128]

[sect. 35] Afterwards, the *ba'al shem* established his household in the city of Tlust. He was also a teacher of small children in Tlust. He used to gather a *minyan* in his courtyard. He did not own more than a camel overcoat, and his shoes were open so that his toes stuck out. He was very poor and used to go to the *mikvah*, even in winter, in the month of Tevet. Nevertheless, during his prayers, drops of sweat the size of beans poured down from him.

[sect. 36] They used to bring sick people to him, but he would not receive them. Once they brought him a madman and a mad woman, and he did not want to receive them. That night, he was notified that his thirty-sixth year had ended, before which he had been prevented from doing *peulot*.[129] In the morning, he realized that this was true, and he received the mad people and did a complete *peulah* and healed them. From then on, he threw away the teaching, hired a scribe who would write amulets. He traveled around with him in all the regions and acquired a reputation as a *ba'al shem* and did *peulot*.

Notes

Introduction

1. The most comprehensive biography of Anski is Gabriella Safran, *Wandering Soul: The Dybbuk's Creator, S. An-sky* (Cambridge: Belknap Press of Harvard University Press, 2010).

2. Concerning Anski's ethnographic expedition, see Nathaniel Deutsch, *The Jewish Dark Continent: Life and Death in the Russian Pale of Settlement* (Cambridge: Harvard University Press, 2011).

3. Gabriella Safran and Steven Zipperstein, eds. *The Worlds of S. An-sky: A Russian Jewish Intellectual at the Turn of the Century* (Stanford: Stanford University Press, 2006). This work contains a collection of studies about the play and its literary and cultural influence. See also Michael C. Steinlauf, "Dybbuk, The." *YIVO Encyclopedia of Jews in Eastern Europe.* 2 vols. (New Haven: Yale University Press, 2008), 1:434–36.

4. *Jewish Mystical Autobiographies: Book of Visions and Book of Secrets* (Classics of Western Spirituality, 94). (New York: Paulist 1999). The *Book of Visions* is divided into four parts, and each section is numbered. References to specific pages will be by part and section number, with page numbers in this edition in parentheses. The part and section numbers are the same in the Hebrew edition.

5. *Sefer Ha-Hezyonot: Yomano ha-Mysti shel Rabbi Hayyim Vital* (Jerusalem: Machon Ben Zvi, 2005).

6. Articles include "Maggidim, Spirits and Women in Rabbi Hayyim Vital's Book of Visions," *Spirit Possession in Judaism: Cases and Contexts from the Middle Ages to the Present*, ed. M. Goldish (Detroit: Wayne State University Press, 2003), 186–96; "The *Dibbuk* in the *Mayse Bukh*," *Shofar* 30, 1 (2011): 94–103; "The Possession of Rabbi Hayyim Vital by Jesus of Nazareth," *Kabbalah: Journal for the Study of Jewish Mystical Texts* 37 (2017): 29–36; "The *Dybbuk*: The Origins and History of a Concept," in *olam ha-zeh v'olam ha-ba: This world and the World to Come in Jewish Belief and Practice* (Studies in Jewish Civilization 28), ed. L. J. Greenspoon (West Lafayette: Purdue University Press, 2017), 135–50.

7. Safran and Zipperstein, *The Worlds of S. An-sky*, is a good starting point for the reception history and continuing influence of the play.

8. Gedaliah Nigal, *Dybbuk Stories in Jewish Literature* (Hebrew) (Jerusalem: Reuben Mass, 1983 [second revised edition, 1994]).

9. J. H. Chajes "*Between Worlds: Dybbuks, Exorcists and Early Modern Judaism* (Philadelphia: University of Pennsylvania Press, 2003). He has also published several related articles, but they do not add anything to his basic arguments.

10. Sara Zfatman, *Leave Impure One: Jewish Exorcism in Early Modern Ashkenaz* (Hebrew) (Jerusalem: Magnes Press, 2015).

11. Examples of Bilu's work include "The Moroccan Demon in Israel: The Case of Evil Spirit Disease," *Ethos* (1980): 24–39; "*Dybbuk* and *Maggid*: Two Cultural Patterns of Altered Consciousness in Judaism," *AJS Review* 21, 2 (1996): 341–66; "The *Dybbuk* in Judaism: Mental Disorder as Cultural Resource" (Hebrew), *Jerusalem Studies in Jewish Thought*, 2, 4 (1982): 529–63. Eli Yassif,'s work includes *The Legend of Safed: Life and Fantasy in the City of Kabbalah* (Detroit: Wayne State University Press, 2019).

12. Moses Gaster, *Ma'aseh Book*. 2 vols. (Philadelphia: Jewish Publication Society, 1934, Story no. 152), 1:301–3.

13. Gershom Scholem, "Dibbuk-Dybbuk," *Encyclopedia Judaica* (Detroit: Macmillan Reference USA, 2007), 5:643–44.

14. Zfatman, *Leave Impure One*, xiv, n. 7.

Chapter 1

1. The term "spirit" (*ruah* in Hebrew) can have three different meanings in this book. When it means a demon or other supernatural evil force, it is written as "spirit." When it refers to the part of the soul, it is written as "Spirit." When it refers to what today we call a *dybbuk*, it is written as "*Spirit*."

2. See the sources cited in Nigal, *Dybbuk Stories*, 265–66. Other Rabbinic sources are Bernard Mandelbaum, ed. *Pesikta de Rav Kahana* (New York: Jewish Theological Seminary, 1962), 1: 74; *Midrash Tanhuma*, *Hukat*, 8; *Midrash Numbers Rabbah*, 19.8.

3. The classic work on this subject is Joshua Trachtenberg, *Jewish Magic and Superstition: A Study in Jewish Folk Religion* (New York: Behrman House, 1939). More recent studies are Gideon Bohak, *Ancient Jewish Magic: A History* (Cambridge: Cambridge University Press, 2008); Yuval Harari, *Jewish Magic before the Rise of Kabbalah* (Detroit: Wayne State University Press 2017).

4. References to demons and their exorcism in the New Testament include the following: Mark 1:34, 1:39, 5:8, 7:26, 16:9; Matthew 4:10, 8:16, 8:31–32, 9:34, 12:24, 12:26–27; Luke 4:35, 4:41, 8:29, 11:14, 11:18–20, 13:32.

5. Flavius Josephus, *Antiquities of the Jews*, 8.45–47.

6. Michael Zellmann-Rohrer, "Hippocratic Diagnosis, Solomonic Therapy, Roman Amulets: Epilepsy, Exorcism, and the Diffusion of a Jewish Tradition in the Roman World," *Journal for the Study of Judaism* 53 (2022): 71–72. The quotation is from Lucian, *Philops.* §16.

7. This incident is discussed at great length below.

8. Two surveys of the history of possession and exorcism in Jewish history are Gedaliah Nigal, *Magic, Mysticism, and Hasidism: The Supernatural in Jewish Thought* (Northvale, New Jersey: Jason Aronson, 1994), 67–133; Yuval Harari, "Practical Kabbalah" and the Jewish Tradition of Magic," *Aries—Journal for the Study of Western Esotericism* 19 (2019): 38–82. Hariri's article contains an excellent bibliography of the major works relating to this subject.

9. The relation of Luria to the question of exorcism and the proper methodology to be used will be discussed below, in the chapter on Safed *dybbuk* exorcisms.

10. This question is discussed in detail in Nancy Caciola, *Discerning Spirits: Divine and Demonic Possession in the Middle Ages* (Ithaca: Cornell University Press, 2003). Chapter five explores the history of exorcism and the origins and description of the ritual.

11. Moshe Hallamish, *An Introduction to the Kabbalah* (Albany: State University of New York Press, 1999), 282.

12. Brian P. Levack, *The Witch-Hunt in Early Modern Europe* (London: Longman, 1987), 167–68.

13. Some recent overviews of this issue are Nancy Caciola, "Spirits Seeking Bodies: Death, Possession, and Communal Memory in the Middle Ages," in *The Place of the Dead: Death and Remembrance in Late Medieval and Early Modern Europe*, ed. Bruce Gordon and Peter Marshall (Cambridge: Cambridge University Press, 2000), 66–86; Caciola, *Discerning Spirits: Divine and Demonic Possession in the Middle Ages*; Moshe Sluhovsky, *Believe Not Every Spirit: Possession, Mysticism, & Discernment in Early Modern Catholicism* (Chicago: University of Chicago Press, 2007); Brian P. Levack, *The Witch-Hunt*.

14. Roni Weinstein, "Kabbalah and Jewish Exorcism in Seventeenth-Century Italian Jewish Communities: The Case of Rabbi Moses Zacuto," in *Spirit Possession in Judaism: Cases and Contexts from the Middle Ages to the Present*, ed. Matt Goldish Detroit: Wayne State University Press, 2003, 237–44.

15. See Paul E. Walker, "The Doctrine of Metempsychosis in Islam," in *Islamic Studies Presented to Charles Adams*, ed. W. B. Hallaq and Donald E. Little (Leiden: Brill, 1991), 219–38.

16. The last chapter of tractate *Sanhedrin* begins with the statement that all of Israel have a share in the World to Come. The Talmud continues with a discussion certain specific people whose sins were so heinous that their punishment is eternal. Other than those discussed in the Talmud, all Jews had a possibility of atonement of sins and redemption. It is noteworthy that a rabbinic

controversy erupted in seventeenth-century Amsterdam about the question of the eternality of punishment. See Alexander Altmann, "Eternality of Punishment: A Theological Controversy within the Amsterdam Rabbinate in the Thirties of the Seventeenth Century," *Proceedings of the American Academy for Jewish Research* 40 (1972): 1–88. One cause of this controversy was the influence of Catholic teachings on some of the formerly Christian participants.

17. Hayyim Vital, *Sefer ha-Gilgulim*, Vilna, 1886, chapter 13. Cited in Moshe Hallamish, *An Introduction to the Kabbalah* (Albany: State University of New York Press, 1999), 283.

18. *Zohar*, II: 96a–98b; Hayyim Vital, *Etz Hayyim*, Jerusalem, 1962, gate 5, chapter, 2.

19. Shyovitz, David I. "You Have Saved Me from the Judgment of Gehenna": The Origins of the Mourner's Kaddish in Medieval Ashkenaz," *AJS Review* 39, 1 (2015): 55–58. He quotes several medieval versions of this story and notes 28–30 cite the previous scholarship regarding this story and lists its various versions.

20. Yehudit Weiss, "Two Zoharic Versions of the Story of 'The Tanna and the Dead Man' (Hebrew)," *Tarbiz* 78, 4 (2009): 521–54.

21. *Kallah Rabbati*, 2.9. Quoted from A. Cohen. *The Minor Tractates of the Talmud*, 2 vols. (London: Soncino, 1965), 2: 434–35.

22. Simhah of Vitry, *Mahzor Vitry*, ed. Aryeh Goldschmidt, 2 vols. Jerusalem: Ozar ha-Poskim, 2004, 1: 223 (this latter text is a later German addition to the originally French compilation). The translation of the passage is quoted from Shyovitz, "You Have Saved Me from the Judgment of Gehenna," 56–58.

23. Two basic studies of the concept of *gilgul* are Gershom Scholem, "Gilgul: The Transmigration of Souls," in Gershom Scholem, *On the Mystical Shape of the Godhead: Basic Concepts in the Kabbalah* (New York: Schocken Books, 1991), 197–250; Hallamish, *Introduction to the Kabbalah*, 281–309.

24. Scholem, "Gilgul," 197–99.

25. Scholem, "Gilgul," 207–8.

26. Scholem, "Gilgul," 209–10.

27. Benjamin was not there and therefore not liable. Concerning the origins of this story, see Ra'anan S. Boustan, "The Contested Reception of *The Story of the Ten Martyrs* in Medieval Midrash." In *Envisioning Judaism: Studies in Honor of Peter Schafer on the Occasion of his Seventieth Birthday*. 2 vols, ed. Ra'anan Boustan, et al. (Tübingen: Mohr Siebeck, 2013), 1: 383–90.

28. Faierstein, *Jewish Mystical Autobiographies*, 4. 1–8 (156–63).

29. Concerning the Jewish turn to kabbalistic thought, see Moshe Idel, "The Magical and Neoplatonic Interpretations of the Kabbalah in the Renaissance," in *Jewish Thought in the Sixteenth Century*, ed. Bernard D. Cooperman (Cambridge: Harvard University Press, 1983), 186–242; Moshe Idel, "Particu-

larism and Universalism in Kabbalah, 1480–1650," in *Essential Papers on Jewish Culture in Renaissance and Baroque Italy*, ed. David B. Ruderman (New York: New York University Press, 1992), 324–44. Concerning the Christian interest in Kabbalah, see Chaim Wirszubski, *Pico della Mirandola's Encounter with Jewish Mysticism* (Cambridge: Harvard University Press, 1989).

30. The controversy was first described and analyzed by Ephraim Gottlieb, "The *Gilgul* Debate in Candia" (Hebrew), *Sefunot* 11 (1971–1978): 43–66. See also Aviezer Ravitzky, "The God of the Philosophers and the God of the Kabbalists: A Controversy in Fifteenth Century Crete," in *History and Faith: Studies in Jewish Philosophy*, ed. Aviezer Ravitsky (Amsterdam: Gleben, 1996), 115–53.

31. Brian Ogren, "Circularity, the Soul-Vehicle and the Renaissance Rebirth of Reincarnation: Marsilio Ficino and Isaac Abarbanel on the Possibility of Transmigration," *Accademia: Revue de la Societe Marsille Ficin* 6 (2004): 63–94; Brian Ogren, *Renaissance and Rebirth: Reincarnation in Early Modern Italian Kabbalah* (Leiden: Brill, 2009).

32. Rachel Elior, *Galya Raza: Critical Edition* (Jerusalem: Research Projects of the Institute of Jewish Studies, Hebrew University, 1981); Rachel Elior, "The Doctrine of Transmigration in *Galya Raza*," in *Essential Papers on Kabbalah*, ed. Lawrence Fine (New York: New York University Press, 1995), 243–69.

33. Melilah Helner, "The Teachings of *Gilgul* in the Kabbalistic Works of R. David ibn Zimra" (Hebrew), *Pe'amim* 43 (1990): 16–50.

34. For an analysis of the early history of this concept, particularly in the writings of Nahmanides, see Moshe Idel, "The Secret of Impregnation as Metempsychosis in Kabbalah," *Verwandlungen*, ed. Aleida and Jan Assmann (Munich: Wilhelm Fink Verlag, 2006), 341–79.

35. *Zohar*, II: 104a–b.

36. *Zohar*, III: 217a.

37. Scholem, "*Gilgul*," 222.

38. This concept is described and illustrated in Faierstein, *Jewish Mystical Autobiographies*, part 4 (156–243); Hayyim Vital, *Sha'ar ha-Gilgulim* (Jerusalem: Ahavat Shalom, 2014).

39. Vital, Hayyim, *Sefer ha-Gilgulim*, Vilna, 1886, 8b.

40. Concerning *ibbur* in Safed, see Menachem Kallus, "Pneumatic Mystical Possession and the Eschatology of the Soul in Lurianic Kabbalah," in *Spirit Possession in Judaism*, ed. M. Goldish, 159–85.

41. The most recent overview of this issue is Moshe Idel, "Revelation and the 'Crisis' of Tradition in Kabbalàh: 1475–1575," in *Constructing Tradition, Means and Myths of Transmission in Western Esotericism*, ed. Andreas B. Kilcher (Leiden: Brill, 2010), 255–92. An earlier treatment of this theme is Gershom Scholem, "Religious Authority and Mysticism," in Gershom Scholem, *On the Kabbalah and Its Symbolism* (New York: Schocken Books, 1965), 5–31.

42. A survey of revelation of Elijah in the Jewish mystical tradition is found in Aharon Wiener, *The Prophet Elijah in the Development of Judaism* (London: Routledge & Kegan Paul, 1978), 78–111.

43. Abraham Joshua Heschel, *Prophetic Inspiration after the Prophets: Maimonides and Other Medieval Authorities*, ed. Morris M. Faierstein (Hoboken: Ktav, 1996).

44. See Moshe Idel, "Prophets and Their Impact in the High Middle Ages: A Subculture of Franco-German Jewry," in *Regional Identities and Cultures of Medieval Jews*, ed. J. Castano, T. Fishman, and E. Kanarfogel (London: Littman Library of Jewish Civilization, 2018), 285–337.

45. A few works on Abraham Abulafia by Moshe Idel include *The Writings and Doctrines of Abraham Abulafia* (Hebrew). PhD diss. Hebrew University of Jerusalem, 1976; *The Mystical Experience in Abraham Abulafia*, trans. Jonathan Chipman (Albany: State University of New York Press, 1987); *Studies in Ecstatic Kabbalah* (Albany: State University of New York Press, 1988).

46. Some basic studies about Nehemiah ben Solomon ha-Navi by Moshe Idel include "Some Forlorn Writings of a Forgotten Ashkenazi Prophet: R. Nehemiah ben Shlomo ha-Navi," *Jewish Quarterly Review* 96 (2005): 188–96; "The Anonymous Commentary on the Alphabet of Metatron—An Additional Treatise of R. Nehemiah ben Shlomo the Prophet" (Hebrew), *Tarbiz* 76 (2006): 255–64; "On R. Nehemiah ben Shlomo the Prophet's 'Commentaries on the Name of Forty-Two' and *Sefer ha-Hokhmah* Attributed to R. Eleazar of Worms" (Hebrew), *Kabbalah* 14 (2006), 157–261.

47. The basic studies of the *Sefer ha-Meshiv* are Gershom Scholem, "The Maggid of Rabbi Joseph Taitazak and the Revelations Attributed to him" (Hebrew), *Sefunot* 11 (1971–1978): 69–112; Moshe Idel, "Studies in the Doctrine of the Author of *Sefer ha-Meshiv*: A Chapter in the History of Sephardic Kabbalah" (Hebrew), *Sefunot* N.S. 2 (1983): 185–266.

48. Biographical information can be found in Louis Isaac Rabinowitz, "Taitaẓak, Joseph," *Encyclopedia Judaica* (Detroit: Macmillan Reference USA, 2007), 19: 439–40.

49. Lawrence Fine, "Maggidic Revelation in the Teachings of Isaac Luria," in *Mystics, Philosophers and Politicians: Essays in Intellectual Jewish History in Honor of Alexander Altmann*, ed. J. Reinharz, J. Swetschinski, and K. Bland (Durham: Duke University Press, 1982), 141–57.

50. There are a number of studies about the women in Safed who had these experiences. They include Morris M. Faierstein, "Women as Prophets and Visionaries in Medieval and Early Modern Judaism," in *Studies in Jewish Civilization* 14: *Women and Judaism*, ed. L. J. Greenspoon, R. A. Simkins and J. A. Cahan (Omaha: Creighton University Press, 2003), 247–62; Morris M. Faierstein, "*Maggidim*, Spirits, and Women in Rabbi Hayyim Vital's *Book of Visions*," in, *Spirit Possession in Judaism*, ed. M. Goldish, 186–96; J. H. Chajes,

"He Said She Said: Hearing the Voices of Pneumatic Early Modern Jewish Women," *Nashim* 10 (Fall, 2005): 99–125; Alexandra Cuffel, "Gendered Visions and Transformations of Women's Spirituality in Hayyim Vital's *Sefer Ḥezyonot*," *Jewish Studies Quarterly* 19, 4 (2012): 339–84.

51. Her name is never mentioned in the sources, and she is always described in this way.

52. The classic study of Karo and his *maggid* is R. J. Z. Werblowsky, *Joseph Karo: Lawyer and Mystic* (Philadelphia: Jewish Publication Society, 1977). See also Moshe Idel, "R. Joseph Karo and His Revelations: Or the Apotheosis of the Feminine in Safedian Kabbalah," Tikvah Center Working Paper, 5/10 (2010), http://www.nyutikvah.org/publications.html.

53. For a brief overview of this ritual, see Morris M. Faierstein, "*Tikkun Leyl Shavuot*," *Conservative Judaism* 61, 3 (2009): 76–79. For an extended study of this ritual, see Moshe Hallamish, "*Tikkun Leyl Shavuot*" (Hebrew), in *Kabbalah in Liturgy, Halakhah, and Customs* (Ramat Gan: Bar Ilan University Press, 2000), 595–612.

54. An English translation of the letter is found in Louis Jacobs, *Jewish Mystical Testimonies* (New York: Schocken Books, 1977), 98–104.

55. Concerning automatic speech, see the valuable discussion of Amos Goldreich, *Automatic Writing in Zoharic Literature and Modernism* (Los Angeles: Cherub, 2010), 141–42, n. 88; see also what Goldreich added to it, in the beginning of his book, 16–17, n. 21 (Hebrew).

56. Scholem, "The Maggid of Rabbi Joseph Taitazak," 84; Werblowsky, *Joseph Karo*, 295.

57. In addition to Scholem, "The Maggid of Rabbi Joseph Taitazak," see Shimon Shalem, "The Exegetical Method of R. Joseph Taitazak and His Circle, Its Nature and Form of Inquiry" (Hebrew), *Sefunot* 11 (1971–1978): 113–34; Joseph B. Sermonetta, "Scholastic Philosophical Literature in Rabbi Joseph Taitazak's *Porat Yosef*" (Hebrew), *Sefunot* 11 (1971–1978): 135–85.

58. Werblowsky, *Joseph Karo*, 4–6, 9–12.

59. Vital had a deeply ambivalent attitude towards Karo. Cf., R. J. Z. Werblowsky, *Joseph Karo,* 142–46; Lawrence Fine, "Recitation of Mishnah as a Vehicle for Mystical Inspiration: A Contemplative Technique Taught by Hayyim Vital," *Revue des Etudes Juives* 141 (1982), 193.

60. These numbers in parentheses are references to part and paragraph numbers that are found in both the Hebrew and English editions of Vital's mystical diary, *Sefer Hezyonot* (Book of Visions).

61. Faierstein, *Jewish Mystical Autobiographies*, introduction, 16.

62. The story is found in Faierstein, *Book of Visions*, 1.22–24 (57–73).

63. Vital was sixty-seven years old when this incident took place. He had been living in Damascus since approximately 1600 and died in Damascus at seventy-seven years of age in 1620.

64. Faierstein, *Book of Visions*, 1.24 (65–73).

65. Werblowsky, *Joseph Karo*, 51–54, describes this practice and its implementation.

66. Lawrence Fine, "Benevolent Spirit Possession in Sixteenth–Century Safed," in M. Goldish, ed., *Spirit Possession in Judaism*, 116–17.

67. Concerning Ashkenazi, see Werblowsky, *Joseph Karo*, 272–73; Gershom Scholem, "New Information Concerning R. Joseph Ashkenazi, the *Tanna* of Safed." *Tarbiz* 28 (1958/59): 59–89, 201–35.

68. The most comprehensive biography of Rabbi Isaac Luria is Lawrence Fine, *Physician of the Soul, Healer of the Cosmos: Isaac Luria and His Kabbalistic Fellowship* (Stanford: Stanford University Press, 2003).

69. Fine, *Physician of the Soul*, 31–32.

70. Shlomo Dresnitz, *Shivhei ha-AR"I*. Jerusalem: Ahavat Shalom, 1998, 11.

71. See the discussion of this issue above.

72. On the history of Elijah in the Jewish tradition, see Aharon Wiener, *The Prophet Elijah in the Development of Judaism* (London: Routledge & Kegan Paul, 1978).

73. Dresnitz, *Shivhei ha-AR"I*, 5–6.

74. Fine, *Physician of the Soul*, 93–97.

75. For a detailed discussion of the theory and practice of *yihudim*, see Fine, *Physician of the Soul*, 259–99; Lawrence Fine, "The Contemplative Practice of *Yihudim* in Lurianic Practice," in *Jewish Spirituality*, ed. Arthur Green. 2 vols. (New York: Crossroads, 1987), 2: 64–98.

76. Shemaya and Avtalyon were early Tannaitic figures, and according to medieval tradition, their grave was in Gush Halav, a village near Safed.

77. According to the *Zohar*, I: 7b, II: 44a–45a, the child that Elisha revived was the prophet Habakkuk. Cited by Fine, *Physician of the Soul*, 433, n. 67.

78. The three parts of the soul.

79. Shlomo Dresnitz, letter 1, in *Sefer ha-AR"I ve-Gurav*, ed. Yaakov Moshe Hillel (Jerusalem: Ahavat Shalom, 1998), 8–9. English translation from Fine, *Physician of the Soul*, 284.

80. Dresnitz, letter 3, 45. English translation from Fine, *Physician of the Soul*, 285.

81. Faierstein, *Book of Visions*, 4.14 (169).

82. I date the beginning of Luria's leadership at the funeral of Rabbi Moses Cordovero (Tammuz 20, 1570) and the end at Luria's death (Ab 5, 1572).

83. Important studies that discuss this topic are Pinchas Giller, "Recovering the Sanctity of the Galilee: The Veneration of Sacred Relics in Classical Kabbalah," *The Journal of Jewish Thought and Philosophy* 4 (1994): 147–69; Boaz Huss, "Veneration of Saints Tombs in the Kabbalah of Safed" (Hebrew,) *Mah-*

anaim 14 (2003): 123–34; Jonathan Garb, "The Cult of the Saints in Lurianic Kabbalah," *Jewish Quarterly Review* 98, 2 (2008): 203–29.

84. Moshe Idel, "Jewish Magic from the Renaissance Period to Early Hasidism," in *Religion, Science, and Magic in Concert and in Conflict*, ed. Jacob Neusner, et al. (New York: Oxford University Press, 1989), 106–8.

Chapter 2

1. Werblowsky, *Joseph Karo*, 241–46.
2. Concerning him and his work, see Moshe Idel, "R. Judah Halliwah and His Book *Zofnat Paneah*," *Shalem* 4 (1984): 119–48. The manuscript is in the library of Trinity College, Dublin, Ms. Number, B.5.27. See T. K. Abbot, *Catalogue of the Manuscripts in the Library of Trinity College, Dublin*, London, 1900, no. 26. This story is found on pages 144a–45a in the manuscript.
3. "Studies in the Doctrine of the Author of *Sefer ha-Meshiv*," 224.
4. The full text of this story is found in the appendix to this chapter.
5. A comprehensive study of this text and its history can be found in Joseph Avivi, *Kabbalat ha-AR"I*. 3 vols. (Jerusalem: Ben Zvi Institute, 2008), 2:713–16.
6. H. Y. D. Azulai, *Sefer Shem ha-Gedolim*, Vilna, 1853, Division Books, *Het*, no. 44.
7. A comprehensive study of this manuscript and its history can be found in Avivi, *Kabbalat ha-AR"I*, 1:126–35.
8. *Sefer ha-Hezyonot*, ed. Aaron Zeev Aescoli (Jerusalem: Mosad Harav Kook, 1954). This edition was published as it was left at Aescoli's death, with no introduction and incomplete annotation. Concerning Aescoli, see Zeev Gries, "The Messiah's Scribe: Aaron Zeev Aescoli," *Pe'amim* 100 (2004): 147–57.
9. A discussion of this incident is found in *Catalog of the Gershom Scholem Library of Jewish Mysticism*, ed. Joseph Dan and Esther Liebes. 2 vols. (Jerusalem: Hebrew University/Jewish National and University Library, 1999), 1:325, no. 4331.
10. Faierstein, *Jewish Mystical Autobiographies*.
11. The whereabouts of the original manuscript are presently unknown. The only remaining reproduction is the photocopy made by Aescoli when he prepared his translation.
12. *Sefer Ha-Hezyonot: Yomano ha-Mysti shel Rabbi Hayyim Vital* (Jerusalem: Machon Ben Zvi, 2005).
13. *Book of Visions*, 1.25–27 (73).
14. Some of Vital's problems with *yihudim* are described in *Book of Visions*, 4.14–5 (169–70).

15. Three of the letters were published in the seventeenth century, and the fourth was not published until the twentieth century.

16. The text of this *yihud* is found in Hayyim Vital, *Sha'ar Ruah ha-Kodesh*, Tel Aviv, 1963, 88d–90d.

17. The first published account of this incident is my study, "The Possession of Rabbi Hayyim Vital by Jesus of Nazareth," *Kabbalah: Journal for the Study of Jewish Mystical Texts* 37 (2017): 29–36.

18. Concerning the messianic expectations relating to Isaac Luria and Hayyim Vital, see David Tamar, The "AR"I" and Rabbi Hayyim Vital as Messiah ben Joseph" (Hebrew), *Sefunot* 7 (1963): 169–77; David Tamar, "Messianic Dreams and Visions of Rabbi Hayyim Vital" (Hebrew), *Shalem* 4 (1984): 211–29.

19. Concerning Vital's efforts to become the leader of Luria's disciples after Luria's death, see Gershom Scholem, "The Document on Solidarity of Luria's Disciples" (Hebrew), *Zion* 5 (1940): 133–60.

20. The events that relate to Vital's possession are found in Faierstein, *Book of Visions*, 1:21–24 (52–73).

21. Faierstein, *Book of Visions*, 1.21 (52).

22. Faierstein, *Book of Visions*, 1.21 (55).

23. Faierstein, *Book of Visions*, 1.22–24 (57–73). This messenger was a *maggid*, not a *dybbuk*. A *maggid* is a positive possession that is for a good purpose and differs fundamentally from a *dybbuk* that is a negative possession.

24. This is a paraphrase of Psalm 84:5, which is cited in the Talmud (B. *Sanhedrin* 91b) as a proof text for the doctrine of the resurrection of the dead.

25. Faierstein, *Book of Visions*, 1.24 (66–67).

26. This may allude to an incident that is mentioned in Hayyim Vital, *Sha'ar ha-Gilgulim* (Jerusalem: Ahavat Shalom, 2014), *Hakdamah* 38, 559. In the *Sha'ar ha-Gilgulim*, it immediately precedes the first incident, the story of Vital's possession.

27. He was also a student of Luria, who had other incidents of tension with Vital.

28. An allusion to II Kings, 4:32–35, the story of Elisha and the son of the Shunamite. Elisha brought him back to life.

29. Hayyim Vital, *Sha'ar ha-Gilgulim*, *Hakdamah* 38, 560 (Jerusalem, 1963, ed. *Hakdamah* 38, 158 a–b).

30. See above, in chapter 1, on the origins of the *Dybbuk* concept.

31. In the next paragraph he explains that this is the name of a stream.

32. Hayyim Vital, *Sha'ar ha-Gilgulim*, *Hakdamah* 37, 500. It is worth noting the *Sha'ar ha-Gilgulim*, Jerusalem, 1963, edition, published by the disciples of Rabbi Ashlag, does not contain the whole *Hakdamah* 37. It is not a printing error since the pagination is continuous. The likeliest explanation is that it was censored because of the Jesus reference.

33. Elhanan Reiner, "From Joshua to Jesus: The Transformation of a Biblical Story to a Local Myth" (Hebrew), in *Sharing the Sacred: Religious Contacts and Conflicts in the Holy Land*, ed. A. Kofsky and G. Stroumsa (Jerusalem: Yad Ben Zvi, 1998), 221–71.

34. B. *Sanhedrin* 107b. See also R. Travers Herford, *Christianity in Talmud and Midrash* (London: Williams & Norgate, 1903), 50–54.

35. Reiner, "From Joshua to Jesus," 268.

36. Vilnay's Hebrew translation is "ancient holy one."

37. Ze'ev Vilnay, *Israel Guide*, 9 vols. (Jerusalem: Tour-Israel, 1954 [4th ed.]), 4:312.

38. Hayyim Vital, *Sha'ar ha-Gilgulim* (2014), *Hakdamah* 37, 500–1.

39. The principle enunciated in B. *Sanhedrin* 44a is "A Jew who sins is still a Jew." This principle was also applied to Jesus in rabbinic literature.

40. Scholem, "The Document of Solidarity"; See also Avivi, *Kabbalat ha-AR"I*, 1:38.

41. The letters of Rabbi Shloimel Dresnitz were first published in J. S. Delmedigo, *Ta'alumot Hokhmah*, Basel, 1629, 46a–b. See also Avivi, *Kabbalat ha-AR"I*, 1: 40–41.

42. Dresnitz's account of this story will be discussed in the next chapter.

43. Weinstein, "Kabbalah and Jewish Exorcism in Seventeenth-Century Italian Jewish Communities," 237–56.

44. Weinstein, "Magic in Jewish Italian Communities: A longue-durée Perspective." In Emma Abate, ed., *L'eredità di Salomone: La magia ebraica in Italia e nel Mediterraneo*. Florence: Giuntina, 2019, 185–202.

45. Weinstein, "Kabbalah and Jewish Exorcism in Seventeenth-Century Italian Jewish Communities," 243–45. The text of the story is found in Nigal, *Dybbuk Stories*, 72–74.

Chapter 3

1. A biographical study of Delmedigo is Isaac Barzilay, *Yosef Shlomo Delmedigo (Yashar of Candia): His Life, Works, and Times* (Leiden: Brill, 1974).

2. Simhah Assaf, "Letters from Safed" (Hebrew). *Kovetz al Yad* N.S. 3 [13] (1940): 117–42. This letter is discussed by Patrick Koch, "Of Stinging Nettles and Stones: The Use of Hagiography in Early Modern Kabbalah and Pietism," *Jewish Quarterly Review* 109, 4 (2019): 534–66.

3. Meir Benayahu, *Toldot ha-AR"I* (Jerusalem: Machon Ben Zvi, 1967), 57–60, is a comprehensive summary of what is known about his biography.

4. Concerning the relationship between Shloimel and Issachar Baer, see Andrea Gondos, *Kabbalah in Print: The Study and Popularization of Jewish Mysticism*

in Early Modernity (Albany: State University of New York Press, 2020, 70–73. There are four letters, and there is no way of knowing if there were more letters.

5. Concerning Bacharach and his writings, see Yehudah Liebes, "The Character, Writings and Kabbalah of the Author of *Emek ha-Melekh*" (Hebrew), *Jerusalem Studies in Jewish Thought* 11 (1993): 101–37.

6. "Bacharach, Naphtali ben Jacob Elhanan," *Encyclopedia Judaica* (Jerusalem: Keter, 1971), 4:49–50.

7. For an extended discussion of the questions relating to Bacharach, see Benayahu, *Toldot ha-Ari*, 60–67. Benayahu analyzes this issue at length and offers possible solutions.

8. For the history and editions of this work, see Meir Benayahu, "*Shivhei ha-AR"I*" (Hebrew), *Areshet* 3 (1961): 144–65; Meir Benayahu, "*Shivhei ha-AR"I* in Yiddish" (Hebrew), *Areshet* 4 (1962): 481–89.

9. Vital, *Sefer Hezyonot*, 1.25 (73). See the discussion of this story in the previous chapter.

10. Concerning Sambari and his version, see below.

11. Both were known figures in Safed, and either one was possible in this context. However, when the name is written as an acronym, the acronym for both names is identical.

12. The last name is found in two forms, Falco or Falcon, depending on the text. The recent scholarly consensus is that Falco is the more accurate version. For what we know about Falco, see Avivi, *Kabbalat ha-AR"I*, 1: 133, 219.

13. The blessing for the dead indicates that they had died before the time Vital was writing this, which was approximately 1610–1612.

14. B. *Sanhedrin* 102a.

15. Vital, *Book of Visions*, 4.58–59 (233–39).

16. The Lurianic method is described in the previous chapter in the long extract from Vital's *Sha'ar Ruah ha-Kodesh*.

17. Harari, "'Practical Kabbalah' and the Jewish Tradition of Magic," 54–56.

18. Hayyim Vital, *Sha'ar Ruah ha-Kodesh*, 41 (Tikkun 3). The translation is from Harari, "'Practical Kabbalah' and the Jewish Tradition of Magic," 55.

19. *Shalshelet ha-Kabbalah*, Venice, 1586, 86b–87a; The source of the letter is unclear. Could it be connected to Rabbi Eliezer Ashkenazi and the reports that he mentions?

20. Ashkenazi, Eliezer. *Ma'ase Adonai*, Venice, 1583, chap. 2, 5b.

21. Benayahu, *Toldot ha-Ari*, 47, 104, n. 6.

22. Sambari, *Divrei Yosef*, 319.

23. I have discussed the *Mayse Bukh* exorcism story in two articles, "The First Published Account of a Safed Exorcism" (Hebrew), *Pe'amim* 104 (Summer, 2005): 11–19; "The *Dibbuk* in the *Mayse Bukh*," *Shofar* 30, 1 (2011): 94–103. These articles are the basis for my discussion of this story.

24. Astrid Starck, *Un beau livre d'histoires/ Eyn Shoen Mayse Bukh*. 2 vols. (Schwabe: Basel, 2004), 1:civ–cvi gives a list of Yiddish and translations. The

standard English translation is Moses Gaster, *Ma'aseh Book*. 2 vols. (Philadelphia: Jewish Publication Society, 1934). The basic scholarly studies are Starck, *Un beau livre* 1:xix–cxxxiii; Jacob Meitlis, *Das Ma'assebuch: Sein Entshehung und Quellengeschichte* (Berlin: R. Mass, 1933); Jean Baumgarten, *Introduction to Old Yiddish Literature* (Oxford: Oxford University Press, 2005), 296–316.

25. A town in Lithuania, not the one in Podolia. For basic biographical data, see Meitlis, *Das Ma'assebuch*, 21–23; Clemens P. Sidorko, *Basel und der jiddische Buchdruck (1557–1612): Kulturexport in der Frühen Neuzeit* (Basel: Schwabe Verlag, 2014), 334–38.

26. For a list of sources from which the stories were taken, see Gaster, *Ma'aseh Book*, 2: 665–94; Starck, *Un beau livre*, 1:cxxv–cxxxiii.

27. This is the title of the story in the Basel 1602 edition. It was changed to "The *Dibbuk*" in a later edition.

28. Gaster, *Ma'aseh Book*, 2:686, no. 152.

29. *Brantshpigl*, Basel, 1602, 25a–26a. Gaster in the notes to this story in his *Ma'aseh Book*, 2: 687, quotes Prof. Louis Ginzberg, saying that to the best of his knowledge, there is no earlier version of this story in Hebrew sources.

30. In addition to the notes in Gaster, an analysis of the sources of the *Mayse Bukh* is found in Meitlis, *Ma'asebuch*, chapters 2–4; Sara Zfatman, *Ketav Yad shel "Ma'ase Bukh"* (Innsbruck 1596). Hebrew University, M.A. thesis, 1973.

31. Biographical data on Ashkenazi is taken from H. H. Ben-Sasson, "Ashkenazi, Eliezer ben Elijah the Physician." *Encyclopedia Judaica*. Keter Jerusalem, 1971, 3:725–26.

32. Gaster, Moses, "The Maasehbuch and the Brantspiegel." *Jewish Studies in Memory of George A. Kohut, 1874–1933* (New York: Alexander Kohut Memorial Foundation, 1933), 270–78.

33. Ibid., 271.

34. Joseph Dan, "Menasseh Ben Israel's *Nishmat Hayyim* and the Concept of Evil in Seventeenth Century Jewish Thought," in *Jewish Thought in the Seventeenth Century*. ed. Isadore Twersky and Bernard Septimus (Harvard Center for Jewish Studies) (Cambridge: Harvard University Press, 1987), 66.

35. Joseph Sambari, *Divrei Yosef*, ed. Shimon Shtober (Jerusalem: Machon Ben Zvi, 1994).

36. Sambari, *Divrei Yosef*, 63–70.

37. Benayahu, *Toldot ha-Ari*, 16–18.

38. David Tamar, "Concerning the Book, *Toldot ha-Ari*," in *Studies in the History of the Jewish People in the Land of Israel and Italy* (Jerusalem: Reuben Mass, 1970), 166–93.

39. Joseph Dan, "Toledot Ha-Ari," in *Encyclopaedia Judaica*, 2nd ed., ed. Michael Berenbaum and Fred Skolnik (Detroit, MI: Macmillan Reference USA, 2007), 20:28.

40. The primary relevant source is *Sha'ar Ruah ha-Kodesh*, which was first published in Jerusalem in 1863.

41. Gentile in this context means Muslim.
42. Faierstein, *Book of Visions*, 1.19 (51–52), 1.21 (52–57), 1.29 (74–75), 3.4 (113–14).

Chapter 4

1. As noted in the introduction, stories that are obviously hagiographic or are not historically verifiable are not included in these discussions.
2. Modern day Mikulov, Moravia.
3. The earliest reference to the term *ba'al shem* is found in *Sifre Zuta*. See Hayyim Liberman, "How Is Hasidism Studied in Israel" (Hebrew). *Ohel RaHaL*, 3 vols. Brooklyn, 1980–1984, 1:5.
4. See the discussion of Immanuel Etkes, *The Besht: Magician, Mystic and Leader* (Waltham: Brandeis University Press, 2005), 259–71.
5. A recent survey of this subject is Yuval Harari, "'Practical Kabbalah' and the Jewish Tradition of Magic," *Aries—Journal for the Study of Western Esotericism* 19 (2019): 38–82. The classic survey of this subject is Joshua Trachtenberg, *Jewish Magic and Superstition: A Study in Jewish Folk Religion* (New York: Behrman House, 1939).
6. Karl E. Grözinger, "Jüdische Wundermänner in Deutschland," in *Judentum im deutschen Sprachraum* (Frankfurt am Main: Surkamp Verlag, 1991), 190–221. The appendix containing the names of the *ba'alei shem* is on pages 209–12.
7. This aspect of the *ba'al shem's* function is the subject of an important study by Nimrod Zinger, *The Ba'al Shem and the Doctor: Medicine and Magic among German Jews in the Early Modern Period* (Hebrew) (Haifa: University of Haifa Press, 2017).
8. Two overviews of the history of *ba'alei shem* are Etkes, *The Besht: Magician, Mystic and Leader*, 7–45; Gedaliah Nigal, *Magic, Mysticism, and Hasidism: The Supernatural in Jewish Thought* (Northvale, NJ: Jason Aronson, 1994), 1–31.
9. *Ma'asei Adonai* was published in two volumes. The first volume was published in Frankfurt am Main in 1691, and the second volume, in Fürth in 1694. The *dybbuk* story is in the second volume, 48a–50b.
10. The relationship between these three figures is described in Zfatman, *Leave Impure One*, 6–12.
11. The account of the *dybbuk* and exorcism is at the end of the small book, 43b–48b. It is also found in Zfatman, *Leave Impure One*, 294–305.
12. The Yiddish text is found in Zfatman, *Leave Impure One*, 306–50. For bibliographical details, see Sara Zfatman, *Yiddish Narrative Prose: An Annotated*

Bibliography (Hebrew) (Monograph Series 6). Research Projects of the Institute of Jewish Studies (Jerusalem: Hebrew University, 1981), 69–71, no. 50.

13. Sarah Zfatman has studied and published the original Yiddish text of this story. My discussion relies on her research, though the focus is somewhat different. See "Tale of an Exorcism in Koretz: A New Stage in the Development of a Folk-Literary Genre" (Hebrew), *Jerusalem Studies in Jewish Folklore* 2 (1982): 17–65.

14. The term is used in a similar way in the "Dybbuk in Prague" story. See Zfatman, *Leave Impure One*, 293.

15. *Jerusalem Studies in Jewish Folklore* 2 (1982): 35–65.

Chapter 5

1. Moshe Rosman, *Founder of Hasidism: A Quest for the Historical Ba'al Shem Tov* (Berkeley: University of California Press, 1996); Immanuel Etkes, *The Besht: Magician, Mystic and Leader* (Waltham: Brandeis University Press, 2005).

2. Etkes, *The Besht*, 46–78, has a full description of the Besht's activities as a *ba'al shem*.

3. The most recent study of the state of research on *Shivhei ha-Besht* is Jonatan Meir, "Jewish Hagiography in Context: Sefer Shivhei ha-Besht and the Formation of the Hasidic Movement" (Hebrew), in *The Way of the Book: A Tribute to Zeev Gries*, ed. Avriel Bar-Levav, Oded Yisraeli, Rami Reiner, Jonatan Meir (Jerusalem: Carmel, 2021), 363–88.

4. The Ostrog edition was considered lost, but it was recently discovered. See Jonatan Meir, "The Lost Yiddish Translation of *Sefer Shivhei ha-Besht* (Ostróg 1815)," *Zutot* 15 (2018): 94–113.

5. The standard English translation of *Shivhei ha-Besht* is *In Praise of the Ba'al Shem Tov*, ed. and trans. Dan Ben-Amos and Jerome Mintz (Bloomington: Indiana University Press, 1970).

6. Concerning these letters and their historical influence, see above in chapter 3.

7. First published in Shklov in 1795 and reprinted in Lvov (Lemberg, Lviv) in 1797.

8. For an examination of these parallels, see Morris M. Faierstein, "From Kabbalist to Zaddik: R. Isaac Luria as Precursor of the Baal Shem Tov," *Studies in Jewish Civilization 13: Spiritual Dimensions of Judaism*, ed. L. J. Greenspoon and R. A. Simkins (Omaha: Creighton University Press, 2003), 95–104.

9. The most comprehensive study of the stories relating to the revelation of the Besht is Abraham Rubinstein, "Stories about the Appearance of the Besht in the "*Shivhei ha-Besht*," *Alei Sefer* 6, 7 (1979): 157–86.

10. The demon exorcism stories are numbers 23 and 84 in Ben-Amos and Mintz, *In Praise of the Ba'al Shem Tov*.

11. Ben-Amos and Mintz, *In Praise of the Ba'al Shem Tov*, numbers, 20 and 22.

12. The connection between *dybbuk* possession and madness, particularly in the case of Hasidism, has been studies by Zvi Mark, "*Dybbuk* and *Devekut* in the *Shivhei ha-Besht*: Toward a Phenomenology of Madness in Early Hasidism," in *Spirit Possession in Judaism: Cases and Contexts from the Middle Ages to the Present*, ed. Matt Goldish (Detroit: Wayne State University Press, 2003), 257–301.

13. Gedalyah Nigal has collected the later Hasidic *dybbuk* stories in his comprehensive survey, *Sipurei Dybbuk*, 229–64.

14. "How Jewish Magic Survived the Disenchantment of the World," *Aires: Journal for the Study of Western Esotericism* 19 (2019): 7–37.

15. Bilu's studies include "The Moroccan Demon in Israel: The Case of Evil Spirit Disease," *Ethos* (1980): 24–39; "The Dybbuk in Judaism: Mental Disorder as Cultural Resource" (Hebrew), *Jerusalem Studies in Jewish Thought* 2, 4 (1982): 529–63.

Conclusions

1. Despite its late emergence, *dybbuk* is the term that best describes the subject of our discussion. It also indicates the distinction between the *dybbuk* and the generic evil spirits that are not of interest here.

2. See the important discussion by Seth Wolitz, "Inscribing An-sky's 'Dybbuk' in Russian and Jewish Letters," in *The Worlds of S. An-sky: A Russian Jewish Intellectual at the Turn of the Century*, ed. Gabriella Safran and Steven Zipperstein (Stanford: Stanford University Press, 2006), 164–202.

Appendices

1. Moshe Idel, "Studies in the Doctrine of the Author of *Sefer ha-Meshiv*: A Chapter in the History of Sephardic Kabbalah" (Hebrew). *Sefunot* 17 (N.S. 2) (1983): 224.

2. The reading of Alenu le-Shabeah seven times appears in magical texts. See, for example, in the section of *Sefer ha-Meshiv* that is preserved in Ms. Warsaw 9, p. 136, and others. (This is footnote no. 205 in Idel's article mentioned above.)

3. Another example of the association of epilepsy with possession by demons or evil Spirits or in Safed with *dybbukim*.

4. Perhaps a reference to Vital's own possession and exorcism?

5. This is a form of letter substitution where the first letter of the alphabet is replaced by the last, and so through the whole alphabet.

6. *Zohar*, II: 41b.

7. Midrash *Tanhuma, Beshallah*, 18.

8. Psalm 109:6.

9. This chronicle was composed in the 1670s in Damascus, and selections from it were published in a variety of sources. However, the Stober edition is the first publication of the complete text.

10. The idea of the pulse point as important in contacting and influencing the *dybbuk* is also found in the *yihud* that Luria taught Hayyim Vital in the story of the widow in Safed.

11. The version of this story in Naphtali Bacharach, *Emek ha-Melekh* Amsterdam, 1648, 16c, gives the name as Rabbi Joseph Arzin. The abbreviations of their names are the same.

12. Most likely they announce for what sin he is being punished.

13. B. *Rosh Hashanah* 17a.

14. B. *Sotah* 8b.

15. Hormuz is a port city in Iran, at the entrance to the straits of Hormuz.

16. This term is a Yiddishism, originally referring to Catholic clergy, but eventually became a generic term for non-Jewish clergy.

17. Some other versions of this story give the name as Rabbi Joseph Arzin.

18. B. *Rosh Hashanah* 17a.

19. Hormuz is a port city in Iran, at the entrance to the straits of Hormuz.

20. Rabbi Isaac Luria.

21. Vital, *Book of Visions*, 4: 42 (201–2).

22. Miry clay is one of the names of Gehenna. See B. *Erubin* 19a.

23. This last paragraph is not found in the Dresnitz letter.

24. These are the page numbers in the Amsterdam, 1651, edition of the text.

25. M. *Avot* 4.22.

26. B. *Berakhot* 55a.

27. Most likely the Tripoli in Lebanon and not the one in Libya.

28. This is a reference to the group of prayers and biblical verses that are the introduction to the penitential (Selichot) prayers on the High Holidays and on fast days.

29. These are two things that are traditionally done by children to raise the soul of their deceased parent to a higher level in heaven or alleviate the sufferings of Gehenna. This passage is similar to the story of Rabbi Akiva and the Dead Man story discussed in chapter 1.

30. The *Sefer Kol Bo* is an important medieval halakhic compendium. The text of the excommunication is found in section 139. It is considered one of the strongest forms of excommunication and was often used.

31. This version was translated and discussed in Raphael Patai, "Exorcism and Xenoglossia among the Safed Kabbalists." In *On Jewish Folklore*. Patai. Detroit: Wayne State University Press, 1983, 314–25. (Originally published in *Journal of American Folklore* 91 [1978]: 823–33.)

32. M. *Avot* 4.22.

33. B. *Berakhot* 55a.

34. Most likely the Tripoli in Lebanon and not the one in Libya.

35. Sambari says "daughters," while Nishmat Hayyim says "wives." From the following sentences, it would appear that "wives" makes more sense.

36. This is a reference to the group of prayers and biblical verses that are the introduction to the penitential (*selichot*) prayers on the High Holidays and on fast days.

37. These are two things that are traditionally done by children to raise the soul of their deceased parent to a higher level in heaven or alleviate the sufferings of Gehenna.

38. According to Sambari, *Divrei Yosef*, 321, n. 19, this was the synagogue of the community of exiles from Castile that had been founded about 1525.

39. The *Sefer Kol Bo* is an important medieval halakhic compendium. The text of the excommunication is found in section 139. It is considered one of the strongest forms of excommunication.

40. The language of the local indigenous Jews called Mustarabim.

41. To prove the truth of what he was saying about his wife and her situation.

42. B. *Ketubot* 30a.

43. B. *Baba Mezia* 96a.

44. Psalm 20.

45. Psalm 90:17.

46. Psalm 92.

47. A mystical meditation called the Prayer of Rabbi Nehuniah ben ha-Kanah.

48. This is a series of six verses where the first letter of each verse when read in a vertical sequence spells out "Destroy Satan." The verses are Lamentations 3:56, Psalm 119:160, 122, 162, 66, 108.

49. Psalm 4.

50. These verses are from Exodus 34:5–7. They form the core of the penitential prayers, called *selichot* in Hebrew.

51. Micah 7:18.

52. Psalm 65:4.

53. Psalm 65:5.

54. Exodus 11:8.

55. This translation is based on the text in Zfatman, *Leave Impure One*, 291–93. The original source is Akiva Baer, *Ma'asei ha-Shem*, vol. 2, Fürth, 1694,

48a–50b. Akiva Baer and Rabbi Hirsch Segal were friends, so it is possible that this account came directly from Rabbi Segal.

56. Perhaps it means Prostitz.

57. Certain Hebrew words in the original text have been placed in parentheses ( ). They have been italicized in this translation.

58. The term means sewer or cesspool in German. Zfatman lists terms used by the various editions of this story. See, Zfatman, *Leave Impure One*, 293.

59. My translation of this text is based on the transcription in Zfatman, *Leave Impure One*, 306–50.

60. The modern name is Mikulov, in the Czech Republic.

61. The only other known published version of this story is Moshe ben Menachem Graf (Prager), *Sefer Zera Kodesh Mazevata*. Fürth, 1696, 43b–48b, reprinted in Zfatman, *Leave Impure One*, 294–305. It is unclear to what this is a reference.

62. These paragraph numbers are found in Sara Zfatman's transcription of the text.

63. He uses *peger*, a term for dying for an animal or a term of disrespect, the first time. The second time, he uses *mavet*, a more respectable term for the death of a person.

64. These two references allude to prayers that are well-known parts of the High Holiday liturgy.

65. This was Rabbi David Oppenheim.

66. This could not be the famous Rabbi Meir Eisenstadt because he was in Worms at the time these events took place. See Aharon Fuerst, "Eisenstadt, Meir (MAHARAM ESH)," *Encyclopedia Judaica* (Keter: Jerusalem, 1971), 6:549–50.

67. This is the province of Styria in Austria. Historically, Jews were banned from living there.

68. This is a reworking of the traditional confession of sins (*ashamnu*). The words in bold are in Hebrew and are taken from the words of the confessional prayer. In Hebrew, it is an alphabetical acrostic. It is also a part of the Yom Kippur liturgy.

69. The section of the morning service (*shacharit*) where people do not speak.

70. B. *Baba Kamma* 50a.

71. Changing one's clothes was a sign of preparing for a festivity or holiday. Thus, people might think that he was preparing to celebrate a Christian holiday. It was a Talmudic tradition (tractate *Avodah Zarah*) that Jews avoided any activities that might indicate they were celebrating Christian holidays.

72. This is an allusion to a discussion in B. *Menahot* 60b about mixing fine flour used for meal offerings in the Temple with coarse flour that is not suitable for meal offerings. In other words, making the holy impure.

73. The sentence is allusive rather than explicit. It would seem to refer to acts of bestiality and the idolator in the Ark. It probably does not mean a person, but something like a crucifix.

74. Concerning the "hollow of the sling," see B. *Shabbat* 152b.

75. Probably a reference to gentile men.

76. These are the opening words of a dirge (*kinah*) for Tisha B'Ab. The first half of the sentence is from Job 4:19.

77. It can be assumed that the term "impure" here means that the traditional purification ritual (*taharah*) was not performed before burial.

78. The term used for "dropped dead" is *pegirah*. It is a term used for the death of an animal or an evildoer.

79. An allusion to Genesis 3:14.

80. An important *piyyut* for the High Holy Days.

81. This and the next two paragraphs refer to phrases from the second half of Netane Tokef, a central *piyyut* for the High Holy Days.

82. Based on the discussion between Rabbi Akiva and Turnus Rufus in B. *Sanhedrin* 65b.

83. This is found in *Zohar* 2:151a.

84. It was published in Dessau, 1699, and contained an account of this incident.

85. Zfatman, *Impure One*, 323 n. 11. The Yiddish edition at the beginning until here is a translation based on the Hebrew edition (Moshe Graff (Prager), *Sefer Zera Kodesh Mazavtah*, Fürth, 1696, 43b–48b). From here on, the text is the Yiddish edition only and not in the Hebrew edition.

86. *Bretel* in Yiddish and German is a small wooden tablet. Here it probably means a tablet with holy names inscribed on it.

87. A paraphrase of I Samuel 17:45. See, Zfatman, *Impure One*, 324 n. 12.

88. Perhaps a reference to the spirit that had been exorcised.

89. A reference to the story about the blood of the prophet Zechariah in B. *Gittin* 57b and B. *Sanhedrin* 96b.

90. Most likely an allusion to a crucifix or other Christian image.

91. The term he uses is '*edah*,' a designation for a quorum of ten men, a minyan.

92. B. *Berakhot* 3a.

93. This plant (*asafetida*) is commonly known as devil's dung because of its strong sulfurous smell.

94. Psalms 120 to 134 begin with the phrase "Song of Ascents."

95. This is the opening phrase of a genre of prayers called *tehinnot*, prayers of petition.

96. Psalm 90:17. This verse begins a series of prayers recited at the end of the Sabbath, marking its separation from the rest of the week, from the holy to the profane.

97. Literally, "broken" is one of the standard *shofar* calls; it consists of three short, broken blasts.

98. This whole prayer of petition (*tehinnah*) is in Hebrew.

99. This tradition of fasting on the eve of the new month is known as Yom Kippur Katan.

100. This tradition entails using candle wicking to measure the dimensions of the cemetery. The wicks are then used to make candles, which are donated to the synagogue. This is considered a form of expiation and remembrance for the dead. For a detailed description, see Chava Weissler, *Voices of the Matriarchs* (Boston: Beacon, 1998), 133–46.

101. A paraphrase of Hosea 2:10.

102. This is mentioned in B. *Sanhedrin* 14a as a metaphorical name for a desolate place. Perhaps this was part of an incantation to send the Spirit back to a desolate place.

103. These are page numbers in the original text.

104. Probably a reference to the Council of the Four Lands.

105. One of the constituents of the Four Lands of Poland.

106. Exodus 20:5.

107. B. *Rosh Hashanah* 17a.

108. The "Name of forty-two letters" is a divine name that has theurgic powers and is mentioned in many mystical and magical sources. See Joshua Trachtenberg, *Jewish Magic and Superstition: A Study in Jewish Folk Religion* (New York: Behrman House, 1939), 90–97.

109. The names of these angels are not mentioned in Reuven Margulies, *Malakhei Elyon* (Jerusalem: Mosad Harav Kook, 1964).

110. B. *Avodah Zarah* 17b–18a.

111. Lamentations 3:44.

112. *Pirke de Rabbi Eliezer*, chap. 32.

113. Genesis 22.

114. Psalms 97:9.

115. An allusion to Genesis 18:32.

116. These are the opening words of a *piyyut* first found in *Mahzor Vitry*, sect. 208. The rest of the opening sentence continues "in my anguish I call to You God, I will not fear." It is a hymn sung after the conclusion of the Sabbath.

117. B. *Baba Mezia* 59a.

118. Psalm 121:4.

119. Proverb 10:2.

120. There is a missing word here.

121. As Sara Zfatman notes, this is the name of the fifth sefira of the negative side, according to Moses Cordovero, *Pardes Rimmonim*. See M. Schwab, *Vocabulaire de l'Angelologie* (Paris, 1897), 94.

122. B. *Shabbat* 152b.

210 | Notes to Appendices

123. As mentioned above, in the Lurianic conception of the *dybbuk*, it is impossible for a woman to be a *dybbuk*.
124. Two prayers in the latter part of the daily morning prayers.
125. Zfatman, *Koretz*, 59 n., discusses the sources that explain these names.
126. Hebrew edition, Abraham Rubinstein, ed. and annotated, *Shivhei ha-Besht* (Jerusalem: Reuben Mass, 1991), 64–65. English edition, Dan Ben-Amos and Jerome Mintz, ed. and trans. *In Praise of the Ba'al Shem Tov* (Bloomington: Indiana University Press, 1970) no. 20 (34–35). Yiddish Edition, Karl E. Grözinger, *Die Geschichten vom Ba'al Schem Tov Schivche ha-Bescht*. 2 vols. (Wiesbaden: Harrassowitz Verlag, 1991), 2: 23–24 (sect. 30).
127. A court of three can annul a vow taken by a person, and in this case, it would free the Besht from his vow not to act as a *ba'al shem* before the age of thirty-six.
128. Hebrew edition, Abraham Rubinstein, ed. and annotated, *Shivhei ha-Besht* (Jerusalem: Reuben Mass, 1991), 66–67. English edition, Ben-Amos and Mintz, *In Praise of the Ba'al Shem Tov*, no. 22 (36). Yiddish edition, Grözinger, *Die Geschichten vom Ba'al Schem Tov Schivche ha-Bescht*, 2: 29 (sect. 35–36).
129. *Peulot* (*peulah* is the singular) is the technical term for engaging in magical activities. The plain meaning of the term is actions or operations.

Bibliography

I. Primary Sources

Rabbinic texts that are cited from standard editions with standard pagination are not listed separately.

Ashkenazi, Eliezer. *Ma'asei Adonai*. Venice, 1583.
Bacharach, Naphtali. *Emek ha-Melekh*. Amsterdam, 1648.
Ben Israel, Manasseh. *Nishmat Hayyim*. Amsterdam, 1652.
Delmedigo, J. S. *Ta'alumot Hokhmah*. Basel, 1629–31.
Dresnitz, Shlomo. *Sefer ha-AR"I ve-Gurav*. Ed. Yaakov Moshe Hillel. Jerusalem: Ahavat Shalom, 1998.
Dresnitz, Shlomo. *Shivhei ha-AR"I*. Ed. Yaakov Moshe Hillel. Jerusalem: Ahavat Shalom, 1998.
Flavius, Josephus. *Antiquities of the Jews*.
Ibn Yahya, Gedaliah. *Shalshelet ha-Kabbalah*. Venice, 1586.
Kallah Rabbati. In A. Cohen. *The Minor Tractates of the Talmud*. 2 vols. London: Soncino, 1965.
Karo, Joseph. *Maggid Mesharim*. Lublin, 1646.
Pesikta de Rav Kahana. Ed. Bernard Mandelbaum. 2 vols. New York: Jewish Theological Seminary, 1962.
Sambari, Joseph. *Divrei Yosef*. Ed. Shimon Shtober. Jerusalem: Machon Ben Zvi, 1994.
Shlomo ben Gabbai. *Sefer Meirat Eyna'im*. Constantinople, 1666.
Simhah of Vitry. *Mahzor Vitry*. Ed. Aryeh Goldschmidt. 2 vols. Jerusalem: Ozar ha-Poskim, 2004.
Vital, Hayyim. *Etz Hayyim*. Jerusalem, 1962.
Vital, Hayyim. *Sefer ha-Gilgulim*. Vilna, 1886.
Vital, Hayyim. *Sefer Hezyonot*. Ed. Aaron Zeev Aescoli. Jerusalem: Mosad Harav Kook, 1954.

Vital, Hayyim. *Sefer Hezyonot: Yomano shel R. Hayyim Vital*. Ed. Moshe M. Faierstein. Jerusalem: Machon Ben Zvi, 2005.
Vital, Hayyim. *Sha'ar ha-Gilgulim*. Tel Aviv, 1963.
Vital, Hayyim. *Sha'ar ha-Gilgulim*. Jerusalem: Ahavat Shalom, 2014.
Vital, Hayyim. *Sha'ar Ruah ha-Kodesh*. Tel Aviv, 1963.

II. Secondary Literature

Abbot, T. K. *Catalogue of the Manuscripts in the Library of Trinity College, Dublin*. London, 1900.
Altmann, Alexander. "Eternality of Punishment: A Theological Controversy within the Amsterdam Rabbinate in the Thirties of the Seventeenth Century." *Proceedings of the American Academy for Jewish Research* 40 (1972): 1–88.
Assaf, Simhah. "*Letters from Safed*" (Hebrew). *Kovetz al Yad* N.S. 3 (13) (1940): 117–42.
Avivi, Joseph. *Kabbalat ha-AR"I*. 3 vols. Jerusalem: Ben Zvi Institute, 2008.
Azulai, H. Y. D. *Sefer Shem ha-Gedolim*, Vilna, 1853.
Barzilay, Isaac. *Yosef Shlomo Delmedigo (Yashar of Candia): His Life, Works and Times*. Leiden: Brill, 1974.
Baumgarten, Jean. *Introduction to Old Yiddish Literature*. Oxford: Oxford University Press, 2005.
Ben-Amos, Dan, and Jerome Mintz, ed. and trans. *In Praise of the Ba'al Shem Tov*. Bloomington: Indiana University Press, 1970.
Benayahu, Meir. "*Shivhei ha-AR"I*" (Hebrew). *Areshet* 3 (1961): 144–65.
Benayahu, Meir. "*Shivhei ha-AR"I* in Yiddish" (Hebrew). *Areshet* 4 (1962): 481–89.
Benayahu, Meir. *Toldot ha-AR"I*. Jerusalem: Machon Ben Zvi, 1967.
Ben-Sasson, H. H. "Ashkenazi Eliezer ben Elijah the Physician." In *Encyclopedia Judaica*. Keter: Jerusalem, 1971, 3:725–26.
Bilu Yoram. "*Dybbuk* and *Maggid*: Two Cultural Patterns of Altered Consciousness in Judaism." *AJS Review* 21, 2 (1996): 341–66.
Bilu Yoram. "The Dybbuk in Judaism: Mental Disorder as Cultural Resource" (Hebrew). *Jerusalem Studies in Jewish Thought* 2, 4 (1982): 529–63.
Bilu Yoram. "The Moroccan Demon in Israel: The Case of Evil Spirit Disease." *Ethos* (1980): 24–39.
Bohak, Gideon. *Ancient Jewish Magic: A History*, Cambridge: Cambridge University Press 2008.
Bohak, Gideon. "How Jewish Magic Survived the Disenchantment of the World." *Aires: Journal for the Study of Western Esotericism* 19 (2019): 7–37.
Boustan, Ra'anan S. "The Contested Reception of *The Story of the Ten Martyrs* in Medieval Midrash." In R. Boustan, K. Hermann, et al. *Envisioning*

Judaism: Studies in Honor of Peter Schafer on the Occasion of his Seventieth Birthday. 2 vols. Tübingen: Mohr Siebeck, 2013, 1: 369–93.

Caciola, Nancy. *Discerning Spirits: Divine and Demonic Possession in the Middle Ages.* Ithaca: Cornell University Press, 2003.

Caciola, Nancy. "Spirits Seeking Bodies: Death, Possession, and Communal Memory in the Middle Ages." In *The Place of the Dead: Death and Remembrance in Late Medieval and Early Modern Europe.* Ed. Bruce Gordon and Peter Marshall. Cambridge: Cambridge University Press, 2000, 66–86.

Chajes, Jeffrey H. *Between Worlds: Dybbuks, Exorcists and Early Modern Judaism.* Philadelphia: University of Pennsylvania Press, 2003.

Chajes, Jeffrey H. "He Said She Said: Hearing the Voices of Pneumatic Early Modern Jewish Women." *Nashim* 10 (Fall, 2005): 99–125.

Cuffel, Alexandra. "Gendered Visions and Transformations of Women's Spirituality in Hayyim Vital's *Sefer Ḥezyonot.*" *Jewish Studies Quarterly* 19, 4 (2012): 339–84.

Dan, Joseph. "Menasseh Ben Israel's *Nishmat Hayyim* and the Concept of Evil in Seventeenth Century Jewish Thought." In *Jewish Thought in the Seventeenth Century.* Ed. Isadore Twersky and Bernard Septimus (Harvard Center for Jewish Studies). Cambridge: Harvard University Press, 1987, 63–75.

Dan, Joseph. "Toledot Ha-Ari." In *Encyclopaedia Judaica*, 2nd ed. Ed. Michael Berenbaum and Fred Skolnik. Detroit: Macmillan Reference USA, 2007, 20:28.

Dan, Joseph, and Esther Liebes, eds. *Catalog of the Gershom Scholem Library of Jewish Mysticism* (Hebrew). 2 vols. Hebrew University/Jewish National and University Library: Jerusalem, 1999.

Deutsch, Nathaniel. *The Jewish Dark Continent: Life and Death in the Russian Pale of Settlement.* Cambridge: Harvard University Press, 2011.

Elior, Rachel. "The Doctrine of Transmigration in *Galya Raza.*" In *Essential Papers on Kabbalah.* Ed. Lawrence Fine. New York: New York University Press, 1995, 243–69.

Elior, Rachel. *Galya Raza: Critical Edition* (Hebrew). Jerusalem: Research Projects of the Institute of Jewish Studies, Hebrew University, 1981.

Etkes, Immanuel. *The Besht: Magician, Mystic, and Leader.* Waltham, MA: Brandeis University Press, 2005.

Faierstein, Morris M. "The *Dibbuk* in the *Mayse Bukh.*" *Shofar* 30, 1 (2011): 94–103.

Faierstein, Morris M. "The *Dybbuk*: The Origins and History of a Concept." In *olam ha-zeh v'olam ha-ba: This World and the World to Come in Jewish Belief and Practice* (Studies in Jewish Civilization 28). Ed. L. J. Greenspoon. West Lafayette: Purdue University Press, 2017, 135–50.

Faierstein, Morris M. "The First Published Account of a Safed Exorcism" (Hebrew). *Pe'amim* 104 (Summer, 2005): 11–19.

Faierstein, Morris M. "From Kabbalist to Zaddik: R. Isaac Luria as Precursor of the Baal Shem Tov." In *Studies in Jewish Civilization 13: Spiritual Dimensions of Judaism*. Ed. L. J. Greenspoon and R. A. Simkins. Omaha: Creighton University Press, 2003, 95–104.

Faierstein, Morris M. *Jewish Customs of Kabbalistic Origin: Their History and Practice*. Boston: Academic Studies, 2013.

Faierstein, Morris M. *Jewish Mystical Autobiographies: Book of Visions and Book of Secrets* (Classics of Western Spirituality 94). New York: Paulist, 1999.

Faierstein, Morris M. "Maggidim, Spirits, and Women in Rabbi Hayyim Vital's Book of Visions." In *Spirit Possession in Judaism: Cases and Contexts from the Middle Ages to the Present*. Ed. Matt Goldish. Detroit: Wayne State University Press, 2003, 186–96.

Faierstein, Morris M. "The Possession of Rabbi Hayyim Vital by Jesus of Nazareth." *Kabbalah: Journal for the Study of Jewish Mystical Texts* 37 (2017): 29–36.

Faierstein, Morris M. *Sefer Ha-Hezyonot: Yomano ha-Mysti shel Rabbi Hayyim Vital*. Jerusalem: Machon Ben Zvi, 2005.

Faierstein, Morris M. "Tikkun Leyl Shavuot." *Conservative Judaism* 61, 3 (2009): 76–79.

Faierstein, Morris M. "Women as Prophets and Visionaries in Medieval and Early Modern Judaism." In *Studies in Jewish Civilization 14: Women and Judaism*. Ed. L. J. Greenspoon, R. A. Simkins and J. A. Cahan. Omaha: Creighton University Press, 2003, 247–62.

Fine, Lawrence. "Benevolent Spirit Possession in Sixteenth–Century Safed." In *Spirit Possession in Judaism: Cases and Contexts from the Middle Ages to the Present*. Ed. Matt Goldish. Detroit: Wayne State University Press, 2003, 101–23.

Fine, Lawrence. "The Contemplative Practice of Yihudim in Lurianic Practice." In *Jewish Spirituality*. Ed. Arthur Green. 2 vols. New York: Crossroads, 1987, 2:64–98.

Fine, Lawrence. "Maggidic Revelation in the Teachings of Isaac Lura." In *Mystics, Philosophers and Politicians: Essays in Intellectual Jewish History in Honor of Alexander Altmann*. Ed. J. Reinharz, J. Swetschinski, and K. Bland. Durham: Duke University Press, 1982, 141–57.

Fine, Lawrence. *Physician of the Soul, Healer of the Cosmos: Isaac Luria and His Kabbalistic Fellowship*. Stanford: Stanford University Press, 2003.

Fine, Lawrence. "Recitation of Mishnah as a Vehicle for Mystical Inspiration: A Contemplative Technique Taught by Hayyim Vital." *Revue des Etudes Juives* 141 (1982): 183–99.

Fuerst, Aharon. "Eisenstadt, Meir (MAHARAM ESH)." *Encyclopedia Judaica*. Keter: Jerusalem, 1971, 6:549–50.

Garb, Jonathan. "The Cult of the Saints in Lurianic Kabbalah." *Jewish Quarterly Review* 98, 2 (2008): 203–29.

Gaster, Moses. *Ma'aseh Book*. 2 vols. Philadelphia: Jewish Publication Society, 1934.
Gaster, Moses. The Maasehbuch and the Brantspiegel." *Jewish Studies in Memory of George A. Kohut, 1874–1933*. New York: Alexander Kohut Memorial Foundation, 1933, 270–78.
Giller, Pinchas. "Recovering the Sanctity of the Galilee: The Veneration of Sacred Relics in Classical Kabbalah." *Journal of Jewish Thought and Philosophy* 4, 1 (1994): 147–69.
Goldish, Matt, ed. *Spirit Possession in Judaism: Cases and Contexts from the Middle Ages to the Present*. Detroit: Wayne State University Press, 2003.
Goldreich, Amos. *Automatic Writing in Zoharic Literature and Modernism*. Los Angeles: Cherub, 2010.
Gondos, Andrea. *Kabbalah in Print: The Study and Popularization of Jewish Mysticism in Early Modernity*. Albany: State University of New York Press, 2020.
Gottlieb, Ephraim. "The *Gilgul* Debate in Candia" (Hebrew). *Sefunot* 11 (1971–78): 43–66.
Gries, Zeev. "The Messiah's Scribe: Aaron Zeev Aescoli" (Hebrew). *Pe'amim* 100 (2004): 147–57.
Grözinger, Karl E. *Die Geschichten vom Ba'al Schem Tov Schivche ha-Bescht*. 2 vols. Wiesbaden: Harrassowitz Verlag, 1991.
Grözinger, Karl E. "Jüdische Wundermänner in Deutschland." In *Judentum im deutschen Sprachraum*. Grözinger. Frankfurt am Main: Surkamp Verlag, 1991, 190–221.
Hallamish, Moshe. *An Introduction to the Kabbalah*. Albany: State University of New York Press, 1999.
Hallamish, Moshe. "*Tikkun Leyl Shavuot*" (Hebrew) *Kabbalah in Liturgy, Halakhah, and Customs*. Ramat Gan: Bar Ilan University Press, 2000, 595–612.
Harari, Yuval. *Jewish Magic before the Rise of Kabbalah*. Detroit: Wayne State University Press 2017.
Harari, Yuval. "'Practical Kabbalah' and the Jewish Tradition of Magic." *Aries—Journal for the Study of Western Esotericism* 19 (2019): 38–82.
Helner, Melilah. "The Teachings of *Gilgul* in the Kabbalistic Works of R. David ibn Zimra" (Hebrew). *Pe'amim* 43 (1990): 16–50.
Herford, R. Travers. *Christianity in Talmud and Midrash*. London: Williams & Norgate, 1903.
Heschel, Abraham Joshua. *Prophetic Inspiration after the Prophets: Maimonides and Other Medieval Authorities*. Ed. Morris M. Faierstein. Hoboken: Ktav, 1996.
Huss, Boaz. "Veneration of Saints Tombs in the Kabbalah of Safed" (Hebrew). *Mahanaim* 14 (2003): 123–34.
Idel, Moshe. "The Anonymous Commentary on the Alphabet of Metatron—An Additional Treatise of R. Nehemiah ben Shlomo the Prophet" (Hebrew). *Tarbiz* 76 (2006): 255–64.

Idel, Moshe. "Jewish Magic from the Renaissance Period to Early Hasidism." *Religion, Science, and Magic in Concert and in Conflict.* Ed. Jacob Neusner, et.al. New York: Oxford University Press, 1989, 82–117.

Idel, Moshe. "The Magical and Neoplatonic Interpretations of the Kabbalah in the Renaissance." In *Jewish Thought in the Sixteenth Century.* Ed. Bernard D. Cooperman. Cambridge: Harvard University Press, 1983, 186–242.

Idel, Moshe. *The Mystical Experience in Abraham Abulafia.* Trans. Jonathan Chipman. Albany: State University of New York Press, 1987.

Idel, Moshe. "On R. Nehemiah ben Shlomo the Prophet's 'Commentaries on the Name of Forty-Two' and *Sefer ha-Hokhmah* Attributed to R. Eleazar of Worms" (Hebrew). *Kabbalah: Journal for the Study of Jewish Mystical Texts* 14 (2006): 157–261.

Idel, Moshe. "Particularism and Universalism in Kabbalah, 1480–1650." *Essential Papers on Jewish Culture in Renaissance and Baroque Italy.* Ed. David B. Ruderman. New York: New York University Press, 1992, 324–44.

Idel, Moshe. "Prophets and Their Impact in the High Middle Ages: A Subculture of Franco-German Jewry." In *Regional Identities and Cultures of Medieval Jews.* Ed. J. Castano, T. Fishman, and E. Kanarfogel. London: Littman Library of Jewish Civilization, 2018, 285–337.

Idel, Moshe. *R. Joseph Karo and His Revelations: Or the Apotheosis of the Feminine in Safedian Kabbalah.* *Tikvah Center Working Paper,* 5/10 (2010), http://www.nyutikvah.org/publications.html.

Idel, Moshe. "R. Judah Halliwah and His Book *Zofnat Pa'aneah*" (Hebrew). *Shalem* 4 (1984): 119–48.

Idel, Moshe. "*Revelation and the 'Crisis of Tradition' in Kabbalah: 1475–1575.*" In *Constructing Tradition: Means and Myths of Transmission in Western Esotericism.* Ed. Andreas B. Kilcher. Leiden: Brill, 2010, 255–92.

Idel, Moshe. "The Secret of Impregnation as Metempsychosis in Kabbalah." *Verwandlungen.* Ed. Aleida and Jan Assmann. Munich: Wilhelm Fink Verlag, 2006, 341–79.

Idel, Moshe. "Some Forlorn Writings of a Forgotten Ashkenazi Prophet: R. Nehemiah ben Shlomo ha-Navi." *Jewish Quarterly Review* 96 (2005): 188–96.

Idel, Moshe. *Studies in Ecstatic Kabbalah.* Albany: State University of New York Press, 1988.

Idel, Moshe. "Studies in the Doctrine of the Author of *Sefer ha-Meshiv*: A Chapter in the History of Sephardic Kabbalah" (Hebrew). *Sefunot* 17 (N.S. 2) (1983): 185–266.

Idel, Moshe. *The Writings and Doctrines of Abraham Abulafia* (Hebrew). PhD diss. Hebrew University of Jerusalem, 1976.

Jacobs, Louis. *Jewish Mystical Testimonies.* New York: Schocken, 1977.

Kallus, Menachem. "Pneumatic Mystical Possession and the Eschatology of the Soul in Lurianic Kabbalah." In *Spirit Possession in Judaism: Cases and*

Contexts from the Middle Ages to the Present. Ed. Matt Goldish. Detroit: Wayne State University Press, 2003, 159–85.

Koch, Patrick. "Of Stinging Nettles and Stones: The Use of Hagiography in Early Modern Kabbalah and Pietism." *Jewish Quarterly Review* 109, 4 (2019): 534–66.

Levack, Brian P. *The Witch-Hunt in Early Modern Europe.* London: Longman, 1987.

Liberman, Hayyim. "How Is Hasidism Studied in Israel?" (Hebrew). *Ohel RaHaL.* 3 vols. Brooklyn, 1980–84, 1:1–11.

Liebes, Yehudah. "The Character, Writings and Kabbalah of the Author of *Emek ha-Melekh*" (Hebrew). *Jerusalem Studies in Jewish Thought* 11 (1993): 101–37.

Margulies, Reuven. *Malakhei Elyon.* Jerusalem: Mosad Harav Kook, 1964.

Mark, Zvi. "*Dybbuk* and *Devekut* in the *Shivhei ha-Besht*: Toward a Phenomenology of Madness in Early Hasidism." In *Spirit Possession in Judaism: Cases and Contexts from the Middle Ages to the Present.* Ed. Matt Goldish. Detroit: Wayne State University Press, 2003, 257–301.

Meir Jonatan. "Jewish Hagiography in Context: Sefer Shivhei ha-Besht and the Formation of the Hasidic Movement" (Hebrew). In *The Way of the Book: A Tribute to Zeev Gries.* Ed. Avriel Bar-Levav, Oded Yisraeli, Rami Reiner, Jonatan Meir. Jerusalem: Carmel, 2021, 363–88.

Meir Jonatan. "The Lost Yiddish Translation of *Sefer Shivhei ha-Besht* (Ostróg 1815)." *Zutot* 15 (2018): 94–113.

Meitlis, Jacob. *Das Ma'assebuch: Sein Entshehung und Quellengeschichte.* Berlin: R. Mass, 1933.

Nigal, Gedaliah. *Dybbuk Stories in Jewish Literature* (Hebrew). Jerusalem: Reuben Mass, 1983 (second revised edition, 1994).

Nigal, Gedaliah. *Magic, Mysticism, and Hasidism: The Supernatural in Jewish Thought.* Northvale, NJ: Jason Aronson, 1994.

Ogren, Brian. "Circularity, the Soul-Vehicle and the Renaissance Rebirth of Reincarnation: Marsilio Ficino and Isaac Abarbanel on the Possibility of Transmigration." *Accademia: Revue de la Societe Marsille Ficin* 6 (2004): 63–94.

Ogren, Brian. *Renaissance and Rebirth: Reincarnation in Early Modern Italian Kabbalah.* Leiden: Brill, 2009.

Patai, Raphael. "Exorcism and Xenoglossia among the Safed Kabbalists." In *On Jewish Folklore.* Patai. Detroit: Wayne State University Press, 1983, 314–25.

Rabinowitz, Louis Isaac. "Taitazak, Joseph." *Encyclopedia Judaica.* In Detroit: Macmillan Reference USA, 2007, 19: 439–40.

Ravitzky, Aviezer. "The God of the Philosophers and the God of the Kabbalists: A Controversy in Fifteenth Century Crete." In Aviezer Ravitsky, *History and Faith: Studies in Jewish Philosophy.* Amsterdam: Gleben, 1996, 115–53.

Reiner, Elhanan. "From Joshua to Jesus: The Transformation of a Biblical Story to a Local Myth" (Hebrew). In *Sharing the Sacred: Religious Contacts and*

Conflicts in the Holy Land. Ed. A. Kofsky and G. Stroumsa. Jerusalem: Yad Ben Zvi, 1998, 221–71.

Rosman, Moshe. *Founder of Hasidism: A Quest for the Historical Ba'al Shem Tov*. Berkeley: University of California Press, 1996.

Rubinstein, Abraham. "Stories about the Appearance of the Besht in the "*Shivhei ha-Besht*" (Hebrew). *Alei Sefer*, 6/7 (1979): 157–86.

Rubinstein, Abraham, ed. and annotated. *Shivhei ha-Besht*. Jerusalem: Reuben Mass, 1991.

Safran, Gabriella. *Wandering Soul: The Dybbuk's Creator, S. An-sky*. Cambridge: Belknap Press of Harvard University Press, 2010.

Safran, Gabriella, and Steven Zipperstein, eds. *The Worlds of S. An-sky: A Russian Jewish Intellectual at the Turn of the Century*. Stanford: Stanford University Press, 2006.

Scholem, Gershom. "Bacharach, Naphtali ben Jacob Elhanan." In *Encyclopedia Judaica*. Jerusalem: Keter, 1971, 4:49–50.

Scholem, Gershom. "Dibbuk-Dybbuk." In *Encyclopedia Judaica*. Detroit: Macmillan Reference USA, 2007, 5:643–44.

Scholem, Gershom. "The Document on Solidarity of Luria's Disciples" (Hebrew). *Zion* 5 (1940): 133–60.

Scholem, Gershom. "Gilgul: The Transmigration of Souls." In *On the Mystical Shape of the Godhead: Basic Concepts in the Kabbalah*. Scholem. New York: Schocken Books, 1991, 197–250.

Scholem, Gershom. "Luria, Isaac ben Solomon." In *Encyclopedia Judaica*. Jerusalem: Keter, 1971, 11: 572–78.

Scholem, Gershom. "The Maggid of Rabbi Joseph Taitazak and the Revelations Attributed to Him" (Hebrew). *Sefunot* 11 (1971–78): 69–112.

Scholem, Gershom. "New Information concerning R. Joseph Ashkenazi, the Tanna of Safed" (Hebrew). *Tarbiz* 28 (1958/59): 59–89, 201–35.

Scholem, Gershom. "Religious Authority and Mysticism." In *On the Kabbalah and Its Symbolism*. Scholem. New York: Schocken Books, 1965, 5–31.

Sermonetta, Joseph B. "Scholastic Philosophical Literature in Rabbi Joseph Taitazak's *Porat Yosef*" (Hebrew). *Sefunot* 11 (1971–78): 135–85.

Shalem, Shimon. "The Exegetical Method of R. Joseph Taitazak and His Circle, Its Nature and Form of Inquiry" (Hebrew). *Sefunot* 11 (1971–78): 113–34.

Shyovitz, David I. "You Have Saved Me from the Judgment of Gehenna": The Origins of the Mourner's Kaddish in Medieval Ashkenaz." *AJS Review* 39, 1 (April 2015): 55–58.

Sidorko, Clemens P. *Basel und der jiddische Buchdruck (1557–1612): Kulturexport in der Frühen Neuzeit*. Basel: Schwabe Verlag, 2014.

Sluhovsky, Moshe. *Believe Not Every Spirit: Possession, Mysticism, & Discernment in Early Modern Catholicism*. Chicago: University of Chicago Press, 2007.

Smythe Palmer, A. *Folk-Etymology: A Dictionary of Words Perverted in Form or Meaning, by False Derivation or Historical Anomaly.* London: George Bell, 1882.

Starck, Astrid. *Un beau livre d'histoires/ Eyn Shoen Mayse Bukh.* 2 vols. Schwabe: Basel, 2004.

Steinlauf, Michael C. "The Dybbuk," In *YIVO Encyclopedia of Jews in Eastern Europe.* 2 vols. New Haven: Yale University Press, 2008, 1:434–36.

Tamar, David. "The "AR"I" and Rabbi Hayyim Vital as Messiah ben Joseph" (Hebrew). *Sefunot* 7 (1963): 169–77.

Tamar, David. "Concerning the Book, *Toldot ha-Ari*" (Hebrew). In *Studies in the History of the Jewish People in the Land of Israel and Italy.* Jerusalem: Reuben Mass, 1970, 166–93.

Tamar, David. "Messianic Dreams and Visions of Rabbi Hayyim Vital" (Hebrew). *Shalem* 4 (1984): 211–29.

Tishby, Isaiah. *The Wisdom of the Zohar.* 3 vols. Oxford: Littman Library of Jewish Civilization, 1991.

Trachtenberg, Joshua. *Jewish Magic and Superstition: A Study in Jewish Folk Religion.* New York: Behrman House, 1939.

Vilnay, Ze'ev. *Israel Guide.* 9 vols. Jerusalem: Tour-Israel, 1954 (4th ed.).

Walker, Paul E. "The Doctrine of Metempsychosis in Islam." In *Islamic Studies Presented to Charles Adams.* Ed. W. B. Hallaq and Donald E. Little. Leiden: Brill, 1991, 219–38.

Weinstein, Roni. "Kabbalah and Jewish Exorcism in Seventeenth-Century Italian Jewish Communities: The Case of Rabbi Moses Zacuto." In *Spirit Possession in Judaism: Cases and Contexts from the Middle Ages to the Present.* Ed. Matt Goldish. Detroit: Wayne State University Press, 2003, 237–56.

Weinstein, Roni. "Magic in Jewish Italian Communities: A longue-durée Perspective." In *L'eredità di Salomone: La magia ebraica in Italia e nel Mediterraneo.* Ed. Emma Abate. Florence: Giuntina, 2019, 185–202.

Weiss, Yehudit. "Two Zoharic Versions of the Story of 'The Tanna and the Dead Man'" (Hebrew). *Tarbiz* 78, 4 (2009): 521–54.

Werblowsky, R. J. Z. *Joseph Karo: Lawyer and Mystic.* Philadelphia: Jewish Publication Society, 1977.

Wiener, Aharon. *The Prophet Elijah in the Development of Judaism.* London: Routledge & Kegan Paul, 1978.

Wirszubski, Chaim. *Pico della Mirandola's Encounter with Jewish Mysticism.* Cambridge: Harvard University Press, 1989.

Wolitz, Seth. "Inscribing An-sky's 'Dybbuk' in Russian and Jewish letters." In *The Worlds of S. An-sky: A Russian Jewish Intellectual at the Turn of the Century.* Ed. Gabriella Safran and Steven Zipperstein. Stanford: Stanford University Press, 2006, 164–202.

Yassif, Eli. *The Legend of Safed: Life and Fantasy in the City of Kabbalah*. Detroit: Wayne State University Press, 2019.
Zellmann-Rohrer, Michael. "Hippocratic Diagnosis, Solomonic Therapy, Roman Amulets: Epilepsy, Exorcism, and the Diffusion of a Jewish Tradition in the Roman World." *Journal for the Study of Judaism* 53 (2022): 63–93.
Zfatman, Sara. *Leave Impure One: Jewish Exorcism in Early Modern Ashkenaz* (Hebrew). Jerusalem: Magnes, 2015.
Zfatman, Sara. "Tale of an Exorcism in Koretz"—A New Stage in the Development of a Folk-Literary Genre" (Hebrew). *Jerusalem Studies in Jewish Folklore* 2 (1982): 17–65.
Zfatman, Sara. *Yiddish Narrative Prose: An Annotated Bibliography* (Hebrew) (Monograph Series 6). Research Projects of the Institute of Jewish Studies. Jerusalem: Hebrew University, 1981.
Zfatman, Sara. *Yiddish Narrative Prose: From Its Beginnings to Shivhei ha-Besht (1504–1814)* (Hebrew). 2 vols. Jerusalem: Hebrew University, 1983.
Zinger, Nimrod. *The Ba'al Shem and the Doctor: Medicine and Magic among German Jews in the Early Modern Period* (Hebrew). Haifa: University of Haifa Press, 2017.

Index

Aaron, 17, 172
Aaron R. Leibush, 131, 143
Abihu, 17
Abraham Baal Shem, 171
Abram son of Rabbi Hayyim/Yetta, 125–126, 135, 140–143, 146–148, 151, 154–158, 160, 164, 166–167
Abulafia, Abraham, 19
Abulafia, Meir, 24
Adam, 23
a-Dimaski, 41
adjurations, 9, 59, 60, 75–76, 93, 99, 102, 106, 109–110, 113–114, 117, 123–124, 126, 141, 143, 148–150, 152, 156–157, 159–160, 171
Adrianople, 21
adultery, 90, 95, 112–115
Aescoli, Aaron Zeev, 33–34
Ahab, 50
Akiva, 4, 12–15, 29, 49, 51, 76, 78
Akiva Baer, 66
Alawites, 11
Alenu le-Shabeah, 82
Alkabetz, Shlomo, 20–22, 24, 32, 59, 77, 100, 105, 107, 111
Almshouse, 127, 130, 134, 140–141, 146, 148–149, 157, 159, 162–164
Amsterdam, 48–49, 56, 98, 112–113
amulets, 66, 76, 93, 102, 104, 107, 111, 187

angels, 12, 39–40, 77, 105, 111, 142, 146, 172
angels of destruction, 90, 92, 96, 121–122, 130, 132, 134, 135, 152, 159, 176
Anski, S., 1–2, 68, 80
Antiquities of the Jews, 7, 76
Aristotle, 10
Aristotelian tradition, 10–11
Arueti, Abraham, 105, 111
Arzin, Joseph, 49–50, 89
Ashkenazi, Bezalel, 25
Ashkenazi, Eliezer, 52–54
Ashkenazi, Joseph, 25, 49, 89, 94
Ashkenazi, Samuel, 47
Austria, 144
Avtalyon, 27
Azulay, Hayyim Joseph, 33

ba'al shem (ba'alei shem), 4, 9, 45, 60, 63–66, 71, 73, 76, 79–80, 126, 128, 139, 146, 153, 171, 180, 186–187
Ba'al Shem of Brisk, 126
Bacharach, Naphtali, 48–49, 58, 89
Barrel, 125, 147, 155, 162, 178–179
Bashkes, Leibele, 130
bat kol, 19
Bar Kochba rebellion, 16
Ben Israel, Menasseh, 49, 52–53, 55–56, 58, 63, 89, 98, 112–113

Index

Benayahu, Meir, 52, 57–58
Bereshit Rabbati, 16
Beth Jacob, 101, 108
Between two Worlds, (play), 1
Bilu, Yoram, 3, 74
Boaz, 17
Bohak, Gideon, 74
Bohemia, 127
Bohemian Leiben, 127
Book of Visions, see *Sefer Hezyonot*.
books, 48, 51–53, 66, 68, 140
Brantshpigl, 54
Brisk, 126, 128
Brod, 139
Buddhism, 11
Bueno, Samuel, 105, 111

Cain, 42
Cairo, 17, 56, 58, 60, 91, 96, 115, 117, 119
Candia, Crete, 16, 47
candles, 103–104, 109–110, 155, 160, 162, 164, 179–180
Catholic, 3, 10, 45
cemetery, 12–13, 25, 91, 160, 162, 164
Chajes, J. H., 2–3
Charity, 85–86, 131, 137, 143, 148, 154, 160, 175–176, 178, 182–183
chastisement, 124
chief rabbi, 140–141
Chmelnik, 69
Christian holidays, 136–138
Christian Kabbalah, 16–17
Christians, 75, 123, 140
Cohen, Isaac, 50
confession, 91, 96, 125, 130, 134, 137, 154
Constantinople, 54–55, 85, 113–115
Cordovero, Moses, 24–25, 51, 77
cow, 113–115, 177
Cracow, 54

Damascus, 21, 24, 36–38, 84
Dan, Joseph, 56–57
Danube, 128
daughter of Daniel Romano, 36
daughter of Raphael Anav, 21–24, 38
David ibn Zimra, 17, 25
De Liriah, Tuviah, 106
Delmedigo, Joseph Samuel, 47–49, 55–56, 78, 89
demons, 4, 7–11, 32–33, 37, 45, 51, 57–61, 64, 67, 72, 75–76, 79, 92, 96, 116, 142, 148–149, 157–158, 167, 170, 176–177
destroyers, 132–135, 142, 148–149 152–153, 159, 161
Detmold, 69
devil, 3, 11, 145, 154, 177
diary, 20–22, 24, 28, 31, 33–34, 37, 48, 78
divination, 20
divine names, 65, 83, 90, 94, 103, 109
Divine Providence, 124
Divrei Yosef, 49, 53, 56, 59, 86, 89, 94, 98, 105, 112, 114
Drasenhofen, 144
dream interpretation, 20
dream, 15, 23, 36–39, 73, 84, 99, 106, 117, 166
Dresnitz, Shloimel, 26–28, 35–36, 42, 44, 47–49, 55–60, 72, 78
Druze, 11
Dybbuk, The (play), 1–2

Egypt, 17, 25, 54, 89, 93–94, 173
Ein Zeitun, 41–42
Eisenstadt, Meir, 129
Eleazar, 7–9
Elijah, 19, 26
Elim, 56
Elisha, 27
Emden, Jacob, 65

Emek ha-Melekh, 48–49, 89
epilepsy, 8, 33, 42–43, 64, 73, 76, 79, 81–82, 170
excommunication, 84, 90, 97, 102, 108, 117, 121, 142–143, 148, 155–157, 160, 165–166, 169–172, 179–180
exorcism, 1, 3–5, 7–11, 31–36, 44–45, 47–48, 51–52, 55, 57–61, 63–69, 72, 75–76, 78–80, 82–83, 165, 169
Eybeschutz, Jonathan, 65

Falco, Elijah, 3, 31–32, 36, 44, 47, 49–55, 57, 59–60, 63, 67, 78–80, 98, 100, 105, 107, 111
Falve, 129
fasting, 14, 123, 142–143, 148–149, 153, 160–161, 164–165, 173, 176, 181, 182
Ficino, Marsilio, 17
Fishoff, Wolf, 127, 136–137
Fürth, 66

Gabriel, Abraham, 50
Galilee, 28, 41, 81
Galya Raza, 17
Gano, Judah, 84
garbage, 125, 133
Garden of Eden, 11, 15, 77, 90
Gaster, Moses, 5, 53, 55
Gaza, 92
Gedaliah ibn Yahia, 45, 52–53
Gehenna, 11–12, 15–16, 49, 61, 76–77, 82, 90–92, 95–96, 117–118, 122, 132–133, 139, 142, 146, 166, 176, 179
gentiles, 39–40, 61, 81, 92, 113, 124, 116–117, 128–131, 144, 160, 168
geomancy, 37
Gerona kabbalists, 15
Gershon of Kutov, 72, 186

ghost story, 10, 45
gilgul, 4, 11–12, 15–18, 29, 31–32, 76–78, 100, 102, 107, 109, 116, 118, 133
Ginzberg, Louis, 53–54
Gnostics, 11
Golahav, 177
Graf, Moshe, 64, 66
grave, 19–20, 24–29, 39–42, 65, 77–78, 91, 96, 100–101, 107, 121, 131, 134–135, 144, 175–176
Grözinger, Karl, 65, 185
Gush Halav, 27

Habakkuk, 27
Ha-Levi, Gedaliah, 50
halizah, 16
Halliwah, Judah, 31–32
Harari, Yuval, 51
Hasidism, 2, 4, 64, 71, 73
hegemon, 132, 134–135, 146–147
Hekhalot, chapters of, 51
Hermeticism, 16
Heschel, Abraham Joshua, 19
Hinduism, 11
hollow of the sling, 91, 96, 122, 132–133, 144
Holy names, 51, 75, 123, 140, 142, 146, 157, 163–164, 171–172, 174, 182, 186
Hormuz, 92, 96
Horowitz, Isaiah, 21
Hungary, 127, 141

ibbur, 12, 17–19, 26, 29, 78
ibn Musa, 102, 109
ibn Tabul, Joseph, 50
Idel, Moshe, 19, 29, 32
Isaac (Itzik) R. Hendel, 131, 143
Ishmael, 51
Islam, Shi'ite, 11
Islam, Sunni, 3, 11

Index

Ismailis, 11
Israel Baal Shem Tov (Besht), 4, 64, 69, 71–73, 80, 186
Issachar Baer of Kremnitz, 48
Italy, 45

Jacob ben Abraham of Mezhirech, 53–54
Jerusalem, 37, 61
Jesus, 7, 9–10, 13, 41–42, 75
Job, 32
Jonah, 40
Joseph's ten brothers, 16
Josephus, Flavius, 4, 7, 9–10, 59, 64, 76
Joshua son of Jehozadak, 41
Joshua son of Perahiah, 41
Joshua bin Nun, 31–32, 36, 41–44, 73, 85–86
Judgment, 15, 90, 95–96, 99, 106, 118, 123, 126, 133, 135, 167, 172

Kabbalat Shabbat, 26
Kaddish, 12, 76, 100, 107, 123, 142, 148, 153, 159, 161–162, 164, 178, 182
Kallah Rabbati, 12–13, 76
karet (being cut off), 16
Kharal, 41
Karo, Joseph, 20–25, 29, 31–33, 43–44, 54, 81
Kfar Akhbara, 39
Kiddush, 136, 138, 157
knife, 126, 130, 139, 141, 144, 146, 151
Kol Bo, 102, 108
Kopust, 71
Koretz, 67–69, 71, 169, 174, 185
Kot, Baruch, 68, 174–176, 178–183
Kotelnia, 169–170

Lahmi, Abraham, 100, 105, 107, 111
Latin, 145

levirate marriage, 15–16, 77
Lucian, 8–9
Luria, Isaac, 1, 9, 15–17, 20, 24–29, 31–44, 48, 50–52, 54, 57–61, 63, 72–73, 77–80, 89–90, 94
Lurianic kabbalah, 26, 28, 42, 48, 63
Lurianic writings, 20

Ma'aseh Book (*Mayse Bukh*), 5, 47, 53–55, 111
Ma'asei Adonai, 52, 54
madman, madwoman, 72–73, 80, 187
magic, 4, 8, 45, 51, 139
magician, 37–38
maggid, maggidim, 20–24, 29, 78
Maggid Mesharim, 20–22, 33, 43
Mahzor Vitry, 13, 76
Mashan (Mishan), Judah, 39, 42, 50
Mattersdorf, 128
Mayse Bukh, see *Ma'aseh Book*.
Menasseh, Shabbetai, 50
mercy, 100, 107, 118, 139, 148, 158, 166, 172, 180
Meron, 20, 26–27, 41, 77
Messiah, 38, 41
metempsychosis, 10
mezuzah, 58, 94, 102, 108
Michelstadt, 65
mikvah, 164, 187
millstone, 133, 135, 143, 167
Mindel 169
Mirapol, Rabi Jacob, 68, 174
Mishnah, 20–22, 24
Moravia, 48, 123, 127
Mourner's Kaddish, 12, 76
Muslims, 61, 75

Nadab, 17
Nahmanides, 19
Nefesh, 27, 39
Nehemiah ben Solomon ha-Navi, 19
Neoplatonism, 10–11, 16–17

Index | 225

Neshamah, 27, 39
New Testament, 7
Nigal, Gedaliah, 2
Nikolsburg, 9, 64, 66–69, 73, 79, 121, 123–124, 127, 130, 139–140, 144, 162–163, 166, 168
Nishmat Hayyim, 49, 52, 55–56, 59, 89, 98, 112–113
noblewoman, 129–130

Oppenheim, David, 79, 127, 139–140
Ostrog, 71, 185
oto ha-ish, 13

Phinehas, 17
phylacteries, 81–82, 125, 131, 149–151, 163
physicians, 65, 85–86
Pico della Mirandola, Giovanni, 17
pig, 132–133, 146, 177
Piso (sage), 23–24, 38
piyyut, 68, 134
Platonists, 10
Poland, 54, 125–126, 130, 139, 153–154, 171
possession, Christian, 3, 10
practical kabbalah, 4, 51, 65
Prager, Moshe, 9, 64, 66, 123–124, 139–161, 163–168
Prague, 54, 64, 66–67, 73, 121, 127, 139
prayers, 26, 75, 118, 123, 155–159, 162, 171, 175, 181
Priluka, 170
Pressburg, 128–129
prophecy, 19
Psalms, 146, 156, 159, 161, 164, 167
punishment, 12, 14–18, 29, 32, 50, 61, 76–78, 81, 83, 90, 95, 100, 107, 112, 115–116, 124–125, 131–133, 135, 147, 149, 154, 156, 158–159, 167–169, 174, 177, 179

Pythagoreans, 10

Rabbi Hayyim, 126
Rabbi Moshe, see Prager, Moshe.
Rapoport, Shlomo Zanvil, 1
reincarnation, 16–17
Reiner, Elhanan, 41
repentance, 123
resurrection, 39
revelation, 19, 20, 22, 26, 77
reward, 125
Romano, Daniel, 84
Rome, 85
Rostitz, 121
ruah, 27, 40

Sabbatean, 79
Sabbath, 26, 38, 81, 127, 131, 135–318, 143, 145, 152, 154, 156–157
Safed, 1–2, 11, 17, 20–26, 28–29, 31–32, 35–37, 40–45, 48, 50–54, 57–60, 63, 68, 75–77, 79–80, 86–87, 93, 98, 115
Sagis, Jonathan, 50
saints, Christian, 10
Salonika, 20, 21, 108
Sambari, Joseph, 49, 53, 56–59, 63, 86, 89, 94, 98, 105, 112, 114
saraflik [money changing], 102, 109
Satan, 3, 7, 10–11, 83, 93, 118
Scholem, Gershom, 5, 15, 17, 21–22, 48, 57–58
Sefer Gerushin (The Book of Wanderings), 24
Sefer ha-Bahir, 15
Sefer ha-Meshiv, 20, 22, 43
Sefer Hezyonot (*Book of Visions*), 1, 20, 22–24, 28, 31–34, 36–37, 39, 42, 44–45, 49–50, 59, 61, 78, 82, 84, 89
Sefer Meirat Eyna'im, 32, 85
Sefer Zerah Kodesh Mazevatah, 66

Segal, Hirsch, 66, 121, 138–139, 154, 156, 158, 161–162, 164
Segura, Jacob, 37
Sha'ar ha-Gilgulim, 39, 41, 61, 115
Sha'ar Ruah ha-Kodesh, 35, 51
Shabbetai Zvi, 65
Shalshelet ha-Kabbalah, 45, 52
Shavuot, 21
Shechem, 101, 107
Shekhinah, 19, 22, 90, 95, 142, 154, 166
Shem ha-Gedolim, 33
Shemaya, 27
Shepish, 125
Shivhei ha-AR"I, 33, 48, 54, 57, 72, 80
Shivhei ha-Besht, 71–73, 80, 185
Shivhei Rabbi Hayyim Vital, 33
Shklov, 48
Shlomo ben Gabbai, 32, 85
Shmuel Bukh, 68
Shnei Luhot ha-Berit, 21
shofar, 83, 100, 107, 118, 143, 155, 179–180
shoresh neshamah, 18
Shulhan Arukh, 22
Sidon, 87
sins, 11, 15–16, 29, 32, 76–78, 83, 90, 92, 95–96, 100, 107, 112–115, 118, 121–122, 125–127, 130, 132, 137, 158, 172–175, 177–178
Simeon bar Yohai, 19–20, 26–29, 77
smoke, 9, 59, 99, 103, 106, 109–110, 146, 154–155, 171, 179
Solomon, King, 7–8
Stampa, 129
Steiermark, 130
stone, 84, 116, 125–130, 134–138 144–145, 147, 149, 152, 156, 177
sulfur, 59, 99, 103, 106, 110, 146, 154, 171, 178–179
synagogue, 13, 101, 108, 127, 129, 131, 137–138, 140, 146–150, 152–157, 159–162, 164–166, 175, 179–182

Ta'alumot Hokhmah, 47–49, 56, 89
Tahanun, 142, 148, 153, 161, 164
Taitazak, Joseph, 20–22
Tamar, David, 57
tehinnah, 68
Ten Rabbinic Martyrs, 16
thorns, 13
Tiberias, 86
Tikkun Leyl Shavuot, 21, 26
Titus, 131
Tlust, 73, 186
Toldot ha-Ari, 52, 57
Torah study, 14, 98, 100, 107, 168
transgressions, 16, 32, 77, 90, 118, 123, 149, 156, 158, 167
transmigration, see *gilgul*.
transmigration, Christian, Islamic, 3, 10–11
Tripoli, 99, 106

unification, see *yihud*.

Veisil, Judah, 116
Venice, 45, 52, 54
Vespasian, 7–8, 76
Vienna, 139, 143, 165
Vilnay, Ze'ev, 41
Vital, Hayyim, 1, 16, 20–24, 28–29, 31–40, 42, 44, 50–52, 58–61, 77–79, 82, 86, 90–91, 94–97
Vital, Moshe, 33
Vital, Samuel, 60–61, 115–116, 119

weiberteitsch, 69
Weinstein, Roni, 45
Werblowsky, R. J. Z., 21

Widishlif, Simeon, 137, 140
widow, 89
witchcraft, 2–3, 10
witches 3
Wormser, Seckel, 65
wormwood, 171, 173–174, 178

Yassif, Eli, 3
Yiddish, 71–72
yihud, yihudim, 18–20, 24–29, 35–36, 39, 51, 60, 63, 67, 77–79, 82–83

Zacuto, Moses, 45
zaddik, zaddikim, 27, 38, 136
Zarfati, Joseph, 106
Zarfati, Samuel, 106
Zechariah, 143
Zellmann-Rohrer, Michael, 8
Zfatman, Sara, 3, 5, 66–67, 69, 79
zizit, 23, 125, 147, 161
Zohar, 12, 15–19, 21, 25–26, 41, 76–77, 83, 137
Zofnat Paneah, 31–32